Jack O'Connell
Seattle
30 octobre 1984

Art in the
Ancient World:

A Handbook of
Styles and Forms

Art in the Ancient World

A Handbook of Styles and Forms

by Pierre Amiet, Christiane Desroches Noblecourt,
Alain Pasquier, François Baratte
and Catherine Metzger

translated by Valerie Bynner

RIZZOLI
NEW YORK

Copyright © 1981   Office du Livre
English translation copyright © 1981 Office du Livre

Published in the United States of America in 1981 by

ℛIZZOLI INTERNATIONAL PUBLICATIONS, INC.
712 Fifth Avenue/New York 10019

Library of Congress Catalog Card Number: 80-54673
ISBN: 0-8478-0370-8

Printed and bound in Switzerland

CONTENTS

There is a list of major museums and a concise bibliography following the introduction to each country.

PREFACE

The first volume in this new series, *Oriental Art: A Handbook of Styles and Forms,* has been enthusiastically received all over the world. Building on our success with that, we are continuing the series with a volume on ancient civilizations.

It seemed logical to group together the many civilizations of the Near and Middle East and the Mediterranean, including those of Egypt, Greece, Etruria and Rome, and adopt a similar geographical and chronological framework. We are fortunate in having been able to draw on the expertise of a team of specialists from the Louvre in Paris in compiling such a volume. They have produced a handbook that is both accessible at a glance and comprehensive in its range, and suitable for travellers, scholars, art-lovers and dealers, among others. As in the first volume, the drawings are an essential feature: each author began with the difficult task of making a selection of subjects, and then went on to have drawings of them made by experts.

By arranging the material in the same order for each civilization, we have made it possible for the reader to compare the evolution of different styles and forms, and so train his eye. A general survey at the beginning of each section enables him both to refresh his memory and to fill in any gaps in his knowledge. Such an approach is of particular value to travellers.

Finally, we thought it would be useful to include lists of the principal museums and collections covering the type of objects reproduced in the book, and a glossary of scholarly and technical terms.

JEAN HIRSCHEN

LIST OF ABBREVIATIONS

Ant.	Antiquities
Antikenmus.	Antikenmuseum
Archaeol. Mus.	Archaeological Museum
Bibliothèque Nat.	Bibliothèque Nationale, Paris
B. M.	British Museum, London
c.	century
c.	*circa*
C.	circumference
cm.	centimetres
coll.	collection
D.	diameter
Dyn.	Dynasty
Gall.	Gallery, Galleries
H.	height
Inst.	Institute
L.	length
Landesmus.	Landesmuseum
m.	metres
Met. Mus.	Metropolitan Museum, New York
Mus.	Museum, Museen, Museo, Musée, Musées
Mus. Royaux	Musées Royaux
Nat.	National, Nationale
Nat. Archaeol. Mus.	National Archaeological Museum
Nat. Mus.	National Museum
No.	number
priv.	private
St.	State, Staatliche
St. Mus.	Staatliche Museen
t.H.	total height
Univ.	University
W.	width
(?)	uncertain, unknown

The Middle East

by Pierre Amiet
Curator, Department of Oriental Antiquities, Louvre

Drawings by Marie-Josèphe Devaux

THE MIDDLE EAST

The area known as the Near and Middle East, or Western Asia, originally consisted of separate cultural entities which gradually merged to assume a common identity. Unified for centuries under the aegis of the Persian empire, its stability reflected its reality as a geographical whole. This vast complex of territories is bounded by the Mediterranean, the Black Sea and the Caucasus, by the Central Asian steppes or deserts, and, to the south, by the seas of the Indian Ocean. Its coherence is related to the fact that it is made up of three concentric zones: the Syrian-Arabian desert, the plains of the Fertile Crescent, and the highlands of Anatolia, Armenia and Iran. The considerable variations in the climate and natural resources of the zones imposed differing ways of life on their inhabitants, who were obliged to go to each other for certain necessities.

The Syrian-Arabian desert is an enormous void which no caravan can cross without camels. Nomads had travelled back and forth along its fringes from time immemorial in search of pasture for their herds. These wanderings brought them together as one huge family, a Semitic community, united by culture and language rather than by race. The nomadic tribes were a continual threat to the sedentary residents of the zone made fertile by rain and irrigation. The Tigris and the Euphrates, the two great rivers coming down from the Armenian mountains, amply watered the territory called Mesopotamia on the eastern horn of the Fertile Crescent. This area also contained desert regions, its north differing greatly from its south.

The southern part of Mesopotamia, near the Persian Gulf, is a marshy low plain with a tropical climate. Irrigation much enriched the land but it also brought up salts from the subsoil, a process which very early on caused a partial return to desert. The country in the south was called Sumer. It was subsequently absorbed into Babylonia—later to be renamed Chaldaea after an Aramaean tribe.

Northern Mesopotamia, with a more continental climate, became Assyria and was dominated by the hills of Kurdistan, fertilized by rain and in no need of irrigation. Here, where there were wild grasses and animals to be domesticated, men very soon discovered that they could produce their own food.

The same was true of the countries of the Levant, the western horn of the Crescent. Part of the prosperity of this region was due to its sea-coast and its situation at the focal point of the trading routes from Asia and Africa. The land in the south was called Canaan; that in the north Amurru, a name which for the peoples of Mesopotamia became synonymous with 'west'.

Above the plains were mountain regions, productive of wood, metal and minerals. This was the land of the Hurrians—neither Semitic nor Indo-European—a people who received the immigrants coming down from the northern steppes.

THE MIDDLE EAST

12

In the 2nd millennium B.C. the Hittite empire sprang up on the Anatolian plateau, while in the east the Iranians gave their name to the vast Mesopotamian plateau. The great deserts in the centre of the plateau, Kevir and Lut—former salt lakes—were hostile to life, and trading routes had to skirt round them. Thus links were formed between distant lands, such as Turkmenistan or Bactria in northern Afghanistan, and western Iran. Here, in a small-scale Mesopotamian extension of Babylonia, was the site of the land of Elam, at the crossroads of the routes by which traders brought their goods down from the plateaux to the great towns of the plains. In Elam, merchants met sailors from the Persian Gulf with their loads of copper and hard stone from Oman, and contact was established with faraway India.

THE IRANIAN WORLD

At least 50,000 years ago, Palaeolithic man, seeking subsistence from hunting or gathering, left chipped stones as evidence of his passage through western Iran. In this high region bordering on the Mesopotamian plain, he found that conditions were suitable for semi-sedentary, then sedentary settlement, and about 10,000 years ago he began to till the soil or herd animals that were easily domesticated. In this way predatory man became a producer of his own food, during what is known as the Neolithic Revolution, not a sudden change but a slow and gradual process spreading over several millennia. By about 7000 B.C. people in Ganj Dareh began to use shaped bricks when building their dwellings. It was then discovered that clay hardened when baked and could therefore be moulded in suitable receptacles. Thus pottery was born, and from 6000 B.C. it spread throughout the Near East. Neolithic artists and their successors in the Neolithic tradition were to exploit this new medium, incising their decorations on the clay surface.

The first potters were content to make simply shaped vases covered with rudimentary geometric designs. From the second half of the 5th millennium a richer style developed on the plateau, at Tepe Siyalk near Kashan and at Ismailabad in the north. Strongly stylized animals were painted in black on huge red glazed vases.

The substantial town of Choga Mish and a few small villages on the Elamite plain lived in fellowship with neighbouring Mesopotamia but managed to retain their own originality. Finally, around 4200, Susa was founded and became the centre of a rich district whose inhabitants strengthened their ties with the plateau-dwellers. The Susian potters made splendid vases on which the ibex was reduced to a simple geometric shape with enormous horns, and salukis and waders were made disproportionately long or tall. The Susians fashioned copper axes and, like their nomad cousins in the high valleys of Luristan, engraved their seals with the very earliest mythological figures: a 'master of animals' with the head and coat of an ibex and accompanied by serpents.

The Susians built their temple on an enormous terrace 10 metres high and 80 metres long: they were ready to shed the Neolithic tradition and move on to a properly urban civilization. They turned away from their kinsmen of the plateau and developed links with the Sumerians in the town of Uruk in Mesopotamia, and in so doing, took on, like them, a historical identity. This was the decisive moment in human history when, about the middle of the 4th millennium, the organized state was created. It was marked by the completion of a system of accountancy designed for the management of considerable wealth, and this development led to the cardinally important invention of writing. At first, numbers existed in material form as little objects or counters made of clay, much like the reckoning pebbles from which our word 'calculus' is derived. These were kept in small clay bags and were certified by the impression on their surfaces of seals shaped like cylinders, 'cylinder-seals'. Later the figures were recorded as notches on clay tablets which were sealed in the same way, before the nature of the commodities was specified by means of graphic signs.

In a time when pottery was no longer being decorated, it was those cylinder-seal impressions that revealed the essence of the period's artistic spirit. These town-dwellers preferred realism to prehistoric abstractions, although it was sometimes blended with extravagant fantasy.

The Susians liked to portray scenes from daily life: hunting, farming, stock-breeding, harvesting, baking, weaving—activities taking place around hand-some buildings that were sometimes built with a second storey—and, already, war. Art was the same as at Uruk but with a different, less religious, inspiration. Then at Susa, as at Uruk, a character appeared who could be recognized by his roles of warrior-chief and religious celebrant—the priest-king, sovereign of a centralized state which still left room for private initiative. It was, indeed, Susian merchants who went off to conquer markets as far away as the future Media and who at Godin Tepe built a small fortress overlooking a native village. They went even further, to Tepe Siyalk, where their archives have been found. The Susians of this period created a very delicate statuary portraying worshippers who were anxious to perpetuate their prayers, along with precious vases depicting sacrificial animals in amusing shapes. Metalwork, too, progressed with the mastering of the 'lost-wax' or *cire perdue* technique.

After a serious crisis around 3100 which also affected the Uruk Sumerians, the Susians turned their backs on Mesopotamia and renewed the links they had forged with the mountain peoples when their city was founded. They invented a script known as Proto-Elamite and created an original art style depicting fables or myths in which animals often played the parts of humans. The Proto-Elamite administration opened a road to serve south-east Iran: it began in the region of present-day Shiraz, called the country of Anshan, where a metropolis was built bearing the same name. Beyond this area, a fortress was built at Tepe Yahya in the province of Kerman and the Susian merchants even crossed over the desert of Lut to found a great city, nowadays called Shahr-i Sokhta, in Seistan.

The brilliance of the Proto-Elamite civilization faded around 2800 after a defeat that was recorded in the Babylonian annals. Susa reverted to the level of the cities common in Mesopotamia, with a temple full of statues of worshippers, provincial versions of the ones in the Diyalan plain or at Mari. Not long afterwards the Luristan valleys became the domain of nomad metalworkers who initiated a series of famous 'bronzes', placing them in their great family tombs alongside painted vases similar to the ones at Susa. These nomads were to become wealthy supplying the plains people with metal. They developed their own special art, carving decorative figures on their tools and weapons.

Simultaneously an independent civilization was flourishing in north-east Iran, in the Gurgan plain. It was characterized by grey polished pottery with very studied forms, while further east the inhabitants of Turkmenistan had revived the tradition of animal-decorated pottery. It was by way of these regions that precious stones such as lapis lazuli were conveyed to Mesopotamia. Gradually an immense trading circuit developed around the central Iranian deserts. In the proximity of the deserts green serpentine quarries were worked for the production of luxury vases which were exported in large numbers to Mesopotamia and to the Arabian coast of the Persian Gulf. Similar vases were still being fashioned at Tepe Yahya, in the Kerman province, during the period when Susa was annexed to the Akkadian empire, between 2340 and 2200. Merchants buried not far from there, on the fringes of the Lut desert, were interred with funerary statues which reflected the extensive influence of Mesopotamia. That influence spread right into Bactria (northern Afghanistan) where composite statues of limestone and serpentine have been found. Compartmented copper stamp-seals have also been discovered there and, indeed, right along the road leading to Susa in one direction and up to the borders of China in the other. An itinerary similar to the Silk Route was, therefore, already in existence around 2000 B.C.

Not long after, however, the relay stages on this route fell into decay and were finally absorbed by the desert. Around 1800 B.C. the settlements on the Gurgan plain were abandoned, as were those in Seistan and Kerman. The Luristan bronze-workers disappeared and the region was characterized by a village economy.

At the beginning of this 2nd millennium Susa had regained its independence by uniting with Anshan, its twin city on the plateau. The rich burghers lived in houses conceived along the lines of palaces, and had themselves buried in vaults with their portraits done in an astonishingly vigorous style. We know that the great god of Anshan, enthroned on a serpent, was honoured in open-air ceremonies held in high, rocky places; but much of the history of this period is lost to us.

Then in the 13th century a new dynasty was founded and Elam came to exert an exceptional influence. King Untash Napirisha built a royal city, not far from Susa, today called Choga Zambil, and crowned it with a great temple. The temple was subsequently transformed into a four-storey tower, probably 54 metres high and decorated with enamelled tiles. During the following century the kings of Elam conquered Babylon and carried away an immense booty: Hammurabi's code of law, the stele of Naramsin and other treasures.

The masterpieces they ordered from their bronze-workers reveal a technology that was then unique. The kings sponsored an art that varied in style from the crude and brutal to the delicate and charming.

The end of this same 2nd millennium was probably the period during which a people speaking the Iranian tongue settled in the northern part of the plateau. Their chiefs were buried at Marlik (near Amlash) with chattels that indicated great wealth: their animal-shaped terracotta vases were extremely original. The gold-work, however, was influenced by the art of the great plains civilizations: the winged bulls on gold vases, for instance, are based on Assyrian models; and the monsters with interlaced limbs, on Mitannian ones.

At the same time, the nomads re-established themselves in Luristan and the 18th-century art of bronze-working was revived. From then on, and especially in the 8th and 7th centuries, the bronze-workers developed a style of extraordinary fantasy. The figures, worked according to their nomadic taste, represented a totally different spirit from that of the Assyrian palace doors. The citadel of Hasanlu, in north-west Iran, contained residences in which the ceiling of the main hall was supported by two rows of wooden columns: in the 9th century they received columned portals inspired by those in the Syrian palaces. Median immigrants, who were first in evidence at this time, adopted these architectural principles. Their eagle's nest at Nash-i Jan consisted of a columned palace, a fortified warehouse and a fire temple.

A bigger palace with a columned hall 25 metres on each side was constructed at Godin Tepe and can be seen as the direct ancestor of the palaces at Pasargadae.

To the region near Hasanlu a Scythian prince appears to have come, travelling via the Caucasus to settle eventually on the hill of Ziwiye. Here his people, influenced by the art of this crossroads region, created a new art style, offering evidence of Scythian art earlier than that known to us from the tombs in Russia. After a long period of eclipse, the Elamites restored their kingdom at the end of the 8th century. They liked to cover their buildings with polychrome enamels. Then in 646 they collapsed again, crushed by the Assyrians. In their hinterland, however, at Izeh (Malamir), an Elamite prince had rock reliefs carved that suggest the presence of Persian immigrants. These people had found their home in the country of Anshan (now Fars). After the fall of Susa, local artists speaking the Elamite language created an art that can be seen on their seals: the finely engraved hunting scenes with their 'aerial gallops' are remarkable pieces of work.

This art was developing from the 7th to the 6th century and it was during that time that Cyrus II, king of Anshan, that is, king of the Persians, overthrew successively the Medes, the Lydians and the Babylonians, thereby creating an empire greater than any other. He furthered his ambitions of universal domination by dealing benevolently with his conquered peoples and so generating peace.

Cyrus summoned Ionian stonemasons for his building works at Pasargadae and they introduced Greek techniques and architectural models, notably columns on torus and stylobate bases. And yet the conception of Cyrus's palaces remained fundamentally Iranian, their columned halls and porticoes and their eclectic decorations reflecting a desire to synthesize the traditions developed in the old Asiatic world.

Persian art received a second, definitive, impulse with the accession of Darius I (521–485), who also established himself in Fars, at Persepolis. Darius began the construction of this city, although it was essentially the work of his son Xerxes. The city spread over the Marv Dasht plain with the citadel built on a terrace at the foot of the mountain. It was a citadel conceived in the style of the Assyrian palaces, with a 'public' front and a 'private' rear part. The former was dominated by the palace known as the Apanada, by analogy with the one of that name at Susa. It was built on a terrace 112 metres across and was flanked by four towers with stairways inside them. Framed by the towers were porticoes which bordered on a hall, 20 metres high and with 36 columns. Never before had such a vast interior been created. It was the culmination of a tradition that included the buildings in Hasanlu and Media, a tradition drawing its origins from the *megaron* of Asia Minor, which was also adopted by the Greeks. The composite columns show the syncretism that Cyrus had already desired: a capital with two protomes of bulls, which were the ancient symbol of stability to the Sumerians and Elamites, then a voluted section borrowed from Levantine art, and a papyriform section derived from Egypt, the whole on an Ionian-type fluted column shaft with a bell-shaped base which shows an original adaptation of Egyptian models. The terrace of the palace had a double stairway which originally framed a huge relief representing Xerxes (not Darius as has long been believed) with his eldest son, protected by a canopy and receiving a dignitary and his retinue. From both sides approach delegations from the peoples of the empire, a constant theme in imperial art, aimed at affirming the universality of the Persian kings' power. A building called the Tripylon served as the audience hall and gave access to the 'private' quarters. These were a grouping of similarly conceived palaces, each with a square columned hall preceded by a portico flanked by towers, an arrangement inspired, as at Hasanlu, by Syrian models.

Darius made Susa his administrative capital. It was dominated by a palace which was entered from the town through a monumental gate. On either side of the gate stood colossal statues of the king, probably carved in Egypt. In the palace two buildings of different styles were juxtaposed: the Apanada, a characteristically Iranian columned hall similar to the one at Persepolis, and the palace proper which revived a layout adopted two centuries earlier by Sennacherib in Nineveh and then by the kings of Babylon. This edifice, of unbaked brick, was faced with polychrome enamelled bricks depicting the Persian army along with terrifying guards in the form of real or fabulous animals.

Achaemenian art represents the final expression of a tradition inaugurated at the end of prehistoric times; even Greek contributions such as the pleating of clothes were assimilated by it. The conquests of Alexander the Great, however, put an end to the tradition by imposing Hellenism on the whole of the former Persian

THE IRANIAN WORLD

1 Bastam	13 Nishapur	25 Choga Zambil (Dur Untash)
2 Tabriz	14 Hamadan (Echatan)	26 Izeh (Malamir)
3 Ardebil	15 Godin Tepe	27 Kurangun
4 Hasanlu	16 Tepe Nush-i Jan	28 Pasargadae
5 Ziwiye	17 Nehavend	29 Persepolis
6 Marlik	18 Tepe Giyan	30 Shiraz
7 Kalardasht	19 Baba-Jan	31 Firuzabad
8 Khurvin	20 Tepe Siyalk	32 Kerman
9 Teheran	21 Isfahan	33 Tell-i Iblis
10 Tepe Hissar	22 Tepe Musiyan	34 Tepe Yahya
11 Turing Tepe	23 Jaffarabad	35 Shahr-i Sokhta
12 Namazga-depe	24 Susa	36 Bampur

empire. It was cultivated not only by the conqueror's heirs, the Seleucids, but also by the Parthians who, in the 2nd century B.C., had come from the steppes to the east of the Caspian Sea.

The Parthian kings aspired to be philhellenic and certainly in their capital of Ctesiphon, near the former Babylon, they patronized an art dominated by Hellenism. But they gave great autonomy to their Iranian subjects, especially to the kings of Elymais in the eastern part of Susiana. These raised temples on vast terraces where Iranian gods in Greek guise were worshipped, for example, Heracles at Masjid-i Solaiman. In sculpture, the Greek tradition had already been considerably obscured by the adoption of Persian costume and the frontality convention, although the latter is thought to have originated in the Greek world.

The Sassanians, whose first king, Ardashir, vanquished his Parthian overlord in A.D. 224, reclaimed the Achaemenian heritage and sponsored a national art. Their architecture was of brick, using light vaults and cupolas, designs which allowed the creation of spacious interiors. *Iwans* opened to the outside in a style that carried over to Islamic architecture. Sumptuous stucco decorations covered the buildings and there were also mosaic decorations, probably made by Roman prisoners. The Sassanid kings resumed the tradition of rock reliefs and liked to depict their victories in vast, highly animated narrative pictures, such as at Firuzabad and close to the royal Achaemenid tombs at Naqsh-i Rustem, where Shapur I was represented triumphant over the Roman emperor Valerian. Again, in the 5th century, King Peroz displayed scenes of his investiture and his hunting exploits at Taq-i Bustan. And finally, like the Achaemenians, the Sassanid kings were great lovers of gold and silver-work. Their gilded silver plates showed royal hunting scenes or 'bacchic' scenes with delightful dancing-girls, and these were integrated into the Persian art tradition during the Islamic period.

MAJOR MUSEUMS

France   Musée du Louvre, Paris
Iran   Archaeological Museum, Teheran
U.S.A.   Metropolitan Museum of Art, New York

CONCISE BIBLIOGRAPHY

AMIET, P.   *Les Antiquités du Luristan.* Collection David Weill. Paris, 1976.
———   *Elam.* Auvers-sur-Oise, 1966.
CAMERON, G.   *Histoire de l'Iran antique.* Paris, 1937. *History of Early Iran* (new éd.). Chicago and London, 1969.
GHIRSHMAN, R.   *L'Iran des origines à l'Islam.* Paris, 1951. *Iran: From the Earliest Times to the Islamic Conquest.* Harmondsworth, 1954.
———   *Parthes et Sassanides.* L'Univers des Formes. Paris, 1962. *Iran: Parthians and Sassanians,* trans. Stuart Gilbert and James Emmons. London, 1962.
———   *Perse, Proto-Iraniens, Mèdes, Achéménides.* L'Univers des Formes. Paris, 1963.
HINZ, W.   *Das Reich Elam.* Stuttgart, 1964.
MOOREY, P. R. S.   *Ancient Persian Bronzes in the Adam Collection.* London, 1974.
POPE, A. U.   *A Survey of Persian Art,* vols. I and IV. Oxford, 1938. *New Studies,* 1938–1960, vol. XIV. Oxford, 1967.
PORADA, E.   *Iran ancien.* Paris, 1963. *Ancient Iran: The Art of Pre-Islamic Times.* London, 1965. *The Art of Ancient Iran: Pre-Islamic Cultures.* New York, 1965.
VANDEN BERGHE, L.   *Archéologie de l'Iran ancien.* Leyden, 1959.

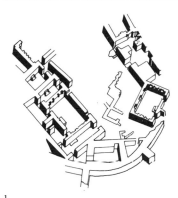

1
Citadel of the Uruk period, c. 3400–
3200 B.C., Godin Tepe (Media)

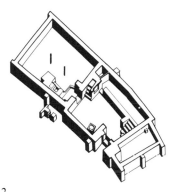

2
'Palace' with cult area, burnt, c. 2000
B.C., Tepe Hissar, near Damghan

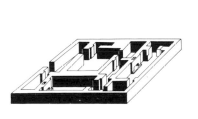

3
House with chapel, Level XV, beginning of the 2nd millennium, Susa

4
Residential palace of Rabibi, 17th c.
B.C., Susa

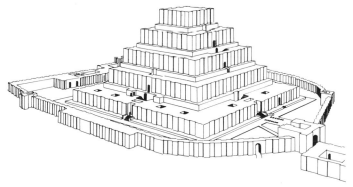

5   Reconstruction of the stepped tower at Dur Untash, now Choga Zambil,
mid-13th c. B.C.

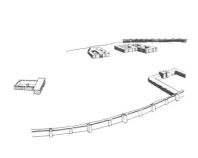

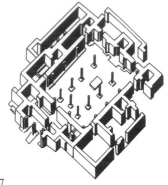

6
Reconstruction of the palace and fire temple at Dur Untash, now Choga Zambil, mid-13th c. B.C.

7
House with columned hall and porticoed entrance added later, 10th–9th c. B.C., Hasanlu (Kurdistan)

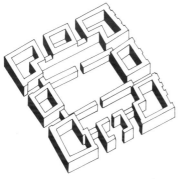

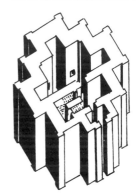

8
Fortified 'manor', 8th c. B.C., Baba-Jan (Luristan)

9
Fire temple in the Median citadel of Tepe Nush-i Jan, 8th c. B.C.

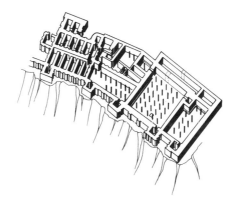

10   Median palace at Godin Tepe (Media), 8th–7th c. B.C.

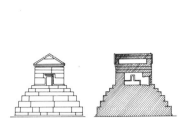

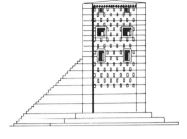

11
Tomb of Cyrus II at Pasargadae, c. 530
B.C.

12
Tower-shaped temple at Pasargadae,
c. 535 B.C.

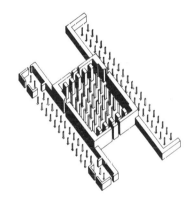

13   Residential palace of Cyrus II at Pasargadae, c. 535 B.C.

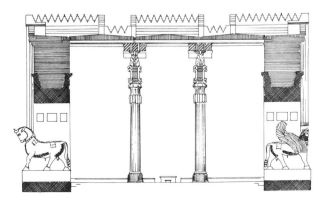

14   'Gate of all countries' built by Darius I and Xerxes at Persepolis, 5th c. B.C.

15   Reconstruction of the north façade of the so-called Apanada palace at
Persepolis, 5th c. B.C., after Krefter

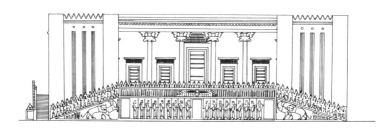

16
Reconstruction of the so-called Tach-
ara, Darius' residential palace at
Persepolis, 5th c. B.C., after Krefter

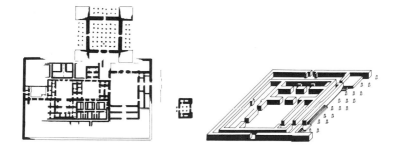

17
Plan of the palace of Darius at Susa
with the Apanada or columned hall to
the north

18
Parthian temple at Masjid-i Solaiman
(Bakhtiari Mountains), 2nd c. B.C.

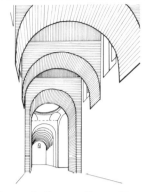

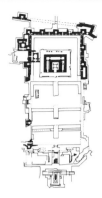

19
Palace of Shapur II at Eivan-e-
Karkha (south-west Iran), interior,
3rd c. A.D.

20
Kushan temple at Surkh-Kotal
(northern Afghanistan), 2nd c. A.D.

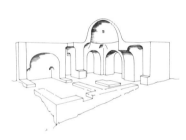

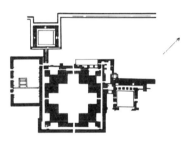

21
Fire temple at Nigar (Kerman province), 5th c. A.D.

22
Palace of Shapur I at Bishapur (Fars),
3rd c. A.D.

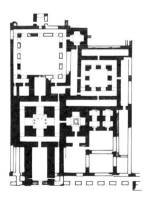

23   Sassanian palace at Takht-i Solaiman (partial view), 4th–5th c. A.D.

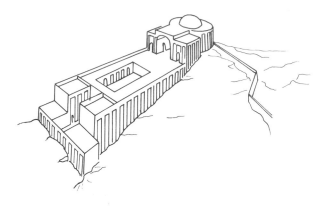

24   Sassanian palace at Qala'ye Dukhtar (Fars), 4th–5th c. A.D.

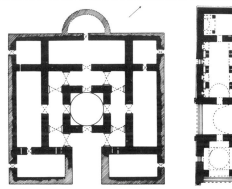

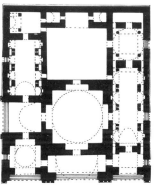

25
Fire temple at Chahar Dih (Fars), 5th
c. A.D.

26
Plan of the palace at Servestan (Fars),
5th c. A.D.

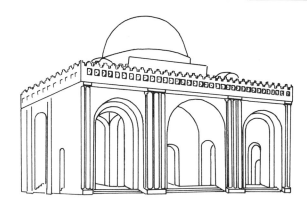

27   Reconstruction of the Sassanian palace at Servestan (Fars), 5th c. A.D.

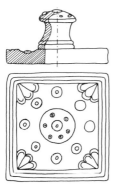

28
Ornamental tile with enamelled pommel, W. 37 cm., *c.* 1250 B.C., temple at Dur Untash, Louvre

29
Moulded brick mural decoration from an Elamite temple, H. 1.370 m., 12th c. B.C., Susa, Louvre

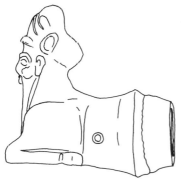

30
Enamelled ornamental tile held in place by a pommel, Neo-Elamite period, 7th c. B.C., Susa

31
Enamelled ornamental tile, H. 25 cm., 7th c. B.C., Susa, Louvre

32
Pommel for holding a tile in place, in shape of a monster, reconstruction, H. *c.* 20 cm., 7th c. B.C., Susa, Louvre

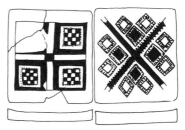

33
Painted ornamental tile from the 'painted room' at Baba Jan (Luristan), 8th–7th c. B.C.

34
Genius conferring blessing, guardian of the passage, monumental gate at Pasargadae, H. 2.75 m., *c.* 535 B.C.

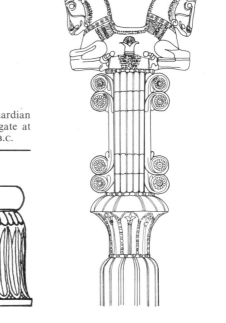

35
Column base from the palace of Darius at Susa, grey limestone, H. 1.140 m., *c.* 500 B.C., Louvre

36
Capital from the palace of Darius at Susa, grey limestone, W. 3.740 m., *c.* 500 B.C., upper part in Louvre

37
Bull in enamelled bricks, H. 1.630 m., beginning of 5th c. B.C., palace of Darius at Susa, Louvre

38
Monster in enamelled bricks, L. 2.520 m., beginning of 5th c. B.C., palace of Darius at Susa, Louvre

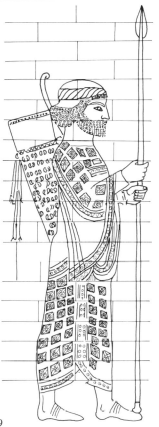

40
Lion in enamelled bricks, H. 2 m., beginning of 5th c. B.C., palace of Darius at Susa, Louvre

39
Archer in enamelled bricks, H. 2 m., beginning of 5th c. B.C., palace of Darius at Susa, Louvre

41
Motif from enamelled decoration, H. 10 cm., beginning of 5th c. B.C., palace of Darius at Susa, Louvre

42   Central relief on the façade of the Apanada at Persepolis: Xerxes I giving audience, L. 6.22 m., transported from the Treasury, Archaeol. Mus., Teheran

43
Relief decorating one of the stairways to the Apanada of Darius and Xerxes at Persepolis, 1st half of 5th c. B.C.

44
Persian and Median nobles, façade of the Apanada at Persepolis, 1st half of 5th c. B.C.

45
Susian tribute-bearer offering two daggers, façade of the Apanada at Persepolis, 1st half of 5th c. B.C.

46
Armenian tribute-bearer leading a horse, façade of the Apanada at Persepolis, 1st half of 5th c. B.C.

47
Syrian tribute-bearer bringing precious vases, façade of the Apanada at Persepolis, 1st half of 5th c. B.C.

48
Ethiopian tribute-bearer, façade of the Apanada at Persepolis, 1st half of 5th c. B.C.

49
Scythian tribute-bearer, façade of the
Apanada at Persepolis, 1st half of 5th
c. B.C.

50
Persian hero fighting a monster, so-
called Tachara palace of Darius at
Persepolis, 1st half of 5th c. B.C.

51
Xerxes entering the throne-room
known as the Tripylon: decoration,
Persepolis, 1st half of 5th c. B.C.

52
Artaxerxes I on his throne: door-jamb
decoration in the Hall of a Hundred
Columns at Persepolis, mid-5th c. B.C.

53
Head of a man, mural painting in the
Parthian palace of Kuh-i Kwadja, 1st
c. A.D., now disappeared

54
Stucco decoration in the Parthian
palace of Kuh-i Kwadja, 1st c. A.D.

55   Mosaic from the floor of the Sassanian palace at Bishapur, H. 86 cm., 2nd
half of 3rd c. A.D., Louvre

56   Mosaic from the floor of the Sassanian palace at Bishapur, 2nd half of 3rd
c. A.D., Louvre

58
Sassanian capital at Bisutun, 5th c.
A.D.

59
Sassanian capital at Bisutun, 5th c.
A.D.

57
Stucco recess in the palace at
Bishapur, 2nd half of 3rd c. A.D.,
Louvre

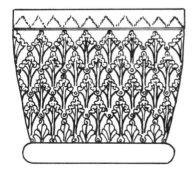

60
Sassanian capital at Venderi, near
Taq-i Bustan, 5th c. A.D.

61
Sassanian capital at Kale-i Kuna, 5th
c. A.D.

62
Fragment of carved vase exported to
Tell Agrab, serpentine, mid-3rd mil-
lennium, Iraq Mus., Baghdad

63
Decoration on a vase exported from
Iran to Mesopotamia in mid-3rd mil-
len., serpentine, H. 11.4 cm., B.M.

64
Continuation of No. 63

65
Continuation of No. 63

66
Punched relief from mid-3rd millen-
nium, H. 17 cm., alabaster, Susa,
Louvre

67
Carved relief from the mid-3rd mil-
lennium, bituminous limestone,
Acropolis at Susa, Louvre

68
Carved support from mid-3rd millennium, H. 18.3 cm., bituminous limestone, Susa, Louvre

69
Carved support from mid-3rd millennium, H. 7.2 cm., bituminous limestone, Susa, Louvre

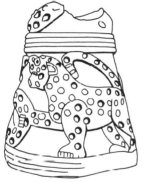

70
Carved support of Iranian origin, found at Nippur, H. 14.2 cm., serpentine, mid-3rd millennium, Iraq Mus.

71
Punched block of Puzur/Kutik-Inshushinak, c. 2150 B.C., H. 55.5 cm., limestone, Susa, Louvre

72   Rock-face relief at Kurangan (western Fars), 17th c. B.C.

73
Bearded Elamite goddess, carved on a 16th-c. B.C. stele, H. (stele) 74 cm., Susa, Louvre

74
Fish-goddess decoration on the stele of Untash-Napirisha, king of Elam, c. 1250 B.C., W. 77.4 cm., Susa, Louvre

75
Moufflon-genius from the stele of Untash-Napirisha, king of Elam, c. 1250 B.C., Acropolis at Susa, Louvre

76
Effigy: king of Elam, Babylonian stele, appropriated in 12th c. B.C., H. (stele) 63 cm., basalt, Susa, Louvre

77
War-god depicted on a Neo-Elamite bronze relief, 8th–7th c., Acropolis at Susa, Louvre

78
Lady spinning, Neo-Elamite relief in bituminous limestone, 8th c. B.C., Acropolis at Susa, Louvre

79
Neo-Elamite victory stele, H. 50 cm.,
8th–7th c., limestone, Acropolis at
Susa, Louvre

80
Neo-Elamite victory stele, H. 50 cm.,
8th–7th c., limestone, Acropolis at
Susa, Louvre.

81
Neo-Elamite stele of Adda-hamiti-
Inshushinak, c. 650 B.C., W. 32.7 cm.,
limestone, Acropolis at Susa, Louvre

82
Protective-genii, fragment of relief,
end of the 7th c. B.C., limestone, Acropolis at Susa, Museum of Susa

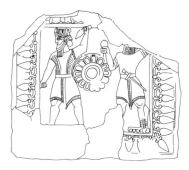

83
Guardian-demons, punched Neo-
Elamite relief, H. 14.5 cm., limestone,
7th c. B.C., Acropolis at Susa, Louvre

84
Rock-face relief of Hanni, Elamite
king of Aiapir, in Izeh (Malamir),
Bakhtiari Mountains, mid-7th c. B.C.

85   Victory relief of Darius I at Bisutun, *c.* 518 B.C.

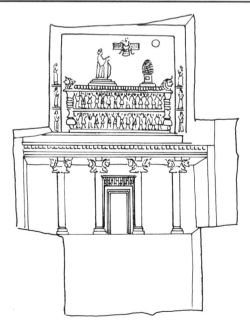

86   Tomb of Darius I at Naqsh-i Rustem, near Persepolis, beginning of 5th c.
B.C.

87
Cult scenes presided over by a king of
Elymais, 2nd c. B.C., Tang-i Sarwak
rock (Bakhtiari Mountains)

88
Cult scenes presided over by a king of
Elymais, 2nd c. B.C., Tang-i Sarwak
rock (Bakhtiari Mountains)

89   Cult scenes presided over by a king of Elymais, 2nd c. B.C., Tang-i Sarwak
rock (Bakhtiari Mountains)

90
Priest of Elymais, altar decoration in
the temple of Bard-e Neshandeh, H.
69 cm., Parthian period

91
Prince of Elymais, temple relief at
Masjid-i Solaiman, Bakhtiari foot-
hills, Parthian period

92
Artabanus V giving audience, lime-
stone, H. 90 cm., *c.* A.D. 215, Susa,
Archaeol. Mus., Teheran

93
Rock-face relief: investiture of
Ardashir I, 1st half of 3rd c. A.D.,
Naqsh-i Rustem, near Persepolis

94   Rock-face relief of Ardashir I at Naqsh-i Rajab

95   Rock-face relief of Shapur I: triumph over the Roman emperors Valerian
and Philip the Arab, 2nd half of 3rd c. A.D., Naqsh-i Rustem, near Persepolis

96
Victory relief of Ardashir I at Darab-
gerd, 1st half of 3rd c. A.D.

97
Rock-face relief of Ardashir II at
Taq-i Bustan, 4th c. A.D.

98   Grotto at Taq-i Bustan: investiture relief and equestrian statue of Peroz,
5th c. A.D.

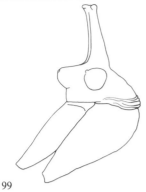

99
Neolithic female idol from Tepe Sarab, terracotta, H. 15 cm., *c.* 6000 B.C., Archaeol. Mus., Teheran

100
Idol from Susa I, painted terracotta, H. 12 cm., *c.* 4000 B.C., Archaeol. Mus., Teheran

101
Female idol, serpentine, H. 27 cm., level VI-D, *c.* 4500/3800 B.C., Tepe Yaha, Archaeol. Mus., Teheran

102
Man's head, sandstone, H. 18 cm., *c.* 3400 B.C., Susa, Uruk period, Mus. of Susa

103
Kneeling worshipper, alabaster, H. 11.8 cm., *c.* 3400 B.C., Acropolis at Susa, Uruk period, Louvre

104
'Cubist' worshipper, limestone, H. 6.7 cm., *c.* 3400 B.C., Acropolis at Susa, Uruk period, Louvre

105
Vase-bearing worshipper, alabaster, H. 12 cm., *c.* 3400 B.C., Acropolis of Susa, Uruk period, Louvre

106
Sitting monkey, alabaster, H. 13.5 cm., *c.* 3400 B.C., Acropolis at Susa, Uruk period, Louvre

107
Vase-bearing bull, silver, H. 15.9 cm., *c.* 3000 B.C., Proto-Elamite period, Metropolitan Mus.

108
Lioness-telamon, magnesite, H. 9 cm., *c.* 3000 B.C., Proto-Elamite period, Brooklyn Mus.

109
Moufflon-genius, copper, H. 14.8 cm., *c.* 3000 B.C., Iran, Brooklyn Mus.

110
Worshipper, pre-Sargonid temple at the Acropolis at Susa, alabaster, H. 14.8 cm., *c.* 2500 B.C., Louvre

111
Archaic statue (*c.* 2700/2600 B.C.)
appropriated *c.* 2270 B.C., alabaster,
H. 30 cm., Louvre

112
Funerary statuette from a tomb in the
desert of Lut, terracotta, *c.* 2600 B.C.,
Archaeol. Mus., Teheran

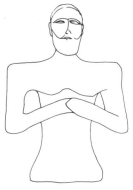

113
Funerary statue from desert of Lut,
painted unbaked clay, H. 45 cm., *c.*
2200 B.C., Archaeol. Mus., Teheran

114
Elamite statuette of a woman, serpentine and white limestone, H. 18.3 cm.,
c. 2300 B.C., Bactria, Louvre

115
Statuette of a scarred genius, serpentine and alabaster, H. 11.7 cm., end of
3rd millennium, western Iran, Louvre

116
Statue of the goddess Narundi, lime-
stone, H. 1.09 m., *c.* 2150 B.C., Susa,
Louvre

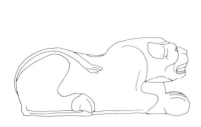

117
Guardian-lion of a temple, limestone, L. 1.101 m., *c.* 2150 B.C., Louvre

118
Female idol placed in a tomb at the end of the 3rd millennium, terracotta, H. 16 cm., Susa, Louvre

119
Bust of a worshipper, alabaster, H. 30 cm., *c.* 2200/2000 B.C., Susa, Louvre

120
Female idol from Tureng Tepe, terracotta, H. 18.5 cm., *c.* 2000 B.C., Archaeol. Mus., Teheran

121
Elamite god, bronze, gold-plated hand, H. 17.5 cm., beginning of 2nd millennium, Susa, Louvre

122
Female statuette, ivory, H. 9.4 cm., beginning of 2nd millennium, Susa, Louvre

123
Funerary portrait of a man, painted unbaked clay, H. 24 cm., 17th–16th c., Susian burial vault, Louvre

124
Funerary portrait of a woman, painted unbaked clay, 17th–16th c., Susian burial vault, Louvre

126
God on a throne guarded by serpents, bronze, H. 5 cm., 17th–16th c., Susa, Louvre

125
Elamite god on a chariot, bronze, H. 15.7 cm., 17th–16th c., Susa, Louvre

127
Fish-goddess, bronze, H. 12 cm., 17th–16th c., Elam, B.M.

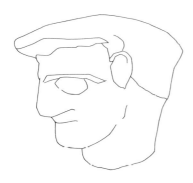

128
Head of a doll, terracotta, H. 7.8 cm.,
mid-2nd millennium, Susa, Louvre

129
Statue of Queen Napir-Asu, bronze,
H. 1.290 m., c. 1250 B.C., Susa, Louvre

130
Guardian-bull, Choga Zambil, enam-
elled terracotta, H. 1.35 m., c. 1250
B.C., Archaeol. Mus., Teheran

131
Guardian-griffin, ziggurat at Choga
Zambil, enamelled terracotta, H. c.
1.30 m., c. 1250 B.C., Mus. of Susa

132   Guardian-lion of the temple of Inshushinak at Susa, enamelled terracotta, L. 1.360 m., 12th c. B.C., Louvre

133
Gold figurine: worshipper carrying a goat, funerary deposit, Susa, H. 7.5 cm., 12th c. B.C., Louvre

134
Elamite worshipper, funerary deposit, Susa, bronze, H. 12 cm., 12th c. B.C., Louvre

135
Royal (?) head, H. 7 cm., 9th c. B.C.,
burnt building at Hasanlu (Iranian
Kurdistan), Archaeol. Mus., Teheran

136
Head of Elamite goddess, enamelled
clay, H. 5.4 cm., 7th c. B.C., Susa,
Louvre

137–138   Neo-Elamite worshipper, enamelled terracotta, H. 5.4 cm., 7th c. B.C.,
Susa, Louvre

139
Luristan god, bronze, H. 37 cm., 8th–
7th c., Archaeol. Mus., Teheran

140
Achaemenian worshipper, silver, H.
14.8 cm., 6th (?) c. B.C., Oxus Treasure
(Bactria), B.M.

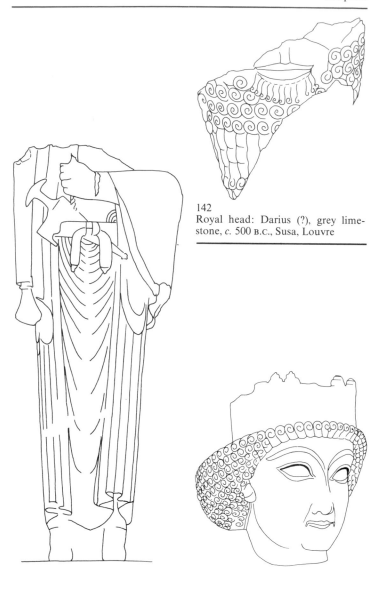

142
Royal head: Darius (?), grey limestone, c. 500 B.C., Susa, Louvre

141
Statue of Darius I, palace at Susa, grey
limestone, H. 1.95 m., c. 500 B.C.,
Archaeol. Mus., Teheran

143
Head of Achaemenian princess, lapis
lazuli paste, H. 6.5 cm., 5th c. B.C.,
Persepolis, Archaeol. Mus., Teheran

144
Statue of a Parthian prince, bronze, H.
1.92 m., 2nd c. B.C., Shami (Bakhtiari
Mountains), Archaeol. Mus., Teheran

145
Head of a man, limestone, H. 26 cm.,
1st–3rd c., Parthian period, Susa,
Louvre

147–148
Head of a man, 1st c. A.D., Parthian
temple of Masjid-i Solaiman

146
Statue of Heracles, limestone, H.
2.40 m., 1st c. A.D.(?), temple of Masjid-i Solaiman, Bakhtiari Mountains

149
Head of a man, limestone, H. 18.5 cm.,
Parthian temple of Masjid-i Solaiman,
Louvre

150   Sassanian royal bust, bronze, H. 32 cm., 6th–7th c. A.D., Louvre

151   Sassanian royal head, silver, 5th c. A.D., Metropolitan Mus.

152
Bowl with horned serpents, H. 14.3 cm., *c.* 4500 B.C., Tepe Bouhallan, near Susa, Louvre

153
Deep bowl, D.⸱*c.* 22.5 cm., *c.* 4000 B.C., Susa I, Louvre

154
Beaker decorated with waders, dogs and ibexes, *c.* 4000 B.C., Susa I, Louvre

155
Painted bowl, *c.* 4000 B.C., Tell-i Bakun, near Persepolis, Archaeol. Mus., Teheran

156
Painted bowl, *c.* 4000 B.C., Tell-i Bakun, near Persepolis, Archaeol. Mus., Teheran

157
Vase in the shape of a chalice, *c.* 3800 B.C., Tepe Hissar, near Damghan, Archaeol. Mus., Teheran

158
Vase in the shape of a chalice (see No. 157)

159
Vase with panthers, *c.* 3600 B.C., Tepe Siyalk, near Kashan, Louvre

160
'Style II' globular vase, *c.* 2500 B.C., Susa, Louvre

161
Vase in the shape of a man offering a libation, *c.* 1200 B.C., Marlik, Archaeol. Mus., Teheran

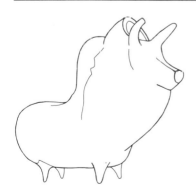

162
Bull-shaped vase, *c.* 1300–1200, Marlik, Archaeol. Mus., Teheran

163
Vase shaped like a man offering a libation, 8th–7th c., Luristan, Archaeol. Mus., Teheran

164   Spouted vase, 9th–8th c., Tepe Siyalk, Necropolis B, Archaeol. Mus., Teheran

165
Neo-Elamite pyxis, H. 17 cm., 7th c. B.C., Susa, Louvre

166
Neo-Elamite pyxis (see No. 165)

167   Neo-Elamite vase decoration, H. 20.5 cm., 7th c. B.C., Susa, Louvre

168
Horse-shaped rhyton (drinking cup),
L. 29.4 cm., 6th c. B.C., Susa, Louvre

169
Parthian rhyton, H. 37 cm., 1st c. B.C.,
Demavend, Archaeol. Mus., Teheran

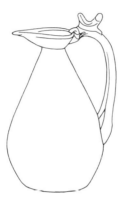

170   Sassanian glass jug, 6th–7th c. A.D., Archaeol. Mus., Teheran

171   Double vase in serpentine, L. 18.3 cm., c. 2500 B.C., Susa, Louvre

172   Bowl with bisons, bituminous limestone, H. 9.6 cm., *c.* 2000/1900 B.C.,
Susa, Louvre

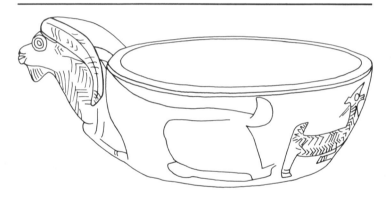

173   Bowl with ibex, bituminous limestone, H. 9 cm., *c.* 2000/1900 B.C., Susa,
Louvre

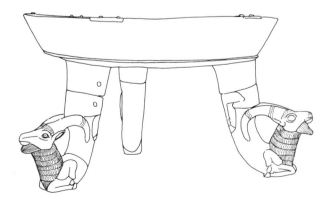

174   Tripod cup, bituminous limestone, H. 28 cm., *c.* 2000/1900 B.C., Susa,
Louvre

175
Copper pin, H. 10.6 cm., *c.* 3400 B.C.,
Uruk period, Susa, Louvre

176
Club decorated with a chariot, copper,
L. 13.4 cm., *c.* 2600 B.C., Luristan,
Louvre

177
Rein-ring from a chariot, early dy-
nastic period, *c.* 2500 B.C., Luristan,
Louvre

178
Dagger, copper, L. 23.3 cm., Luristan,
Louvre

179
Silver votive hammer, H. 9 cm., *c.* 2000
B.C., Susa, Archaeol. Mus., Teheran

180
Copper 'standard', W. 23.4 cm., *c.*
2100 B.C., tomb in the desert of Lut,
Teheran

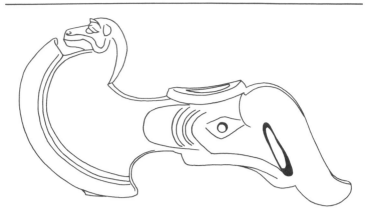

181   Axe-insignia of office, L. 15 cm., *c.* 2000/1900 B.C., Bactria, Louvre

182
Axe-insignia of office, L. 11.1 cm., *c.*
1900/1800 B.C., Luristan, Louvre

183
Disc-shaped pinhead of gilded silver
on bitumen, D. 8.3 cm., 14th c. B.C.,
Susiana, Louvre

184   Electrum vase, H. 11 cm., 13th–12th c., Marlik civilization, Louvre

185
Gold vase, H. 12 cm., 13th–12th c.,
Marlik civilization, Archaeol. Mus.,
Teheran

186
Gold vase, H. 12.5 cm., 12th–11th c.,
Kalardasht, Archaeol. Mus., Teheran

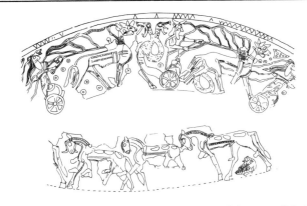

187   Mythological vase decoration in silver-plated bronze, 13th–12th c.,
H. 20.1 cm., Marlik region, Louvre

188   Mythological decoration on the gold vase of Hasanlu (Iranian Kurdistan),
H. 20.6 cm., 13th c. B.C., Archaeol. Mus., Teheran

61

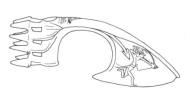

189
Digitated axe, L. 25.5 cm., 9th–8th c.,
Luristan, Former David Weill Coll.

190
Halberd with lion head in Chinese
Tao Tieh style, L. 11.1 cm., 8th c. B.C.,
Luristan, Former David Weill Coll.

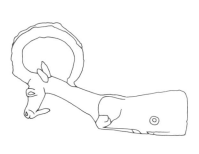

191
Handle of a whetstone, L. 9.2 cm., 11th
c. B.C., Luristan, Former David Weill
Coll.

192
Portable 'idol', H. 19.4 cm., 8th–7th c.,
Luristan, Former David Weill Coll.

193
Pin-head, H. 12.9 cm., 7th c. B.C.,
Luristan, Louvre

194
Pin-head, D. 10.9 cm., 7th c. B.C.,
Luristan, Louvre

195   Horse's cheekpiece, 8th–7th c., Luristan, Louvre

196
Decoration on the rim of a funerary
vessel, H. 4.5 cm., 7th c. B.C., Ziwiye
(Iranian Kurdistan), Louvre

197
Gold plaque, 7th c. B.C., Ziwiye,
Archaeol. Mus., Teheran

198   Gold plaque, L. 27.7 cm., 7th c. B.C., Ziwiye, Archaeol. Mus., Teheran

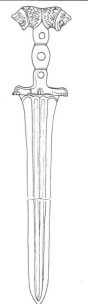

199
Achaemenian gold sword, L. 10.5 cm.,
5th c. B.C., Hamadan (?), Archaeol.
Mus., Teheran

200
Inlaid armlet, D. 12.3 cm., 5th–4th c.,
Oxus Treasure, B.M.

201
Achaemenian gold rhyton, H. 17.1
cm., 5th–4th c., Hamadan (?), Metropolitan Mus.

202
Achaemenian silver vase, H. 37 cm.,
private coll.

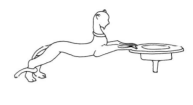

203
Gold plaquette with Achaemenian worshipper, H. 15 cm., Oxus Treasure, B.M.

204
Parthian incense-burner, bronze, H. 11.6 cm., 1st c. A.D., Cleveland Mus.

205
Sassanian throne leg, bronze, H. 32 cm., 4th–5th c., Louvre

206
Gilded silver ewer, 5th c. A.D., Bibliothèque Nat.

207
Sassanian shallow bowl, silver, 5th c.
A.D., Hermitage

208
Silver shallow bowl of Khusraw I,
beginning of 7th c. A.D., Hermitage

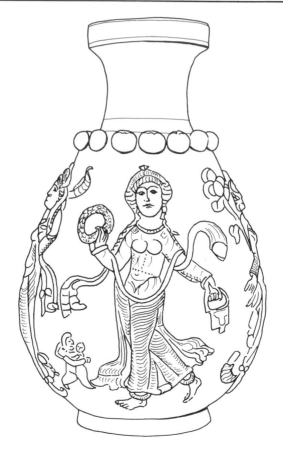

209   Silver ewer, 5th–6th c., Louvre

210
Archaic stamp-seal with master of
animals, *c.* 4000 B.C., Luristan, B.M.

211
Archaic stamp-seal (as No. 210),
Louvre

212
Susa I stamp-seal, cult scene, *c.* 4000
B.C., Louvre

213
Susa I stamp-seal, master of animals,
c. 4000 B.C., Louvre

214
Susa I stamp-seal, cruciform motif,
c. 4000 B.C., Louvre

215
Susa II stamp-seal, Uruk period, *c.*
3500 B.C., Louvre

216
Cylinder-seal from Susa II, Uruk
period, *c.* 2400 B.C., Louvre

217
Cylinder-seal from Susa II, Uruk
period, *c.* 3200 B.C., Louvre

218   Cylinder-seal from Susa II, Uruk period: temple on a terrace and priest-
king, *c.* 3200 B.C., Louvre

219
Proto-Elamite cylinder-seal, Susa III,
c. 3000 B.C., heulandite, Archaeol.
Mus., Teheran

220
Proto-Elamite cylinder-seal: lionesses
supporting mountains, Susa III, *c.*
3000 B.C., Louvre

221
Proto-Elamite cylinder-seal: animals imitating farmers, *c.* 3000 B.C., St. Mus., E. Berlin

222
Cylinder-seal: musician-genii, Susa IV, early dynastic period, *c.* 2700 B.C., Louvre

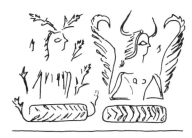

223
Cylinder-seal: goddesses, *c.* 2300 B.C., Tepe Yahya IV B (Kerman province), Archaeol. Mus., Teheran

224
Cylinder-seal: mythological scene, *c.* 2300 B.C., Kerman province, private coll.

225   Compartmented copper stamp-seal, 18th c. B.C., Bactria, Louvre

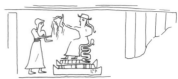

226
Seal of Idadu II: the king hands over
the axe to the chancellor, *c.* 1950 B.C.,
Susa, Louvre

227
Seal of Tan-uli: the prince worship-
ping the great god of Elam, 17th c.
B.C., Louvre

228
Elamite seal, 13th c. B.C., Susa, Louvre

229
Elamite seal: sacred fire cult, mid-13th
c. B.C., Susa, Louvre

230
Seal of Kurash: probably Cyrus I, end
of 7th c. B.C., Persepolis, Oriental Inst.
of Chicago

231
Seal of Darius I (521–485 B.C.), B.M.

232
Sacred fire cult, Achaemenian seal,
5th–4th c., Louvre

233
Achaemenian cult scene, cylinder-
seal, 5th–4th c., Louvre

234
Coin of Shapur I (A.D. 241–272),
silver, Bibliothèque Nat.

235
The fire god on an altar, Sassanian
intaglio, agate, 4th–5th c., Bibliothèque Nat.

MESOPOTAMIA

SUMER, BABYLONIA, ASSYRIA

The variable flow of the rivers on the Babylonian plain rendered it an inhospitable region for a long time. Palaeolithic hunters, at least from Mousterian times, found more favourable terrain in the Kurdistan foothills, whence they could easily cross over to the Iranian plateau. Here and there plants grew, and gathering them gave rise to the idea of cultivation, just as the hunting of wild sheep and goats preceded their domestication. This process was taking place from the 10th millennium B.C., at a time when the Shanidar cave was inhabited, not far from the Zawi Chemi encampment. It was not until the 7th millennium, however, that the village of Qalaat Djarmo was established, and here in about 6000 B.C. pottery was introduced, an 'invention' originating in Iran. At the same time at Umm Dabaghiyah, in the steppe to the west of the Tigris, onager hunters were building great warehouses to store the skins of the beasts they traded in. Soon after, in the same region, the farmers of Hassuna inaugurated what was to become a long-lived village tradition, when they began to make crudely decorated vases. The transition to organized farming, made possible by irrigation techniques, took place after 5500 B.C. at Tell es-Sawwan on the banks of the Middle Tigris. True architecture came into being, with houses containing bedrooms arranged on either side of communal halls. Alabaster vases and statuettes with simplified human features were placed in tombs. Not long afterwards pottery was widespread, richly decorated with whirling designs of people or animals; it has been classified in the town of Samarra. Then, about 5000, the development of this civilization was interrupted by the spread of the so-called Tell Halaf culture which reached as far as the Mediterranean, carried perhaps by nomads, to judge from their poor round houses. But the continuing ceramic tradition, of pure form and dense design, of monochrome and, later, polychrome decoration, represents one of the pinnacles in the history of art. Finally, around 4500, the 'Ubaid culture, elaborated at first in Eridu in southern Mesopotamia, began to spread throughout the region, the first sign of the primacy of the future land of Sumer. The architectural tradition of Tell es-Sawwan, with its central cella, remained dominant for Assyrian houses and temples, such as at Tepe Gawra near Nineveh, and in the temple at Eridu—which was built on a terrace and was the forerunner of the stepped 'towers'. The population of pre-Sumerian Eridu knew little of figurative art, other than in their strongly stylized idols. At Tepe Gawra, however, as at Susa and Luristan, the art of seal decoration gave rise to an iconographic repertoire depicting the mythical master of animals.

Around 3600 the inhabitants of the south abandoned the painting of ceramics and the prehistoric traditions bound up with it and began the massive production of pottery, a trend which also spread across Susiana and right into Syria. In about 3400 the town of Uruk created a theocratic state, its inhabitants raising great temples with central cellas measuring up to 76 metres long, and inventing a script to keep their temple accounts. They thus took on their historical identity as Sumerians. With the adoption of the cylindrical form for their seals they developed a new artistic tradition, depicting cult scenes but based on realism. The new style had already been used on huge monuments, a striking example being a basalt stele with two pictures of the priest-king as huntsman.

After they had survived a crisis around 3100 B.C., the Sumerians were able to continue their artistic development. One notable theme was the marriage of the royal couple, who seem to have represented the divine couple. At Uruk and further north, at Tell 'Uqair, they built small temples on one or even two superimposed terraces. The plain to the east of Baghdad, watered by the Diyala, became a cultural centre at this time and its art continued to develop throughout the 3rd millennium, in what is known as the early dynastic period.

This was at first the period of the legendary hero-kings including Gilgamesh and Enmerkar. Then, around 2500, came the truly historical kings of the first dynasty of Ur and of Mari, Lagash, and so on. The god and clergy of the holy city of Nippur patronized the monarchy and a sort of concert of nations was set up, which extended as far as Mari, now in Syria, and to Susa in Iran. The earliest known palaces date from this period, the one at Mari including a 'sacred enclosure', apparently for the royal cult. The largest known temple, the so-called Oval Temple at Khafaje, consisted of a small shrine on a terrace within a court formed by an oval wall, outside of which was another wall encircling the first. Within the second wall was a temple-house, evidently designed for a high-ranking official. The devout came in large numbers to offer their effigies in the temples and this became the golden age of statuary. The sculptures were clumsy and angular to begin with, with strangely stylized faces. Then, after 2500, they took on a new look of smiling realism. Bas-reliefs depicting the ritual meal were stylized in a similar way. In about 2450 the prince of Lagash had his victories commemorated on a large stele, the 'Vultures Stele', the first great page of pictorial history accompanied by a text. This final period saw the splendour of Ur and Mari, cities enriched by their mutual trade, as evidenced by the golden treasures in the 'royal tombs' at Ur on the one hand, and the rich offerings in the Mari temples on the other. Mesopotamian civilization even penetrated as far as Ashur on the Middle Tigris, Tell Chuera on the Turko-Syrian borders and into Syria itself at Ebla to the south of Aleppo. Political organization in this time of greatness remained archaic with a mosaic of independent city-states weakened by continual wars. Eventually around 2340 a Semitic conqueror, Sargon, from the old city of Kish to the south of Baghdad, annexed all of the Sumerian-type city-states and organized the first real empire by creating a totally new administration. He set up his capital at Akkad, and the art that he patronized and that his successors perpetuated symbolized his claims to universal domination. Most of the examples of this 'imperial art' have been found at Susa, where they were carried as spoils of war some 1100 years later. Royal victory was almost the only theme, and it was rendered with notable realism both in anatomy and in the postures of the subjects. The theme was usually treated in the conventional way with registers into which the various episodes were distributed; but around 2250 it received a grandiose interpretation on the stele of Naramsin, fourth king of the dynasty, when the whole story was combined in a single scene. Statuary lost some of its former spontaneity and became a court art. The cylinder-seals, on the other hand, depicted mythological themes with a predilection for war-gods, worthy patrons of a military monarchy. A favourite subject was Nergal, the summer sun, destroyer of vegetation.

The Akkadian dynasty was overthrown around 2200 by wild mountaineers, the Guti. This cleared the way for a Sumerian revival which first manifested itself in the state of Lagash. Gudea, the chief or *ensi* of this city, was typical of the new ideal of a prince who was no longer the universal emperor as in the Akkadian period, but a scholarly leader at a time when literature was beginning to flower. His numerous statues portray confident devotion towards his gods and carry the text of hymns composed to commemorate the construction of temples, the main activity of the reign. Soon after Gudea, the third dynasty of Ur organized the 'Neo-Sumerian' empire which was more or less modelled along the old Akkadian lines. Its kings restored the great Sumerian temples: that of Nanna, moon-god at Ur; that of Inanna, the planet-goddess Venus, at Uruk; that of Enlil, god of air, at Nippur and of Ea, god of the deep, at Eridu. Each of these temples was given a ziggurat which was not so much a tower as a mighty terrace—62.50× 43 metres at Ur—surmounted by one or two smaller terraces and topped by a temple as if it were reaching into the heavens. Three great stairways, comparable to Jacob's Ladder, converged on the temple. Urnammu, founder of the third dynasty of Ur, erected a stele of which fragments survive and which commemorated the building of the great temple of Ur. The execution of this temple was perfect although its rigorously academic symmetry makes it somewhat monotonous.

The Ur empire was destroyed around 2000 b.c. Its downfall more or less coincided with the disappearance of the Sumerians. Their language was retained for religious use but was otherwise replaced by the Semitic Akkadian tongue. Semitic nomads coming from the west, the Amorites, adopted this language and founded a series of rival kingdoms at Isin, Larsa, Eshnunna and then at Babylon and in the north at Ashur and Mari.

At Mari the princes erected a sumptuous palace, decorated with paintings, a wonder of the world at that time. The earliest paintings, executed under the influence of the suzerains of Ur, show signs of Neo-Sumerian affinities. The most recent depicts the 'investiture' of Zimrilim, last king of Mari, in the presence of the war-goddess Ishtar whose temple door is guarded by river-goddesses and in a garden peopled by mythological figures. The kings of the other capitals had similarly conceived palaces, though not so large, with the broad throne-room opening onto the audience chamber and giving access to the inner apartments where, at Mari, a temple, probably dynastic, was constructed. It was here that the statue of Ishtup-ilum, one of the predecessors of Zimrilim, was found: a cruder version of the Gudea statues.

The temples were usually arranged along an axis, with a succession of rooms: a vestibule, then the open-air court where religious ceremonies took place, then an antechamber or antecella, and finally the holy of holies or cella. In the provincial town of Shadduppum (Tell Harmal, on the outskirts of Baghdad) the entrances were guarded by terracotta lions. In the town of Karana (Tell el Rimah) in the west of Assyria, the cella was cut into the body of the ziggurat with a temple backing onto it, the whole forming a monumental complex.

The initially modest dynasty of the city of Babylon, which was previously virtually unknown, ended by defeating its rivals during the reign of its sixth king, Hammurabi (1792–1750 b.c.), who restored a united empire to Mesopotamia. This prince is remembered for his legal code engraved on a stele, which was discovered in Susa with other monuments taken by the Elamites in the 12th century. The Neo-Sumerians had, in fact, already promulgated collections of comparable laws, but Hammurabi's laws were superior both in their range and in the classical purity of their Semitic language. At the top of the stele is carved an effigy of the king praying before Shamash, the sun-god and god of justice. Shamash can be recognized by the flames leaping from his shoulders, a symbolism inherited from Akkadian times. Contemporary with or slightly earlier than this stele is a royal head, identifiable as such by the rimmed cap and long beard, which illustrates the new conception of the enlightened king-lawgiver in contrast to the pious Gudea and the haughty Akkadian emperors.

Slowly the Babylonian empire declined, and at the beginning of the 16th century it was destroyed by raiding Hittites from Asia Minor. Then a foreign dynasty, the Kassites, ruled, without great distinction, until the 12th century. They have left us title deeds engraved on boundary stones or *kudurru,* which were placed under the protection of the gods. The latter were not represented in human form but rendered by emblems which, although of great interest to religious historians, are artistically sterile.

At Uruk a Kassite king erected a temple, whose decoration symbolized the cosmic domain of the goddess; on its façade moulded bricks formed a frieze of mountain gods alternating with river-nymphs. In this period the empire of the Mitanni, encircled by Indo-Europeans, extended from Syria to Iran. Near Kirkuk was a Mitannian city called Nuzi and in the centre was a palace next to a temple decorated with terracotta animals. In the 14th century the Assyrians broke away from the Mitannian yoke and gave birth to a new art movement which revived the earliest traditions in a beautiful naturalistic style.

Assyrian expansion was interrupted at the end of the 2nd millennium by the incursion of Aramaean nomads coming from the fringes of the Syrian desert. The invaders came close to subjugating the whole of Mesopotamia and when, eventually, in the 9th century, the Assyrians had overcome the danger, their kings turned to conquest in order to prevent insurrection. They pushed their borders further and further out, until their collapse in 612.

In the 9th century the capital was Kalakh, the modern Nimrud, south-east of Nineveh, while further south Ashur remained the religious centre. Ashurnasirpal II (884–859) constructed his palace according to what was to become the regular pattern: a 'public' forecourt onto which the throne-room opened, and an inner court containing the residential and reception rooms. Inspired by Hittite models, the Assyrians decorated the entrances with colossal figures, intimidating to an adversary but reassuring to the inhabitants. The throne-room was completely covered in reliefs illustrating on one or two levels the king's victories and his hunting exploits. The palace stood next to a temple so that the king could fulfil his role of priest. Sometimes the temple was even incorporated into the palace. Ashurnasirpal II and his son Shalmaneser III (858–824) alone among the Assyrian kings had their statues sculpted in the hieratic style. At Balawat they covered the temple doors with embossed bronze sheets depicting their feats of courage as in a strip cartoon. After Shalmaneser III Assyria went through a long period of decline until a revival under Tiglathpileser III. One of his successors, Sargon II (721–705), shifted his capital to the new city of Dur-Sharrukin (Khorsabad). The palace, which stood astride the city wall, covered an area of 10 hectares (25 acres). Its layout resembled that of the Nimrud palace, but the outside walls were covered with huge decorations. The decorations inside, portraying incidents in the king's life, showed a greater feeling for nature than had been seen before.

Sargon's successors made Nineveh their capital. Sennacherib (704–681) had his palace laid out along different lines, nearer to the style of the Babylonian residences. He patronized an art that reached its peak under his grandson Ashurbanipal (669–627). During this period, the sculptors alternated between creating vast frescoes to portray great events on the largest scale and chronicling episodes in miniature, on registers with accompanying inscriptions. Sennacherib's campaign against Judah and Ashurbanipal's against the Elamites were depicted with documentary precision and a feeling for nature that were only surpassed in hunting scenes where the Oriental artist's traditional sympathy towards animals is manifested. The Assyrian kings imported ivory inlaid furniture from the Levant as spoils of war, or had it made by expatriate ivory-workers who introduced an artistic cosmopolitanism with marked Egyptian affinities.

Undermined by civil war, the Assyrian empire was eventually destroyed by an alliance of Medes and Babylonians. The palaces of the Babylonian kings Nabopolassar and, above all, Nebuchadnezzar II (604–562) were really groups of palaces in a complex which included a great warehouse, mistakenly thought to

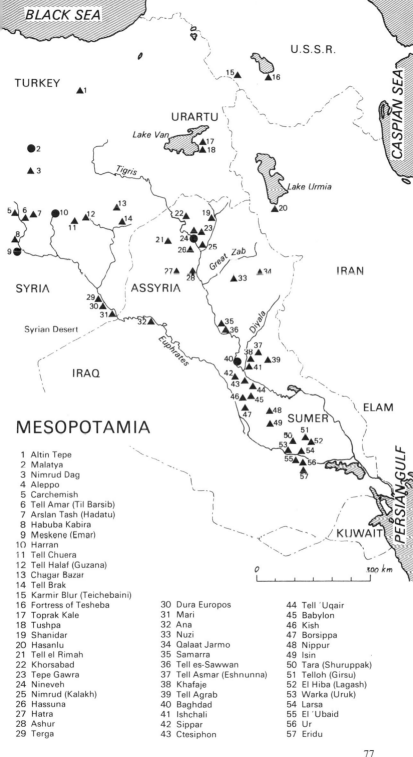

MESOPOTAMIA

1 Altin Tepe
2 Malatya
3 Nimrud Dag
4 Aleppo
5 Carchemish
6 Tell Amar (Til Barsib)
7 Arslan Tash (Hadatu)
8 Habuba Kabira
9 Meskene (Emar)
10 Harran
11 Tell Chuera
12 Tell Halaf (Guzana)
13 Chagar Bazar
14 Tell Brak
15 Karmir Blur (Teichebaini)
16 Fortress of Tesheba
17 Toprak Kale
18 Tushpa
19 Shanidar
20 Hasanlu
21 Tell el Rimah
22 Khorsabad
23 Tepe Gawra
24 Nineveh
25 Nimrud (Kalakh)
26 Hassuna
27 Hatra
28 Ashur
29 Terga

30 Dura Europos
31 Mari
32 Ana
33 Nuzi
34 Qalaat Jarmo
35 Samarra
36 Tell es-Sawwan
37 Tell Asmar (Eshnunna)
38 Khafaje
39 Tell Agrab
40 Baghdad
41 Ishchali
42 Sippar
43 Ctesiphon

44 Tell 'Uqair
45 Babylon
46 Kish
47 Borsippa
48 Nippur
49 Isin
50 Tara (Shuruppak)
51 Telloh (Girsu)
52 El Hiba (Lagash)
53 Warka (Uruk)
54 Larsa
55 El 'Ubaid
56 Ur
57 Eridu

be 'hanging gardens'. The ramparts were placed close by the town's main gate, a gate dedicated to Ishtar formed by glazed bricks decorated with animals in white and yellow on a blue ground. In the heart of the town was the double temple of Bel Marduk: one building contained the shrines of the god and his court of lesser divinities, and quite separate from it was the high temple, on top of the famous Tower of Babel, 91 metres high and resembling, on a larger scale, the Neo-Sumerian ziggurats.

Babylon continued to be an important city after the Persian conquest, but it went into decline when the capital was transferred first to Seleucia and then, during the time of the Parthians, to Ctesiphon. From the 1st to the 3rd century A.D., under the vassal princes of the Parthians, a remarkable renaissance took place in the former Assyria. At Ashur a Persian-type palace was erected of brick, containing *iwans,* rooms like enormous niches which opened onto the façades. At Hatra, a holy city situated in the steppe to the west of Ashur, similar structures were built next to columned buildings of Hellenistic type. Arab princes such as Sanatruq were virtually independent of Parthian suzerainty and provided for their temples richly robed statues of themselves in Persian costume with pleated trousers and long tunic. The most impressive sculpture is of the goddess Allat, successor to the Assyro-Babylonian Ishtar. Like Ishtar she is carried by a lion, but she is dressed like Athena and is accompanied by two minor goddesses: a good illustration of the perennial nature of religious tradition.

In the 3rd century the Sassanid Persians destroyed the Parthian empire and its vassal kingdoms and took possession of the whole of Mesopotamia. Their palace at Ctesiphon is evidence of Iranian primacy. An immense *iwan* opens between façades made up of a series of columned arcades in an arrangement quite unlike anything in Roman architecture. And so a new tradition was born, the basis of later developments in Islamic civilization.

MAJOR MUSEUMS

East Germany	Staatliche Museen, East Berlin
France	Musée du Louvre, Paris
Great Britain	British Museum, London
	Ashmolean Museum, Oxford
Iraq	Iraq Museum, Baghdad
U.S.A.	University Museum, Philadelphia

CONCISE BIBLIOGRAPHY

AMIET, P. *L'Art antique du Proche-Orient.* Paris, 1977.

FRANKFORT, H. *The Art and Architecture of the Ancient Orient.* 4th ed. London, 1970.

MOORTGAT, A. *Die Kunst Vorderasiens.* Cologne, 1967.

ORTHMANN, W. *Der alte Orient.* Propyläen Kunstgeschichte, vol. 14. Berlin, 1975.

PARROT, A. *Archéologie mésopotamienne.* 2 vols. Paris, 1946 and 1953.

——————— *Assur.* L'Univers des Formes. Paris, 1961.

——————— *Sumer.* L'Univers des Formes. Paris, 1960. *Sumer,* trans. Stuart Gilbert and James Emmons. London, 1960.

STROMMENGER, E., and HIRMER, M. *Fünf Jahrtausende Mesopotamien. Die Kunst von den Anfängen bis zu Alexander dem Grossen.* Munich, 1962. *The Art of Mesopotamia,* trans. Christina Haglund. London, 1964.

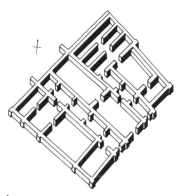

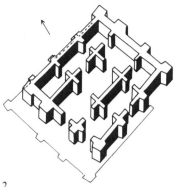

1
Level I house, Tell es-Sawwan, near
Samarra, *c.* 6000/5500 B.C.

2
House of the Samarra period at Choga
Mami, to the north-east of Baghdad,
c. 5500 B.C.

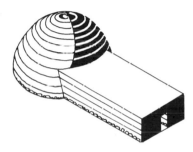

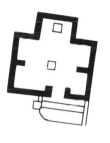

3
Round house, Tell Arpachiyah, near
Nineveh, Tell Halaf period, *c.* 4000
B.C.

4
Level XVI temple, Eridu, southern
Mesopotamia, between 5500 and 5000
B.C.

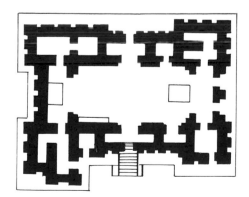

5   Temple on a terrace from Level VII, Eridu, end of 'Ubaid period, *c.* 4200 B.C.

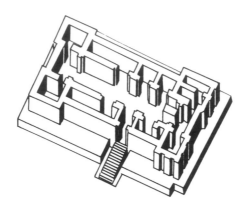

6   Temple on a terrace from Level VI, Eridu, end of 'Ubaid period, *c.* 4000 B.C.

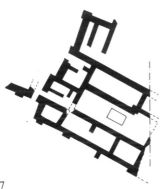

7
Level XVIII temple, Tepe Gawra, to the north-east of Nineveh, beginning of 'Ubaid period, *c.* 4500 B.C.

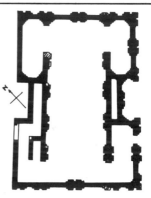

8
Level XIII, north temple, Tepe Gawra, end of 'Ubaid period, *c.* 4000 B.C.

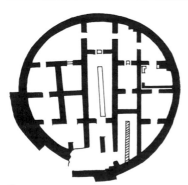

9
Level XI, 'round house', Tepe Gawra, beginning of Gawra period, *c.* 3800 B.C.

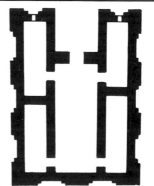

10
Level VIII, south-west temple, Tepe Gawra, end of Gawra period, *c.* 3000 B.C.

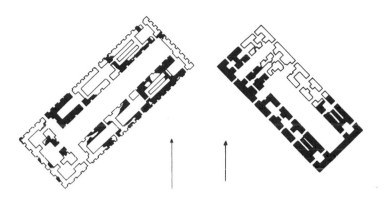

11
Eanna temple of the goddess Inanna,
Level V, 'Limestone Temple', Uruk,
c. 3400 B.C.

12
Eanna temple, Level IV Q, 'Temple
C', Uruk, c. 3200 B.C.

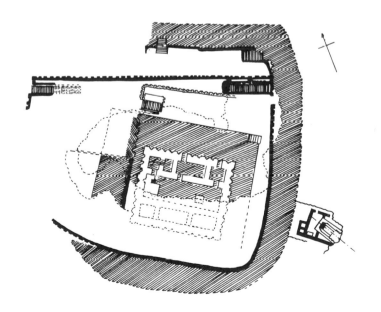

13   Painted temple, on a terrace, Tell 'Uqair, to the east of Babylon, c. 3200 B.C.

14   Ziggurat of Anu, god of the heavens, Uruk, Jemdet Nasr period,
c. 3100 B.C.

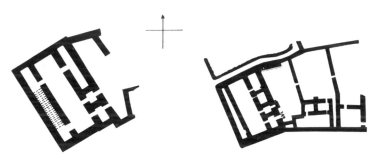

15
Temple of Sin, Level I, Khafaje,
Diyala region, to the east of Baghdad,
c. 3100 B.C.

16
Temple of Sin, Level IV, Khafaje, end
of Jemdet Nasr period, *c.* 2900 B.C.

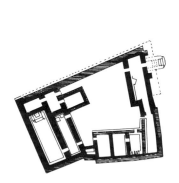

17
Temple of Sin, Level VIII, Khafaje,
c. 2700/2600 B.C.

18
'Square Temple' of the god Abu, Tell
Asmar, formerly Eshnunna, *c.* 2750
B.C.

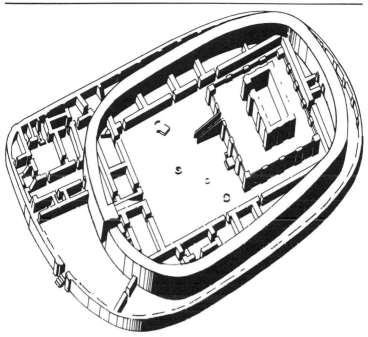

19 'Oval Temple', Khafaje, *c.* 2650 B.C.

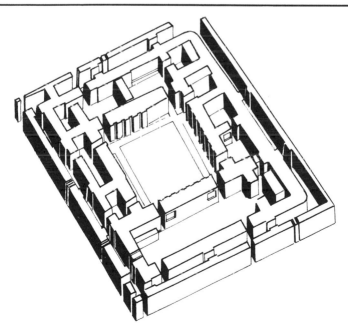

20 'Sacred zone' of the pre-Sargonid palace, Mari (Middle Euphrates),
c. 2500 B.C.

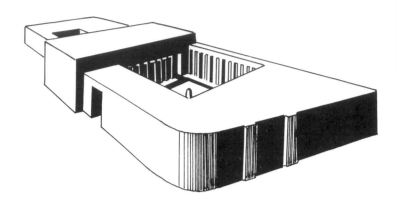

21   Temple of the goddess Ninni-Zaza, Mari, *c.* 2400 B.C.

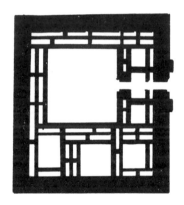

22   Palace-fortress of Naramsin, Tell Brak (western Syria), *c.* 2250 B.C.

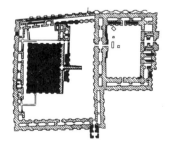

23   Temple with ziggurat of Nanna, Ur, 3rd dynasty of Ur period, *c.* 2100 B.C.

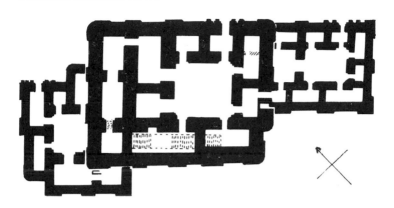

24   Temple covering the royal hypogea of the 3rd dynasty, Ur, *c.* 2050/2000 B.C.

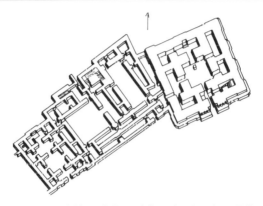

25   Temple of the deified king of Ur, and the prince's palace, Tell Asmar, formerly Eshnunna, *c.* 2050/1950 B.C.

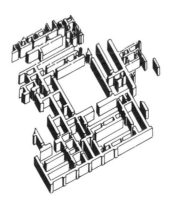

26   Unfinished palace, Larsa, beginning of the 2nd millennium

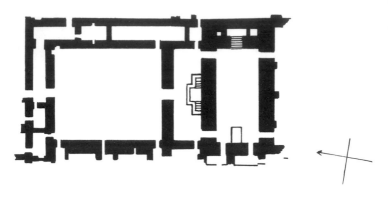

27   Official part of the palace of Zimrilim, Mari, 1st half of the 18th c. B.C.

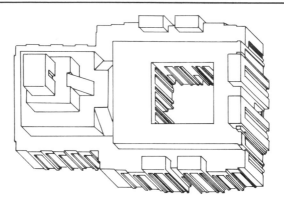

28   Temple with ziggurat, Tell el Rimah, formerly Karana, to the west of
         Nineveh, 19th c. B.C.

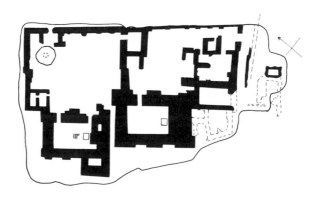

29   Double temple at the 15th-c. B.C. Mitannian city of Nuzi, near Kirkuk

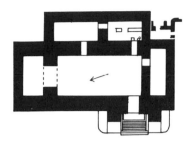
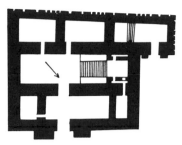

30
Temple of the goddess Ishtar, Level E,
Ashur, on the Tigris, period of the
kings of Ur, c. 2100/2000 B.C.

31
Ishtar temple at Ashur rebuilt by
Tukulti-Ninurta I in the 13th c. B.C.

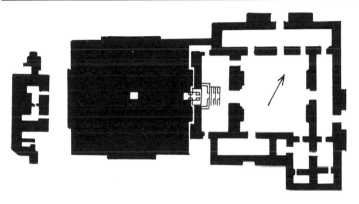

32   Temple with ziggurat at Kar-Tukulti-Ninurta, royal city built near Ashur
in the 13th c. B.C.

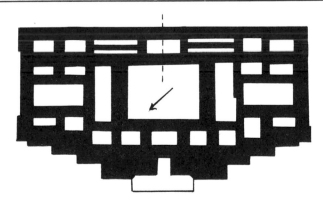

33   Twin temples of Sin (the moon-god) and Shamash (the sun-god), Ashur,
16th c. B.C.

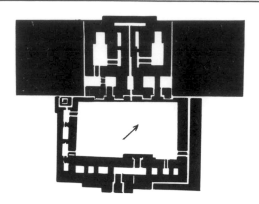

34   Twin temples with ziggurats of Anu (god of the heavens) and Adad (god
of the hurricane), Ashur, 12th c. B.C.

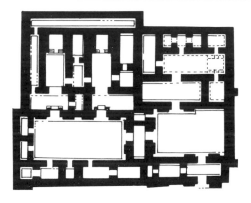

35   Twin temples of Nabu (god of writing) and Ishtar (goddess of war), Ashur,
9th c. B.C.

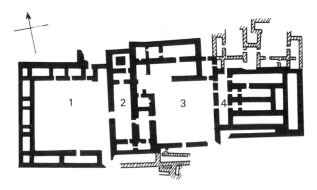

36   Assyrian palace, comprising from left to right (1) the forecourt, (2) the
throne-room, (3) the private inner court, (4) the temple, Arslan Tash
(northern Syria), 8th c. B.C.

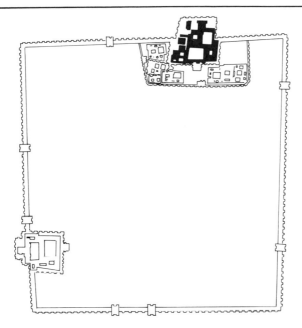

37 Plan of the city with the citadel-palace, Khorsabad, to the north-east of Nineveh, formerly Dur-Sharrukin, capital of Sargon II, end of the 8th c. B.C.

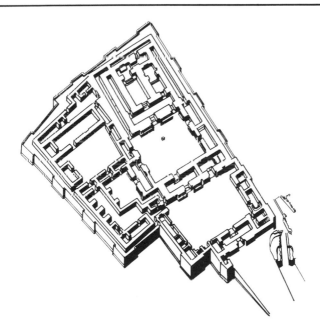

38 Temple of the god Nabu, built next to the citadel, Khorsabad, formerly Dur-Sharrukin, end of the 8th c. B.C.

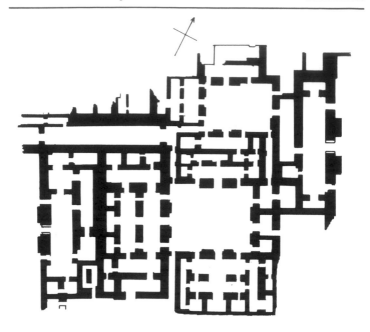

39   Plan of the palace of Sennacherib, Nineveh, beginning of the 7th c. B.C.

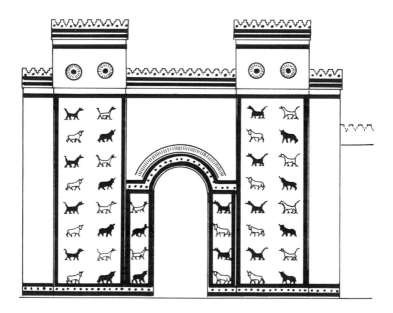

40   Ishtar Gate, built by Nebuchadnezzar II, Babylon, 1st half of 6th c. B.C.

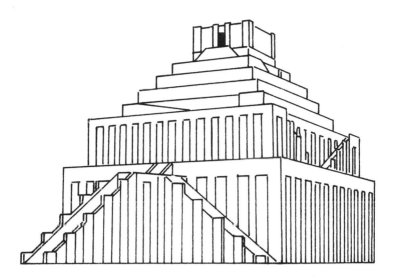

41 Reconstruction of the ziggurat or 'Tower of Babel' in Babylon as it was
    rebuilt in the 6th c., H. c. 90 m., equal to a side of the square base

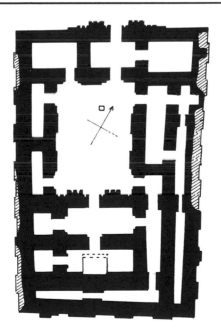

42 Temple of the goddess Ninmah, Babylon, 6th c. B.C.

43   Façade with *iwan*, an arcade opening onto the court, at the Parthian palace, Ashur, 1st/2nd c. A.D.

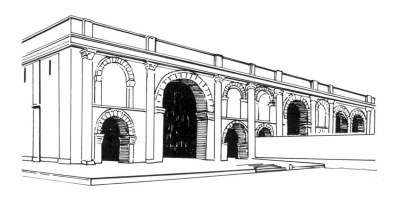

44   Temple with *iwans*, Hatra, in the desert to the west of Ashur, 2nd/3rd c. A.D.

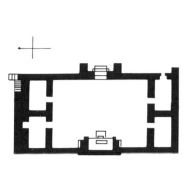

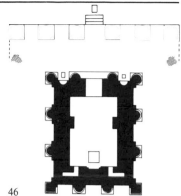

45
Parthian temple built of unbaked bricks, Hatra, 2nd–3rd c. A.D.

46
Plan of the temple of the god Gareus, Uruk (modern Warka), Parthian period

47
Sassanian palace attributed to Shapur I, Ctesiphon, near Babylon, mid-3rd c. A.D.

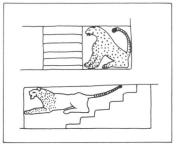

48
Mosaic facing of clay cones, Uruk,
Uruk period, *c.* 3200 B.C., Iraq Mus.,
Baghdad

49
Paintings from the temple podium,
Tell 'Uqair, Uruk period, *c.* 3200 B.C.,
Iraq Mus., Baghdad

50
Central panel of the painting called
the Investiture, Mari, palace of Zimrilim, *c.* 1760 B.C., Louvre

51
Mask of Humbaba decorating a door-
jamb, Tell el Rimah, limestone, *c.*
1800 B.C., Mosul Mus.

52
Moulded brick decoration, temple of
King Kara-indash, Uruk, H. 2.05 m.,
15th c. B.C., Iraq Mus., Baghdad

53
Painting from the palace, Nuzi,
Mitannian city near Kirkuk, 15th c.
B.C.

54
Painting from the terrace of the
palace, Kar-Tukulti-Ninurta near
Ashur, 13th c. B.C.

55
Enamelled clay wall tile, Ashur, 9th c. B.C., St. Mus., E. Berlin

56
Enamelled brick from the palace of Tukulti-Ninurta II (888–884 B.C.), Ashur, B.M.

57
Jamb from a gate in the palace of Sargon II (721–705 B.C.), Khorsabad, ancient Dur-Sharrukin, H. c. 4 m.

58
Caryatid-statue from a temple integrated into the palace of Sargon II, Khorsabad, gypsum

59   Painting from the Assyrian palace, Tell Ahmar, ancient Til Barsip (northern
Syria), 8th c. B.C.

60   Painting from the Assyrian palace, Tell Ahmar, ancient Til Barsip (northern
Syria), 8th c. B.C.

61
Ishtar Gate: enamelled bull, associated with Adad, Babylon, H. 1 m., 1st
half of 6th c. B.C., St. Mus., E. Berlin

62
Ishtar Gate: enamelled lion, Babylon,
H. 1 m., 1st half of 6th c. B.C., St. Mus.,
E. Berlin

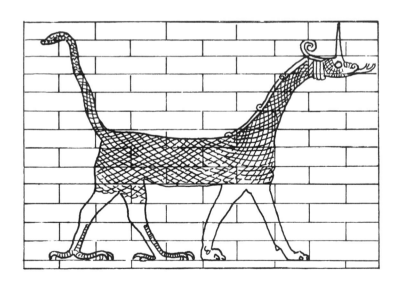

63   Ishtar Gate: dragon-serpent, Babylon, H. 1 m., 1st half of 6th c. B.C.,
St. Mus., E. Berlin

64
Stucco relief of the Sassanid palace at Kish, near Babylon, 5th c. A.D., Chicago Mus.

65
Stucco relief of the Sassanid palace at Kish (see No. 64)

66
Royal bust from No. 64

67
Profile of No. 66

68   Stele with hunting scene, Uruk, basalt, H. 80 cm., Uruk period, *c.* 3200 B.C.,
     Iraq Mus., Baghdad

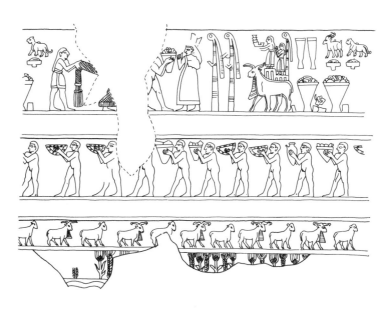

69   Cult vase, Uruk, low-relief decoration, alabaster, Jemdet Nasr period, *c.*
     3000 B.C., Iraq Mus., Baghdad

70
Punched relief, Khafaje, gypsum, H. 32 cm., *c.* 2700 B.C. (fragment at bottom from Ur), Iraq Mus., Baghdad

71
Punched relief with banquet scene, Khafaje, ancient Tutub, gypsum, H. 20 cm., *c.* 2700 B.C., Chicago Mus.

72
Relief with victory scene, Telloh, ancient Girsu, limestone, H. 18 cm., 1st half of 3rd millennium B.C., Louvre

73
War-god, Khafaje, ancient Tutub, alabaster, H. 10 cm., *c.* 2600 B.C., Iraq Mus., Baghdad

74
Mace-head of Mesalim, king of Kish, Telloh, ancient Girsu, limestone, H. 19 cm., *c.* 2600/2550 B.C., Louvre

75
Top view of No. 74: lion-headed eagle

76 Relief of Ur-Nanshe, king of Lagash, Telloh, ancient Girsu, limestone,
H. 40 cm., *c.* 2550/2500 B.C., Louvre

77
Relief of Ur-Nanshe, king of Lagash,
Telloh, ancient Girsu, gypsum, H.
15 cm., *c.* 2550/2500 B.C., Louvre

78
Stele of Ur-Nanshe, king of Lagash, El
Hiba, limestone, H. 91 cm., *c.* 2550/
2500 B.C., Iraq Mus., Baghdad

79 'Vultures Stele' raised by Eannatum, Telloh, ancient Girsu, limestone, H. 1.80 m., *c.* 2500–2450 B.C., Louvre

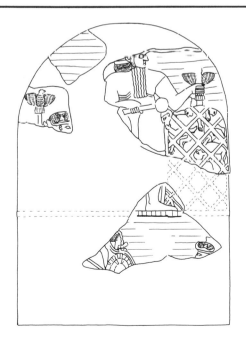

80 'Vultures Stele', reverse, Telloh, ancient Girsu

81
Punched relief: libation to a goddess, Telloh, ancient Girsu, limestone, H. 12 cm., *c.* 2400 B.C., Louvre

82
Plaque engraved with a cult scene, Nippur, schist, H. 19 cm., *c.* 2400 B.C., Mus. of Istanbul

83   Mosaic shell decoration: milking, temple of the goddess Ninhursag, El 'Ubaid, near Ur, H. 23 cm., first dynasty of Ur, *c.* 2450 B.C., Iraq Mus., Baghdad

84
Mythological relief, El 'Ubaid, near Ur, limestone, H. 14.5 cm., *c.* 2450 B.C., University Mus., Philadelphia

85
Fragment of a mythological relief, Mari, gypsum, H. 13.5 cm., *c.* 2540 B.C., Nat. Mus., Damascus

86   Stele of Sargon of Akkad brought from Babylonia, Susa, diorite, H. *c.* 50 cm., *c.* 2300 B.C., Louvre

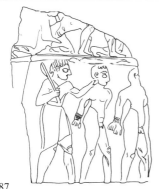

87
Fragment of stele of Sargon of Akkad brought from Babylonia, Susa, diorite, H. 46 cm., *c.* 2300 B.C., Louvre

88
Disc of Enkheduanna, Ur, calcite, D. 26.5 cm., *c.* 2300 B.C., University Mus., Philadelphia

89
Fragment of stele, Lower Mesopotamia, green alabaster, *c.* 2300/2250 B.C., Iraq Mus., Baghdad

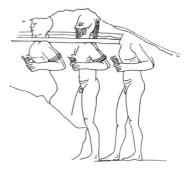

90
Fragment of green alabaster stele of the Akkadian period, *c.* 2300/2250 B.C., H. 21 cm., Iraq Mus., Baghdad

91   Stele of Naramsin, 4th king of Akkad, brought from Babylonia to Susa, reddish sandstone, H. 2 m., *c.* 2250/2200 B.C., Louvre

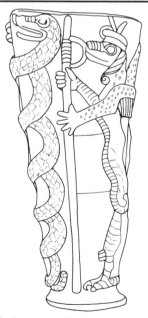

92
Libation vase of Gudea, prince of Lagash, Telloh, ancient Girsu, steatite, H. 23 cm., *c.* 2150 B.C., Louvre

93
Fragment of a relief from the Gudea period, Telloh, ancient Girsu, steatite, H. 14 cm., *c.* 2150 B.C., Louvre

94   Register from the stele of Urnammu, founder of the 3rd dynasty of Ur,
     limestone, *c.* 2100 B.C., University Mus., Philadelphia

95
Embossed plaquette, Babylonia, terracotta, H. 12 cm., beginning of 2nd
millennium B.C., Louvre

96
Upper part of code of Hammurabi,
brought as spoils to Susa, basalt, t. H.
2.25 m., 1792–1750 B.C., Louvre

97
Relief found in the temple of the god Ashur, Ashur, gypsum, H. 1.22 m., 15th–14th c., St. Mus., E. Berlin

98
Altar of Tukulti-Ninurta I (1241–1205 B.C.), Ashur, limestone, H. 57.5 cm., St. Mus., E. Berlin

99
Kudurru (boundary-stone) of Melishi-pak II, Susa, black limestone, H. 68 cm., early 12th c. B.C., Louvre

100
Kudurru (boundary-stone) of Mar-duknadinakhe, limestone, H. 61 cm., beginning of 11th c. B.C., B.M.

101   Relief of Nabupaliddina, Sippar (Babylonia), limestone, H. 18 cm., 9th c. B.C., B.M.

102   Relief from the throne-room of Ashurnasirpal II (884–859 B.C.), Nimrud, ancient Kalakh, gypsum, H. 1.78 m., B.M.

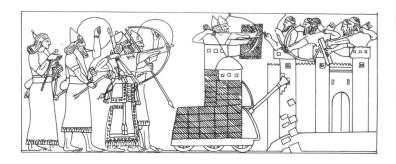

103   Relief from the palace of Ashurnasirpal II (884–859 B.C.), Nimrud, ancient
         Kalakh, gypsum, H. 98 cm., B.M.

104   Relief from palace of Ashurnasirpal II, Nimrud (see No. 103)

105   Relief from palace of Ashurnasirpal, Nimrud (see No. 103), H. 92 cm.

106
Relief from palace of Ashurnasirpal,
Nimrud (see No. 103), H. 2.44 m.

107
Relief from the temple of Ninurta,
Nimrud, ancient Kalakh, gypsum,
9th c. B.C., B.M.

108
Detail from the bronze door of Shal-
maneser III (858–824 B.C.), Balawat
(Assyria), H. 28 cm., B.M.

109
Detail from the obelisk of Shalmaneser III (858–824 B.C.), Nimrud,
ancient Kalakh, black alabaster, B.M.

110
Sargon II (721–705 B.C.) and a noble-
man, Khorsabad, gypsum, H. 2.98 m.,
Louvre

111
Genius conferring blessing, palace of
Sargon II (721–705 B.C.), Khorsabad,
gypsum, H. 3.06 m., Louvre

112   Palace of Sennacherib (704–681 B.C.): the king at the siege of Lachish, Nineveh, gypsum, B.M.

113   Rock-relief at Bavian (northern Assyria), beginning of the 7th c. B.C., H. (figures) 1.48 m.

114   Palace of Ashurbanipal (668–627 B.C.): the king in his chariot, Nineveh, gypsum, Louvre

115
Warriors in chariots, Nineveh (as No.
114), gypsum, Louvre

116
Arab cameleers in flight, Nineveh (as
No. 114), gypsum, B.M.

117
Deported Elamites, Nineveh (as No.
114), gypsum, Louvre

118
The king and queen's victory banquet,
Nineveh (as No. 114), H. 55 cm., B.M.

119   The king hunting, Nineveh (as No. 114), B.M.

120
Wounded lioness, Nineveh (as No. 114), B.M.

121
Wounded lion, Nineveh (as No. 114), B.M.

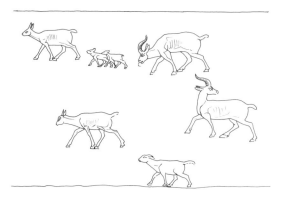

122   Animals in the Assyrian steppe, Nineveh (as No. 114), B.M.

123   *Kudurru* (boundary-stone) of Marduk-apla-iddina II (721–710 and 703 B.C.), Babylonia, limestone, H. 46 cm., St. Mus., E. Berlin

124
Votive stele of the Parthian period, Ashur, 1st–2nd c. A.D.

125
Altar with an infernal god, Hatra, alabaster, 2nd–3rd c. A.D., Iraq Mus., Baghdad

126   The goddess Ellat between two minor goddesses, Hatra, limestone, H. 1.15 m., 2nd–3rd c. A.D., Iraq Mus., Baghdad

127   The god Nergal, master of the underworld, Hatra, limestone, H. 90 cm.,
2nd–3rd c. A.D., Iraq Mus., Baghdad

128   Relief with three goddesses, Hatra, alabaster, Mosul Mus.

129
Statuette of naked woman, Tell es-Sawwan, alabaster, 1st half of 6th millennium, Iraq Mus., Baghdad

130
Figurine of naked woman, Ur, terracotta, H. 16 cm., 'Ubaid period, c. 4000 B.C., Iraq Mus., Baghdad

131
Figurine of mother with child, Ur, terracotta, H. 14 cm., 'Ubaid period, c. 4000 B.C., Iraq Mus., Baghdad

132
'Eye' idol with child, from Tell Brak, west of Assyria, alabaster, c. 3200 B.C., Nat. Archaeol. Mus., Aleppo

133
Statuette of naked priest-king, Uruk region, limestone, H. 29.5 cm., Uruk period, c. 3200 B.C., Louvre

134
Marble head of woman, Uruk, H. 20 cm., Jemdet Nasr period, c. 3000 B.C., Iraq Mus., Baghdad

135
Worshipper, temple of Sin, Khafaje, limestone, H. 11 cm., *c.* 3000/2900 B.C., Iraq Mus., Baghdad

136
Tall worshipper, square temple of Abu, Tell Asmar, gypsum, H. 72 cm., *c.* 2800/2700 B.C., Iraq Mus.

137
Tall worshipper, square temple of Abu, Tell Asmar, gypsum, H. 59 cm., *c.* 2800/2700 B.C., Iraq Mus., Baghdad

138
Vase-bearing genius, square temple of Abu, Tell Asmar, alabaster, H. 21 cm., *c.* 2800/2700 B.C., Iraq Mus., Baghdad

139
Head of worshipper, temple of Sin IX,
Khafaje, limestone, H. 8 cm., *c.* 2700
B.C., Oriental Inst. of Chicago

140
Back view of No. 139

141
Vase-bearing genie, temple of Shara,
Tell Agrab, limestone, H. 10 cm., *c.*
2700 B.C., Chicago Mus.

142
Naked worshipper, temple of Nintu,
Khafaje, alabaster, H. 24.5 cm., *c.*
2700 B.C., Iraq Mus., Baghdad

143
Squatting worshipper, temple of
Nintu, Khafaje, marble, H. 15.5 cm., *c.*
2700/2600 B.C., Iraq Mus., Baghdad

144
Standing worshipper, temple of
Nintu, Khafaje, alabaster, H. 30 cm.,
c. 2700 B.C., Worcester Art Mus.

145
Pair of wrestlers bearing vases, temple of Nintu, Khafaje, copper, H. 10.2 cm., *c.* 2700/2600 B.C., Iraq Mus.

146
Model of a chariot, temple of Shara, Tell Agrab, copper, H. 7.2 cm., *c.* 2700 B.C., Iraq Mus., Baghdad

147
Support in the shape of a naked man, 'Oval Temple', Khafaje, copper, H. 55.5 cm., *c.* 2700 B.C., Iraq Mus.

148
Statuette of a worshipper, Eridu, alabaster, H. 16 cm., *c.* 2600/2500 B.C., Iraq Mus., Baghdad

149   Worshipper, temple of Nintu, Khafaje, alabaster, H. 30 cm., *c.* 2500 B.C.,
         University Mus., Philadelphia

150
Worshipper, temple of Sin IX, Kha-
faje, limestone, H. 14.9 cm., *c.* 2600
B.C., Iraq Mus., Baghdad

151
Profile of No. 150

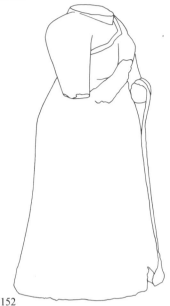

152
Worshipper, temple of Nintu, Khafaje, alabaster, H. 30.8 cm., *c.* 2600/
2500 B.C., University Mus., Phila.

153
Head of a worshipper, temple of
Shara, Tell Agrab, limestone, H.
12 cm., *c.* 2600 B.C., Iraq Mus.

154
Worshipper, temple of Nintu, Kha-
faje, limestone, H. 41.5 cm., *c.* 2500
B.C., Oriental Inst. of Chicago

155
The Intendant Ebikh-il, temple of Ishtar Virile at Mari, alabaster, H.
52.5 cm., *c.* 2450 B.C., Louvre

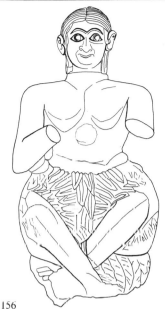

156
Statuette of Ur-Nanshe, the great singer, Mari, gypsum, H. 26 cm., *c.* 2450/2400 B.C., Nat. Mus., Damascus

157
Naked goddess, Mari, bronze, silver and gold, H. 11.3 cm., *c.* 2400 B.C., Nat. Mus., Damascus

158
Naked woman, pre-Sargonid palace at Mari, ivory, H. 8.4 cm., *c.* 2400 B.C., Nat. Mus., Damascus

159
Copper bull, El 'Ubaid near Ur, H. 62 cm., *c.* 2450 B.C., B.M.

160
Statue of a prince in the Akkadian
period, Ashur, diorite, *c.* 2300/2250
B.C., St. Mus., E. Berlin

161
Statue of a prince, back view (see No.
160)

162   Royal head of the Akkadian period, Nineveh, bronze or copper, H. 30 cm.,
       c. 2250/2200 B.C., Iraq Mus., Baghdad

163   Mythological group, Tell Asmar, ancient Eshnunna, alabaster, H.
          10.2 cm., c. 2300/2200 B.C., Iraq Mus., Baghdad

164   Mythological group, back view (see No. 163)

165   Head of prince from Adab, gypsum, H. 9 cm., end of the 3rd millennium,
          Oriental Inst. of Chicago

166
Head of Gudea, prince of Lagash, Telloh, ancient Girsu, diorite, H. 23 cm., *c.* 2150 B.C., Louvre

167
Statue of Gudea as architect, Telloh, ancient Girsu, diorite, H. 93 cm., *c.* 2150 B.C., Louvre

168
Statue of Gudea with flowing vase, Telloh, ancient Girsu, calcite, H. 63 cm., *c.* 2150 B.C., Louvre

169
Woman with shawl, Telloh, ancient Girsu, steatite, H. 17 cm., time of Gudea, *c.* 2150 B.C., Louvre

170
Bust of Ur-Ningirsu, son of Gudea, Telloh, ancient Girsu, dolerite, H. 20 cm., *c.* 2100 B.C., St. Mus., E. Berlin

171
Lower part of statue of Ur-Ningirsu, son of Gudea, Telloh, ancient Girsu, brown alabaster, *c.* 2100 B.C., Louvre

172   Androcephalous bull, Telloh, ancient Girsu, steatite, H. 12 cm., time of Gudea, *c.* 2150/2100 B.C., Louvre

173
Swimmer, Tell Asmar, ancient Eshnunna, bronze, H. 6.7 cm., beginning of 2nd millennium, Iraq Mus.

174
Swimmer (see No. 173)

175
Four-faced god from Ishchali (?),
bronze, H. 17.3 cm., beginning of 2nd
millennium, Oriental Inst. of Chicago

176
Four-faced goddess from Ishchali (?),
bronze, H. 16.2 cm., beginning of 2nd
millennium, Oriental Inst. of Chicago

177
Statue of Puzur-Ishtar, from Babylon,
limestone, H. 1.75 m., 19th c. B.C.,
Berlin and Istanbul

178
Goddess with flowing vase, Mari,
limestone, H. 1.49 m., 1st half of 18th
c. B.C., Nat. Archaeol. Mus., Aleppo

179
Royal head of Hammurabi (?), Susa, from Babylonia, diorite, H. 15 cm., 19th/18th c. B.C., Louvre

180
Bronze dedicated to Hammurabi, Larsa, bronze and gold, H. 19.5 cm., 18th c. B.C., Louvre

181
Guardian-lion of a temple, Tell Harmal, ancient Shaduppum, terracotta, 19th c. B.C., Iraq Mus., Baghdad

182
Hurrian goddess in ivory, Nuzi, near Kirkuk, H. 8.2 cm., 15th c. B.C., Iraq Mus., Baghdad

183
Statue of Ashurnasirpal II (884–859
B.C.), Nimrud, ancient Kalakh, ala-
baster, H. 1.06 m., B.M.

184
Head of an Assyrian (?) princess,
Nineveh, limestone, 8th–7th c. B.C.,
B.M.

185   The demon Pazuzu, Assyria, bronze, H. 14.5 cm., 8th–7th c. B.C., Louvre

186
God with lion's cub, Hatra, alabaster,
H. 90 cm., 3rd c. A.D., Iraq Mus.,
Baghdad

187
Statue of a goddess, Hatra, alabaster,
H. 84 cm., 3rd c. A.D., Iraq Mus.,
Baghdad

188
The king of Hatra presenting a
statuette of a young god, limestone,
H. 1.97 m., 3rd c. A.D., Iraq Mus.

189
Head of a statue of a nobleman from
Hatra, limestone, 2nd–3rd c. A.D., Iraq
Mus., Baghdad

190   Pottery with incised ornament, Hassuna (Assyria), Hassuna period, begin-
      ning of 6th millennium, Iraq Mus., Baghdad

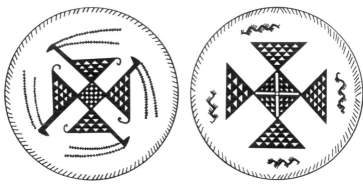

191
Painted   bowl,   Samarra   (Middle   192
Tigris), Samarra period, *c.* 5000 B.C.   Painted bowl (see No. 191)

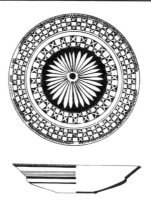

193   Polychrome painted bowl, Arpachiyah, to the east of Nineveh, Tell Halaf
      period, *c.* 5000/4500 B.C., Iraq Mus., Baghdad

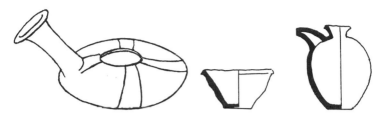

194
'Tortoise' jar, Tepe Gawra, to the
north-east of Nineveh, 'Ubaid period,
end of 5th millennium

195
Pottery of the Uruk period, 2nd half of
the 4th millennium

196   Painted vase, Jemdet Nasr, to the east of Babylon, c. 3000 B.C.

197
Carved cult vase, temple of Inanna, Uruk, limestone, *c.* 3000 B.C., Iraq Mus., Baghdad

198
Royal tomb, Ur, reconstructed lyre, wood, head of bull in gold, *c.* 2500 B.C., Iraq Mus., Baghdad

199
Shell mosaic decorating the front of a lyre, Ur, *c.* 2500 B.C., University Mus., Philadelphia

200
'Standards', detail from shell-mosaic picture, Ur, *c.* 2500 B.C., B.M.

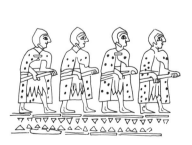

201
'Standards', detail (see No. 200)

202
Pendant in the shape of a lion-headed eagle, Mari, lapis lazuli and gold, *c.* 2400 B.C., Nat. Mus., Damascus

203
Engraved shell plaquette: Syrian
goddess, Mari, *c.* 2400 B.C., Louvre

204
Ivory plaquette, Nimrud, ancient
Kalakh (Assyria), 8th c. B.C.

205
Stamp-seal with genius, master of animals, Tepe Gawra, 'Ubaid period, *c.*
4000 B.C., University Mus., Phila

206
Cylinder seal impression, Uruk,
temple of Inanna, Level IV, Uruk
period, *c.* 3300 B.C.

207
Cylinder-seal impression, Uruk (see
No. 206)

208
Cylinder-seal impression, Uruk (see
No. 206)

209   Cylinder-seal, Uruk, Level III, Jemdet Nasr period, St. Mus., E. Berlin

210   Cylinder-seal (as No. 209), Iraq Mus., Baghdad

211
'Brocade' style cylinder-seal, Khafaje (Diyala region), early dynastic I, *c.* 2800 B.C.

212
Cylinder-seal impression, Ur, early dynastic I, *c.* 2800 B.C.

213   Cylinder-seal with a frieze of animals and heroes, Mesopotamia, early
dynastic II, *c.* 2700/2600 B.C., Louvre

214   Cylinder-seal with combat between herbivores and beasts of prey, Ur,
royal tomb, *c.* 2500 B.C., Iraq Mus., Baghdad

215
Cylinder-seal of the Lady Pu-abi, Ur,
royal tomb, lapis lazuli, *c.* 2500 B.C.,
B.M.

216
Cylinder-seal: boat-god and stepped
building, Kish, near Babylon, *c.*
2500/2400 B.C., Iraq Mus., Baghdad

217
Cylinder-seal with mythological sub-
ject, Mesopotamia, *c.* 2400/2350 B.C.,
B.M.

218
Cylinder-seal of the Akkadian period:
sun-god coming out of mountains,
Susa, *c.* 2300 B.C., Louvre

219
Cylinder-seal: the god of the deep
with guardians, Mesopotamia, Akkadian period, Bibliothèque Nat.

220
Cylinder-seal: sun-gods paying homage to the god of the deep, Ur, Akkadian period, *c.* 2250 B.C., Iraq Mus.

221   Seal of the governor of the city of Ishkun-Sin, Mesopotamia, *c.* 2100 B.C.,
B.M.

222   Cylinder-seal of the period of the first dynasty of Babylon, Susa, *c.* 1800
B.C., Louvre

223
Cylinder-seal with Sumerian prayer,
Babylonia, Kassite period, 14th–13th
c. B.C., Louvre

224
Renaissance-period cylinder-seal, As-
syria, 14th–13th c., Pierpont Morgan
Library, N.Y.

225   Cylinder-seal with mythological subject, Assyria, period of the neo-Assyrian empire, 8th c. B.C., B.M.

226   Rock-crystal cylinder-seal with mythological subject, Assyria, end of the
period of the neo-Assyrian empire, Louvre

227
Cylinder-seal: Ishtar, goddess of war,
Assyria, 7th c. B.C., B.M.

228
Cylinder-seal: a genius bearing the
winged disc of the sky, Assyria, 7th c.,
B.M.

229
Cylinder-seal: a god killing a dragon,
Assyria, 7th c. B.C., Pierpont Morgan
Library, N.Y.

230
Impression from the seal of Sen-
nacherib, Nimrud, beginning of 7th c.
B.C., Iraq Mus., Baghdad

THE LEVANT

SYRIA AND PALESTINE

The favourable climate of Asia's Mediterranean seaboard has encouraged man to settle since earliest times, the pluvial ages there coinciding with the glacial ages of Europe. The inhabitants of the Mount Carmel caves, to take a notable example, were related to Neanderthal man. Thus, it is not surprising that from the 10th millennium B.C. onwards a long process known as the Neolithic Revolution had been taking place, continuing through the Natufian period, from Palestine to the Euphrates. Characteristic of this period are minute microlithic tools, beautiful naturalistic bone carvings and strongly stylized work in calcite. In the tropical climate of the lower Jordan valley was to be found the ancient site of Jericho. The villagers who dwelt there were to turn it into a substantial town covering ten acres, dominated by an extraordinary tower with an internal staircase.

In the 7th millennium, a new village was built at Jericho of massive bricks: the houses surrounded a little sanctuary with an antechamber preceded by a portico. The dead were buried in two stages, the head being detached from the body, stripped to the bone and then covered with clay plaster so that the facial features could be modelled and likenesses made—they were painted and had eyes inset with shells. There is evidence of a similar funeral custom in Syria during the period in which pottery was introduced. Then, as in most of the Palestinian sites, a climatic change caused Jericho to be abandoned. Byblos, however, now rose up on the Lebanese coast and developed along with other sites such as Ras Shamra in the north, facing the isle of Cyprus.

During the course of the 4th millennium Palestine was resettled by newcomers who had to learn to adapt to different ecological conditions. At Beersheba, in the southern desert (the Negev), several agricultural and stockbreeding villages with dwelling-places cut out of the ground, like caves, were taken over by artisans who specialized in the making of basalt vases, in copper-working and in the use of ivory.

Some characteristics of the vigorously styled statuettes of naked men and women have parallels in Amratian Egypt. Further north, particularly near Tel Aviv, burial caves were dug out to store masses of terracotta funerary urns shaped, apparently, to represent houses on supports, and sometimes given animal forms. At the same time, several pottery traditions began to emerge, probably corresponding to different groups of people, some of whom imitated basalt vases with a fenestrated base. Chalcolithic Palestine was the melting-pot of urban civilization and the population that inspired it were the first Canaanites, a sedentary Semitic people who were to establish contact with first-dynasty Egypt.

141

The Canaanites organized themselves into small warrior kingdoms with towns protected by enormous ramparts. At Ai, the prince occupied a palace which contained a large hall with pillars of wood. At Megiddo, in the Esdraelon plain, the simple temple was composed of one chamber with two pillars, in accordance with the prevailing tradition in the Levant. It backed onto a 'high place' shaped like a truncated cone, a great altar open to the sky.

The Egyptians made a sort of protectorate out of Byblos, through which they imported the timber they needed from the Lebanon. The pharaohs sent quantities of offerings there to be consecrated in the temple to the Lady of Byblos, the goddess Isis-Hathor. They also honoured the kings of Ebla, capital of a powerful kingdom to the south of Aleppo which, in the middle of the 3rd millennium, had adapted the cuneiform script to the language of the western Semites. Subsequently, Syria and Palestine fell prey to invaders—Amorite nomads who ended by establishing a series of dynamic dynasties during the 2nd millennium. The temples of the restored Ebla guarded great sacred basins with sculpted decorations which made an original interpretation of Mesopotamian models. It was during this period that the princes of Byblos had themselves buried in the Egyptian manner, with grave furnishings imported from Egypt or modelled on Egyptian lines. A temple was laid out around a huge obelisk symbolizing the god. Scattered in the courtyard around the obelisk were a great many smaller obelisks, representing statues of worshippers, in accordance with ideas peculiar to the western Semites.

The 18th century saw the birth of Syrian classicism, well represented in the little kingdom of Alalakh in the lower Orontes valley. Its king, Yarimlim, built a terraced palace with columns and painted decorations, adjoining a temple of the same simple conception as the one at Megiddo. Some of the statues consecrated there show Egyptian affinities but others have a vigorous originality that can be seen again in the cylinder-seals—which reflect a mythology dominated by the storm-god Hadad or Baal, and the naked or unveiling goddess Ashera, or Anat the goddess of war. Baal was depicted on a monumental stele set up in the main temple at Ugarit (Ras Shamra): he is brandishing a spear symbolizing lightning, its shaft ending in a leafy stem to indicate the happy results of his intervention. This was the golden age in Canaan, the future Palestine, whose princes, the Hyksos, invaded Egypt. At the beginning of the 16th century the Egyptians took their revenge by annexing the whole country. They even penetrated into northern Syria, where they came up against the Mitannian empire in which an Indo-European aristocracy ruled over native Hurrians and Semites.

The sturdy 'cubist' statue of King Idrimi of Alalakh, with his fantastic biography inscribed on it, is a typically clumsy example of one trend in Syrian sculpture of the period. Then, in the 14th and 13th centuries, when the Hittites of Asia Minor had supplanted the Mitanni, Aegean seafarers, Cretans and above all Mycenaeans and Cypriots, distributed their beautiful painted wares throughout the Levant. At this time a new cosmopolitanism became evident, illustrated at Ugarit by the multiplicity of written languages. To them the Canaanite tongue was added, which used a cuneiform alphabet that was the direct ancestor of our own. In art, this cosmopolitanism brought together contributions from Egypt, the Aegean, Mesopotamia and sometimes from the Hittites too. These mingling influences can be seen in the contemporary showpieces, especially the ivories—either making up individual items such as boxes, or inlaid into precious furniture. In the poorer land of Canaan in the south, archaic cults were mixed with mainly Egyptian influences. The temples of Hazor, the metropolis of Upper Galilee, are typical of this so-called Late Bronze Age civilization. In the smallest of the temples, steles symbolizing worshippers were ranged in a half-circle next to a solitary statue and a monolithic door-jamb. On the door-jamb, a lion was carved in bas-relief with its head done in the round, in line with the tradition already seen in Ebla.

This, therefore, was the environment into which the Hebrews came. Their Exodus almost certainly took place in the 13th century, just before the devastation wrought first by the 'Sea Peoples' and then by the Aramaean nomads. The Aramaeans profited from the decline of the great powers to found warlike kingdoms and drive the autochthones back onto the coast, which thus acquired its Phoenician identity. From that time on, the Phoenicians turned to the colonization of the western Mediterranean, bringing with them their alphabet, then only recently invented, and their divinity cults which were often symbolized by steles or baetyls and solemnized by infant sacrifice. The Aramaeans, grown rich from trading with the powers to the east, adopted the alphabet and most of the Phoenician artistic conventions. They spread the building of the type of palace known as *hilani*, characterized by a columned portico with animal-sculpted door-jambs. The lower part of the walls was faced with sculpted slabs or orthostats which, although heavy in style, were vividly diverse in conception. The most impressive *hilani* is the palace of a minor king called Kapara at Guzana (Tell Halaf), near the source of the Habur, where the columns were in the form of heavy statues of deities. Behind a similar palace at Tell Tayanat, a small temple was built with a porch of two columns leading into a large central room, at the end of which was the holy of holies. This traditional Syrian layout was precisely that of the Temple of Solomon, which, according to the pictures on ivory inlays, must have been decorated in much the same way. The Phoenicians and Aramaeans developed ivory-work to its artistic pinnacle. Their style was extremely eclectic, though the strongest influence was that of the Egyptians whose attractive iconographic themes were appropriated without always being understood. Ivories like these have been found in Samaria, although those from other Israelite towns, such as Megiddo, with their enormous royal warehouses (long mistaken for stables), are better known to us.

The countries of the Levant were in time annexed by the Persian empire which, however, respected their individuality. Their art they preserved, while gradually absorbing ideas from Greece. The 4th-century anthropoid sarcophagi at Sidon, although Egyptian in style, often had faces carved by Ionian artists. With the domination of Rome, Hellenism triumphed, and the best symbol of it is without doubt the enormous complex at Baalbek (2nd century A.D.), consecrated to the storm-god in his new guise as the sun-god, Jupiter Heliopolitanus.

During this period the nomads, whose caravans brought goods from the east, were also becoming wealthy. The Nabataeans, who were spread throughout Transjordan and Arabia, made Petra their trading post. Tombs carved in the rocks above the town imitated the façades of Roman palaces; but here the souls of the dead were symbolized, in the Semitic tradition, by great pyramidal steles or obelisks. In the heart of the Syrian desert stood Palmyra, a caravan site already known from the Mari texts. Its inhabitants raised a Semitic-type temple, standing alone, like the one in Jerusalem, in the centre of an esplanade, but covered with decoration of Hellenistic inspiration. The gods, like the dead, were represented either in the Roman style or in Persian costume—but always in front view, so conforming to the 'frontality' law characteristic of the hieratic preoccupations of the Parthian world. Further east, in the Roman fortress of Dura on the Euphrates, this law was applied consistently. Dura was a sanctuary for many diverse beliefs, and within its walls were a Syrian temple, a Mithraic temple, a synagogue and a Christian chapel. In the synagogue, the Old Testament illustrations prefigure early Christian art.

ASIA MINOR

Asia Minor, an area consisting mainly of the Anatolian plateau, was the cradle of another Neolithic Revolution, of great originality in comparison with developments elsewhere in the Orient. About 6500 B.C. a substantial settlement called Çatal Hüyük grew up on the Konya plain. Its size gave it the look of a town, even if the term should really be reserved for a specific social and administrative organization that was inconceivable at that time. The houses, built so closely together that they had no doors, were entered from the roof. They were decorated with polychrome paintings and unbaked clay reliefs of deer and 'goddesses'. Modelled bulls' heads were incorporated into the decoration, although their significance is hard to determine. The supernatural powers represented by the statuettes can in any event be seen as remote ancestors of the deities known in the historic period. Pottery made a tentative appearance during the 1,000-year existence of this settlement. When Çatal Hüyük was destroyed around 5700, the very different village of Hacilar was established further west. Alongside richly decorated painted vases, the potters of Hacilar fashioned idols. These works, which show exceptional freedom in attitudes, represent the 'mother goddess', usually accompanied by a male partner—husband or child—and smaller in size, or else nursing an animal like a child. It is surprising that such promising beginnings should have proved abortive; after Hacilar was destroyed there seems to have been no sustained cultural development until the beginning of the 3rd millennium—during the period when Troy was being founded on the Aegean coast. From this time on, the plateau was divided into compartments with a series of more or less independent cultures.

Around 2400 B.C. a race of people who were the ancestors of the Indo-European Hittites invaded Anatolia. They appear to have been responsible for the rich royal tombs at Alaça, where the biers were protected by beams and flanked by bronze standards in the form of animals or pierced discs. The first known dagger comes from these tombs, made out of terrestrial as opposed to meteoric iron.

A decisive factor in the integration of the country into the rest of the Near East was the arrival of Assyrian merchants, who in the 20th and 19th centuries organized trading with the small Anatolian kingdoms. The merchants established small communities called *karum* (quay), and these trading quarters were situated on the outskirts of the indigenous agglomerations, the best known of which is Kültepe, the former Kanesh, near Kayseri. Their language and cuneiform script became known to us from their abundant correspondence and their cylinder-seals. They assumed the Anatolian way of life and adopted, in particular, their beautiful zoomorphic vases. The autochthones, in turn, profited from their contact with the Assyrians by appropriating the cylinder-seal and creating an iconography that illustrated their Syrian-related mythology. At the end of the 18th century, during the wars that created the Hittite empire, the Assyrian colonies were destroyed and abandoned. The Hittite empire took a long time to establish itself and even in the 15th century its art was still strongly dependent on Syrian models, as can be seen from the cylinder-seals and from the little bronzes representing gods. One of the most typical examples of the cylinder-seal shows the storm-god Teshub in his chariot approaching the supreme goddess who is opening her robes to be fertilized by the god-sent rain.

Not until the 14th century could the Hittite kings be sure of the coherence of their composite kingdom and enter into competition with Egypt for the control of Syria, the crossroads of the Near East. They had adapted the Babylonian script to their Latin-related Indo-European language, but they had also created their own hieroglyphic script. With the help of foreign artists they developed and patronized an imperial art.

Hattusas, the capital (modern Boghazköy), was enlarged and a citadel was built. The buildings inside were each adapted to a specific function and spread out around colonnaded courts: a library, a throne-room with wooden columns supporting a vast inner area, and a building with a porticoed gateway set between two towers. In many respects this architecture can be seen as the precursor of the style that subsequently developed on the Iranian plateau. The ramparts were pierced by corbelled gates which had monolithic door-jambs carved partly in low relief and partly in high relief, a style inaugurated in Syria and revived by the Assyrians. The best known of these gates was guarded by a war-god carved in vigorous relief on one of the jambs. In the neighbouring fortress of Alaça was a gate decorated in the same spirit, with a sphinx whose head shows Egyptian influence next to reliefs covering the lower part of the walls. For the first time, people are shown in true profile: priests are leading victims and, ahead of them, the king and queen officiate before an altar with a bull perched on it, symbolizing the storm-god.

Not far from the capital lay Yazilikaya, a double rock gorge worked into an open-air sanctuary and shut off by a temple preceded by a propylaeum. Two processions of divine figures from the Hurrian pantheon were carved on the walls of the rocks. They meet at the rear of the main chamber in such a way as to suggest that this is the marriage celebration of Teshub the storm-god, who is supported by mountain-gods, and Hepat, who is standing on a lioness and followed by her son-god.

With the dawning of the 12th century the Hittite empire collapsed, but some of the Hittite principalities in the east of the country survived: Malatya, where the pantheon was also portrayed, and an area on the Syrian borders that had been invaded by Aramaeans. And so it happened that a mixed art developed in this region, while in the 8th century the Phrygians built their grandiose capital of Gordion. The tomb presumed to be that of King Midas contained bronze treasures with affinities to those found at Urartu.

URARTU

Urartu, with a population based on Hurrian stock, spread out around Lake Van and Mount Ararat in Armenia. From the 9th to the 6th century its kings were formidable enemies of the Assyrians, whom they survived by a score or so years. Their fortresses were economic centres and military bases. They contained enormous warehouses and encompassed simple temples: little, one-roomed buildings covered, it would seem, by a roof pitched on four sides and standing in the middle of a porticoed court. In them were dedicated great cauldrons and ceremonial weapons, products of a remarkable metallurgy whose decoration of great originality evokes the cosmopolitanism of the period.

MAJOR MUSEUMS

France	Musée du Louvre, Paris
Great Britain	British Museum, London
Israel	Israel Museum, Jerusalem
Lebanon	National Museum, Beirut
Syria	National Archaeological Museum, Aleppo
	National Museum, Damascus
Turkey	National Museum, Ankara

CONCISE BIBLIOGRAPHY

AKURGAL, E. *Die Kunst Anatoliens von Homer bis Alexander.* Berlin, 1961.
──────────── *Die Kunst der Hethiter.* Munich, 1961. *The Art of the Hittites,* trans. Constance McNab. London, 1962.
──────────── *Orient und Okzident. Die Geburt der Griechischen Kunst.* Baden-Baden, 1966. *Orient et Occident. La Naissance de l'art grec.* Paris, 1969. *The Birth of Greek Art: The Mediterranean and the Near East,* trans. Wayne Dynes. London, 1968.
BOSSERT, H. *Altanatolien.* Berlin, 1942.
──────────── *Altsyrien.* Tübingen, 1951.
DUPONT-SOMMER, A. *Les Araméens.* Paris, 1949.
KENYON, K. *Archaeology in the Holy Land.* 4th ed. London, 1979.
LLOYD, SETON. *Early Highland Peoples of Anatolia.* London, 1967.
MATTHIAE, P. *Ars Syra.* Rome, 1962.
MOSCATI, S. *The World of the Phoenicians.* London, 1973.
PARROT, A., CHEBAB, M., and MOSCATI, S. *Les Phéniciens. L'Expansion phénicienne. Carthage.* L'Univers des Formes. Paris, 1975.
VAN LOON, M. *Urartian Art: Its Distinctive Traits in the Light of the New Excavations.* Istanbul, 1966.
de VAUX, R. *Histoire ancienne d'Israël.* 2 vols. Paris, 1971 and 1973. Vol. 1. *The Early History of Israel,* trans. David Smith. London, 1978.

THE LEVANT

1 Troy	14 Kayseri	27 Ras Shamra (Ugarit)
2 Pergamon	15 Mersin	28 Ebla
3 Smyrna	16 Kition	29 Meskene (Emar)
4 Ephesus	17 Karatepe	30 Tortosa
5 Miletus	18 Marash	31 Hama
6 Hacilar	19 Malatya	32 Byblos
7 Ankara	20 Zinjirli	33 Beirut
8 Alaça Hüyük	21 Carchemish	34 Damascus
9 Yazilikaya	22 Tell Amar (Til Barsib)	35 Sidon
10 Boghazköy (Hattusas)	23 Alalakh	36 Tyre
11 Konya	24 Antioch	37 Jericho
12 Çatal Hüyük	25 Ain Dara	38 Jerusalem
13 Kültepe	26 Aleppo	39 Lachish

BLACK SEA

1

2
3
4
5
6

7

8
9
10

11
12

13
14

15

17
20

18

19

16 CYPRUS

MEDITERRANEAN SEA

23
24
27

25
26
28

21
22

29

30
31

LEBANON

32
33
35
36

34

SYRIA

JORDAN

37
38 DEAD SEA
39

EGYPT

SINAI

Nile

SAUDI ARABIA

0   300 km

Halys

Euphrates

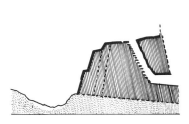

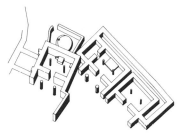

1
Section of a Neolithic stone tower,
Jericho, 8th millennium

2
Plan of the three temples at Megiddo
(Palestine), end of the Early Bronze
Age, *c.* 2000 B.C.

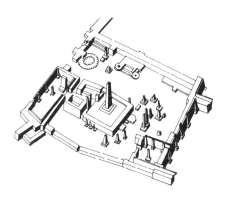

3   Obelisk temple, Byblos (Lebanon), beginning of 2nd millennium

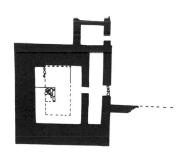

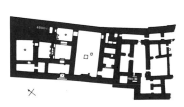

4
Level VII temple, Alalakh, modern
Tell Atchana on the lower Orontes,
18th/17th c. B.C.

5
Palace of King Yarimlim, Alalakh,
modern Tell Atchana, 18th/17th c.
B.C.

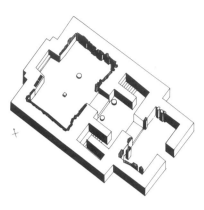

6   14th-c. B.C. temple, Hazor (Palestine)

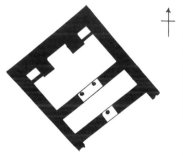

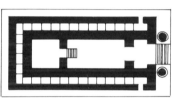

7
13th-c. B.C. temple, Alalakh, modern
Tell Atchana

8
Reconstructed plan of the temple built
by Solomon, Jerusalem, mid-10th c.
B.C.

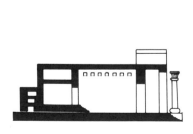

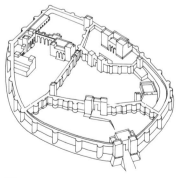

9
Section of No. 8

10
9th-c. B.C. citadel, Sam'al, modern
Zinjirli (northern Syria)

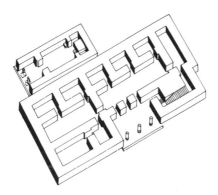

11 *Hilani* palace and temple, Tell Tayanat (northern Syria), 9th c. B.C.

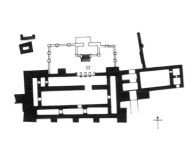

12
Palace of Kapara, Tell Halaf, ancient
Guzana (northern Syria), 9th c. B.C.

13
Meghazil tomb, Amrit, near Tartus
(Lebanon), 4th c. B.C.

14
4th-c. B.C. temple, Amrit, near Tartus
(Lebanon)

15
'Tomb of Absalom', Jerusalem,
mid-1st c. B.C.

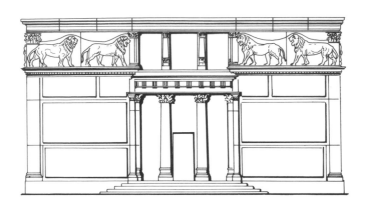

16   Façade of the tomb of the Tobiades, Araq el Emir (Transjordan), *c.* 175 B.C.

17   Rock tomb, Petra, 1st c. A.D.

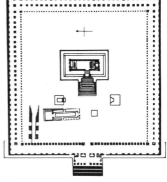

18
Rock tomb surmounted by obelisks,
Petra, 1st c. A.D.

19
Plan of the temple of Bel, Palmyra
(Syria), 1st–3rd c. A.D.

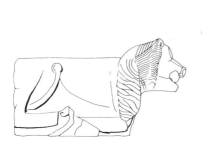

20
Guardian-lion at the gate of a temple, Alalakh, modern Tell Atchana (northern Syria), basalt, 14th c. B.C.

21
Basalt door-jamb, Hazor (Palestine), Israel Mus., Jerusalem

22   Capitals of engaged columns, Samaria (Palestine), limestone, 9th–8th c. B.C.

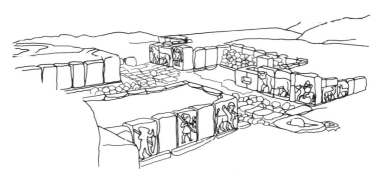

23   Orthostats decorating the southern gate, Sam'al, modern Zinjirli (northern Syria), 9th c. B.C.

153

24   Guardian-lion of a gate and orthostats, Sakjegözü (northern Syria), 8th c.
B.C.

25   Decorations at the entrance of the palace of Kapara, Tell Halaf, ancient
Guzana, 9th c. B.C.

26   Lintel at the temple of Baalshamin, Palmyra (Syria), 3rd c. A.D.

27   Synagogue mosaic: the temple of Solomon, Beth Alpha (Palestine), 5th c.
A.D.

28   Synagogue mosaic: the sacrifice of Abraham, Beth Alpha (No. 27)

29   Synagogue painting: the vision of Ezekiel, Dura Europos (Middle Euphrates), 3rd c. A.D., Nat. Mus., Damascus

30
Decoration on basalt cult basin, Ebla (Syria, south of Aleppo), early 2nd millennium, Nat. Mus., Damascus

31
Stele: Baal with lightning, Ugarit, modern Ras Shamra (Syria), limestone, H. 1.4 m., Louvre

32
Stele symbolizing a worshipper, Hazor (Palestine), basalt, H. 45 cm., 14th c. B.C., Israel Mus., Jerusalem

33
Stele: the cult of the god El, Ugarit, H. 47 cm., 13th c. B.C., Nat. Archaeol. Mus., Aleppo

34   Sarcophagus of the king Ahiram, with alphabetic inscription, Byblos (Lebanon), 10th c. B.C., Nat. Mus., Beirut

35
Cover of No. 34

36
Stele of Tukulti-Ninurta II, Syria (Middle Euphrates region), basalt, 9th c. B.C.

37
Large orthostat, Tell Halaf, ancient Guzana (northern Syria), basalt, H. 1.2 m., Nat. Archaeol. Mus., Aleppo

38
Small orthostat: telamon-genius, Tell Halaf, ancient Guzana, basalt, H. 60 cm., 9th c. B.C., Louvre

39
Small orthostat: slaying of Humbaba, Tell Halaf, ancient Guzana, basalt, 9th c. B.C.

40
Orthostat (as No. 39): genius with three pairs of wings, Tell Halaf, basalt, 9th c. B.C.

157

41
Stele: god of war, Shihan (Transjordan), basalt, H. 1.03 m., 9th–8th c. B.C., Louvre

42
Funerary stele, Marash (south-east Turkey), limestone, H. 80 cm., 8th c. B.C., Louvre

43
Stele: god of war, Amrit (Lebanon), limestone, H. 1.80 m., 6th c. B.C., Louvre

44
Tomb of Antiochus of Commagene: Persian ancestor, Nimrud Dagh (south-east Turkey), mid-1st c. B.C.

45
Tomb of Antiochus (No. 44): stars conjoined in the constellation of Leo, Nimrud Dagh

46
Relief of the god Arsu, Dura Europos (Middle Euphrates, Syria), 3rd c. A.D.

47   Sacrifice offered to the six geniuses of Bet-Phasil, Palmyra region (Syria), limestone, 2nd–3rd c. A.D.

48
Relief depicting the funeral banquet of Maliku, at Palmyra, limestone, c. 200 A.D., Louvre

49
Funerary bust, limestone, H. 40 cm., c. 200 A.D., Louvre

50   Triad: the moon-god Aglibol, Baalshamin master of the heavens and Iarhibol the sun-god, Palmyra, limestone, H. 57 cm., Louvre

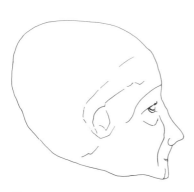

51
Neolithic modelled skull, Jericho, *c.*
7000 B.C., Israel Mus., Jerusalem

52
Neolithic terracotta idol, Munhatta
(Palestine), 5th millennium, Israel
Mus., Jerusalem

53
Neolithic idol, Munhatta (No. 52)

54
Idol from the Tell Halaf period,
northern Syria, terracotta, H. 8 cm.,
c. 5000 B.C., Louvre

55
Naked worshipper in gilded bronze,
Byblos, H. 34 cm., beginning of 2nd
millennium, Nat. Mus., Beirut

56
Statuette of a man in pure copper,
Lebanon, H. 28 cm., beginning of 2nd
millennium, Louvre

57
Plumed god, Syria, bronze, H. 12.5 cm., beginning of 2nd millennium, Louvre

58
Head of a god, Djabbul (Syria), basalt, H. 35 cm., 18th c. B.C., Louvre

59
Deified king, Mishrife, ancient Qarna (Syria), bronze, H. 17.5 cm., Louvre

60
Goddess of war, Syria, bronze, H. 12.5 cm., 15th c. B.C., Louvre

61
Royal head, Alalakh, modern Tell Atchana, Level VII temple, limestone, 17th c. B.C.

62
Enthroned goddess, Ugarit, modern Ras Shamra, bronze, H. 24 cm., 18th c. B.C., Louvre

161

63
Statue of King Idrimi, Alalakh, modern Tell Atchana, limestone and basalt, H. 1.40 m., 15th c. B.C., B. M.

64
Weight in the shape of a head, Ugarit, modern Ras Shamra, bronze, H. 5 cm., 13th c. B.C., Louvre

65
Statue of a worshipper, Hazor (Palestine), basalt, 14th-c. B.C. temple, Israel Mus., Jerusalem

66
Royal statue, Amman (Jordan), limestone, H. 54 cm., 9th–8th c. B.C., Amman Mus.

67
Statue of Minerva, Hauran, basalt, H. 1.59 m., Roman period: 1st–2nd c. A.D., Nat. Mus., Damascus

68
Statuette of Jupiter Heliopolitanus, god of Baalbek, Syria, bronze, H. 47 cm., 2nd c. A.D., Louvre

69
Mitannian footed vase, Tell Billa (Assyria), 15th c. B.C.

70
Enamelled faience vase, Ugarit, modern Ras Shamra, H. 16.5 cm., 14th–13th c. B.C., Louvre

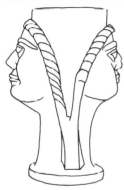

71
Enamelled faience vase, Ugarit, modern Ras Shamra, H. 12.5 cm., 14th–13th c., Louvre

72
Painted pottery decoration, Palestine, 13th–12th c.

73   Gold pectoral from royal tomb, Byblos, W. 20.5 cm., 19th c. B.C., Louvre

74
Dish with hunting scene, Ugarit, modern Ras Shamra, gold, D. 19 cm., 14th c. B.C., Louvre

75
Gold pendant, Minet el Beida, port of Ugarit, H. 6.5 cm., 14th–13th c., Louvre

76   Ivory plaque of Mycenaean inspiration, Megiddo (Palestine), H. 3 cm., 13th c. B.C.

78
Ivory lid of Mycenaean inspiration, Minet el Beida, port of Ugarit, H. 13.7 cm., 13th c. B.C., Louvre

77
13th-c. B.C. ivory, Byblos (Lebanon), Nat. Mus., Beirut

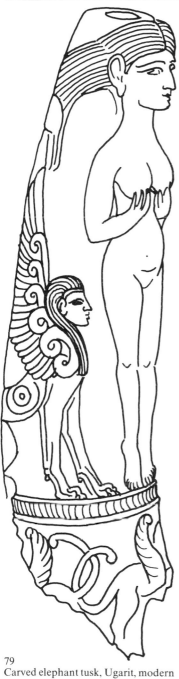

80
Part of the ivory decoration on a bed for lying in state, Ugarit, 13th c. B.C., Nat. Mus., Damascus

79
Carved elephant tusk, Ugarit, modern Ras Shamra, H. 25 cm., 14th–13th c., Nat. Mus., Damascus

81
Box carved in high relief, Megiddo (Palestine), 13th c. B.C., Israel Mus., Jerusalem

82
Phoenician ivory, Nimrud, ancient
Kalakh (Assyria), 8th c. B.C., B.M.

83
Phoenician ivory (No. 82), Nimrud

84
Phoenician ivory, Arslan Tash, an-
cient Hadatu (Syria), H. 7.8 cm., 8th c.
B.C., Louvre

85
Ivory encrusted with coloured paste,
Nimrud, ancient Kalakh, H. 60 cm.,
8th c. B.C., Iraq Mus., Baghdad

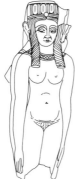

86
Handle in the form of a female
statuette, Nimrud, ancient Kalakh,
8th c. B.C.

87
Phoenician ivory: birth of Horus,
Nimrud, ancient Kalakh, 8th c. B.C.

88
Sphinx-decorated ivory, Samaria, 8th
c. B.C., Israel Mus., Jerusalem

89
Syrian dignitary, Arslan Tash, ancient
Hadatu (Syria), ivory, H. 20.7 cm.,
8th c. B.C., Louvre

90
Panel from a Syrian bed for lying in
state, Nimrud, ivory, H. 11.5 cm., 8th
c. B.C., Iraq Mus., Baghdad

91
Panel, Nimrud (see No. 90)

92
Syrian cylinder-seal: the storm-god and unveiling goddess, 8th c. B.C., Pierpont Morgan Coll., N.Y.

93
Cylinder-seal impression: the god of the deep, unbaked clay, 8th c. B.C., Mari, palace of Zimrilim

94
Syrian cylinder-seal: circle of four geniuses personifying water, 8th c. B.C., Newell Coll.

95
Cylinder-seal showing Aegean influence: hunting scene, 7th c. B.C., Louvre

96
Seal of Shema, official of King Jeroboam II of Israel, 8th c. B.C.

97
Stamp-seal of Yaazanyahu, royal official, Tell en-Nasbeh, to the north of Jerusalem, end of 7th c. B.C.

98   Reconstruction of the Neolithic shrine of Çatal Hüyük near Konya,
     c. 6000 B.C.

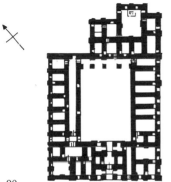

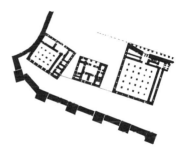

99
Plan of the great temple of Hattusas,
capital of the Hittite empire, 14th–
13th c. B.C.

100
Plan of the north part of the citadel of
Hattusas, 14th–13th c. B.C. (to the
right, columned throne-room)

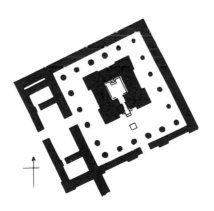

101   Plan of the temple of Altin Tepe (Urartu), east Turkey, 7th c. B.C.

102
Sphinx decorating door-jamb on the
ramparts of Hattusas, limestone, 13th
c. B.C., St. Mus., E. Berlin

103
Guardian-god of the Royal Gate at
the ramparts of Hattusas, H. 2 m., 13th
c. B.C., Nat. Mus., Ankara

104   Central relief panel of the open-air sanctuary of Yazilikaya, near Hattusas: meeting of the supreme Hittite gods, 13th c. B.C.

105   Mythological relief at Malatya (eastern Turkey): libation to the Hittite
gods, basalt, H. 86 cm., 11th–10th c., Nat. Mus., Ankara

106
Relief on the gate of Karatepe (south-east Turkey): goddess suckling, end of 8th c. B.C.

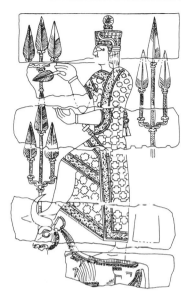

107
Low relief from Adilcevas near Lake Van: Urartian goddess carried by a bull, H. 2.80 m., 7th c. B.C.

108
Cult relief discovered at Ankara: Phrygian goddess, andesite, H. 1.75 m., Nat. Mus., Ankara

109
Neolithic statuette in terracotta: woman suckling, c. 5300 B.C., Hacilar, Nat. Mus., Ankara

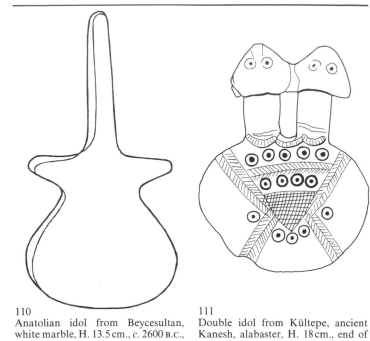

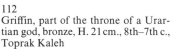

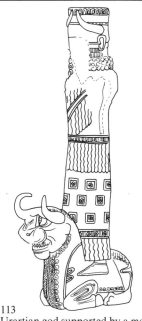

110
Anatolian idol from Beycesultan, white marble, H. 13.5 cm., *c.* 2600 B.C., Nat. Mus., Ankara

111
Double idol from Kültepe, ancient Kanesh, alabaster, H. 18 cm., end of 3rd millennium B.C., Louvre

112
Griffin, part of the throne of a Urartian god, bronze, H. 21 cm., 8th–7th c., Toprak Kaleh

113
Urartian god supported by a monster, detail from a throne, bronze, H. 30 cm., 8th c. B.C., Stoclet Coll.

114
Hittite jug, H. 38.4 cm., 18th c. B.C.,
Hattusas, Nat. Mus., Ankara

115
Bronze standard with stag ornament,
H. c. 30 cm., c. 2300 B.C., royal tomb at
Alaça Hüyük, Nat. Mus., Ankara

116
Bull-shaped standard, bronze and
silver, H. 37 cm., royal tomb at Alaça
Hüyük, Nat. Mus., Ankara

117
Bull-shaped standard, bronze and
silver, H. 36.5 cm., c. 2300 B.C., tomb at
Alaça Hüyük, Nat. Mus., Ankara

118   Bronze tripod cauldron, Altin Tepe (Urartu), 8th c. B.C., Nat. Mus.,
Ankara

173

Egypt

by Christiane Desroches Noblecourt
Curator-in-chief, Department of Egyptian Antiquities, Louvre

Drawings by Chantal Dulos and
Guy Lecuyot (sketches and plans)

EGYPT

No land of remote antiquity has been so well described as the Egypt of the pharaohs. In the last forty years, its fascinating and evocative remains have been the subject of splendidly illustrated books whose photographs range from the gentle colours of the Nile valley to the brilliance of Theban paintings and the gold and semi-precious stones of funerary treasures. Ancient Egypt has left evidence of its art in imposing 'pylons' or monumental gateways, forests of columns with flowered capitals, statues of its rulers and their courtiers, and beautiful princesses; and in conceptions of the divine materialized in objects of human or animal form. The uninitiated may be tempted to see Egyptian art as both hieratic and static throughout the millennia. However, an orderly and gradual evolution is discernible in the artistic achievements of this remarkably gifted people, who expressed through line and colour a whole system of metaphysics shaped by laws dating back, as the texts say, to 'the time of the gods'.

What were the laws applied to Egyptian art that gave it such originality and character, and a perfection so rapidly achieved that it still moves our modern world to admiration and wonder? They sprang directly from the physical phenomena which created and moulded that extraordinary country. For thousands of years this part of Africa—situated almost on a straight line drawn from the south-east coast of the Mediterranean to the site of the modern capital of the Sudan—was dominated by an enormous gulf which caught the tropical rains and carried them out to sea. As it diminished in breadth, it slowly shaped the bed of what was to become one of the oldest and longest rivers in the world. Meanwhile, on its banks, the contemporaries of the Australopithecines and the men of the Omo Valley (Ethiopia), whose remains are being found more and more frequently in Africa and western Asia, began to flake pebbles to make the first implements of *homo habilis*. All this took place 3 or 4 million years ago.

In the Palaeolithic period the men of the Nile basin, hunters and nomads still, continued to advance: picking out the pale desert flints, they fashioned them in the characteristic 'international' style common to all prehistoric productions. However, as their skills developed and the chipping became more delicate, they came to evolve their own techniques and art. By the end of this long, formative period they were using stone burins to engrave the rocky cliffs overhanging the river with pictures of the herds of animals they hunted—elephants, giraffes, ostriches, antelopes and ibexes. Some of the nomads eventually managed to settle on the banks of the menacing river, and the Neolithic period began. There quickly followed a host of innovations to serve and protect them in their daily lives, and their harsh existence was sublimated in the elaboration of beliefs in

177

an after-life. Everything around them predisposed the Nile people to create a unique way of life, based on a philosophy and ethic inspired by the great laws of nature.

In fact, men could only exist on this desert soil—in the most inhospitable place in the whole of Africa—because of an astonishing yearly phenomenon, the inundation of the Nile. It was produced by the tropical rains of Africa which fed its two tributaries: the White Nile, which had as its source Lake Albert at the foot of the 'Mountains of the Moon', and the Blue Nile originating in Ethiopia, both meeting at the level of Khartoum. The flood came regularly to water the two long strips of soil that were built up by its deposits of richly fertile alluvium. It also irrigated the river delta which was steadily formed as the torrent met the Mediterranean; and three of its principal outlets which reached the sea still existed in the last century. That major axis of the flood—from its sources in the south to its outlets in the north—was for the Egyptian world its main 'orientation' and in addition the visible manifestation of the concept of regeneration. To men barely subsisting in a cramped and periodically desiccated land, it brought hope and life.

Around 4000 B.C., astronomers fixed the start of the year at the time when the swollen White Nile, coloured green by papyrus heads torn from the great swampy stretches through which it hurtled, turned red with the ferruginous alluvium carried by the Atbara as it joined the Nile. Wise men had also observed that this regular rise of the Nile, the return of life, was marked by the reappearance of the dog-star Sirius-Sothis after seventy days' occultation, not far from where the sun would rise. The solar year of twelve thirty-day months was created. Five extra days were added (later to be called the *epagomenae* by the Greeks) at the turn of the year, falling regularly around what became the Julian 18 July. A colour symbolism was created, too, with specific meanings attributed to the green and the red waters: hope associated with death, followed by an expression of regeneration. Nature's annual rebirth after long days of trial must have given the Nile people the near-certainty of an after-life, which would follow the desolation and apparent sterility of death as surely as the grain from ripe, cut corn would live again when planted and watered by the river. In such a framework an agrarian religion could hardly fail to be born and to flourish. Thus the annual cycle was symbolized by the overflowing river that gave life to Egypt, as in the celebrated phrase, repeated by Herodotus, of Hecataeos of Miletos: 'Egypt, the gift of the Nile'. If this annual flooding of the Nile is another major axis measuring out the infinite succession of the years, the minor corresponding axis is the sun—whose appearance bringing life and hope is followed by its setting and disappearance—which gave man the rhythm of his days of activity succeeded by his nights of rest, the 'little death' when he temporarily entered a world in which he could renew his vital energies. The expectation of the sun's reappearance each day gave an assurance of continuity to a precarious life, but at the same time caused anxiety about anything which might interfere with its periodicity. These two phenomena, especially perceptible in a world of luminous desert horizons where man is close to the elements, gave birth not only to confused beliefs that developed into myths, but to a whole moral discipline. Parallel to that moral discipline was a material discipline which grouped the inhabitants of the river banks around a master or ruler who could coordinate their vital common efforts. An essential task was to prepare and clean out the canals that were needed to hold back as much water as possible before it ran away to the sea; and it was also necessary for them to join together in the struggle against the 'bad Niles'—too strong or too weak—in order to control famine and epidemics. To avoid upsetting the cosmic balance (a general preoccupation throughout Africa) was the Egyptians' main concern, and their antidote was order and the maintenance of established rules. The latter could be translated by *Maat*, 'the beloved daughter of the Sun', a notion expressing at once the cosmic harmony that the

Egypt

pharaoh had to maintain on earth, and the driving force behind all things, the *eros* that urges action and creation.

Close to the impact of cosmic forces and attentive to the phenomena all around him, the Egyptian was dimly aware of their blind benevolence and, at the same time, their hostile ill will. And so he tried to conform to the rhythms of the beneficent forces, trusting to their earthly protection and to hope of an immortality obtainable only on condition that he did not break the laws of morality and order that were his salvation. In order to achieve this there were rites that reflected actions, reinforced possibilities and helped in the accomplishment of cycles. Religion—a set of practices and beliefs—was a function of the quest for survival of a people who, dreaming only of eternal life, came to create their own immortality.

Never art for art's sake, the craftsmen's work was intended to express the various forms of the divine and of eternal life after death. Of course, the Nile dwellers also fashioned objects for daily use: to eat with, defend themselves with, sleep on; furniture of grandeur; boxes for linen and utensils; clothes—and all these things were usually made with a sure aesthetic sense combined with a refined sobriety. But above all else their work was designed to ensure the clemency and protection of the pharaoh and the superior forces for which he was the mediator. It constituted the means for the achievement of personal immortality.

Deeply attached to his river and his vast desert and rock horizons and extremely sensitive to nature, which was above all the immanent proof of the divine, the Egyptian architect, early or late, strove to blend his creations into their geographical framework, to unite them with the environment. The pyramid shape of the most ancient royal tombs and the flattened trapezium of the *mastabas* which covered the necropolises of the sands of Memphis were in tune with the horizontal bars of sandy cliffs and the contours of rocky terraces. In response to the countryside around, the overseer modified both the monuments themselves and the general lay-out of their temples for the divine pharaoh cult. During the Middle Kingdom, tomb entrances were cut into the cliffs; then, during the same period and in the New Kingdom, the funerary temples ('houses of eternity') of Mentuhotep and Hatshepsut were set into marvellous rocky amphitheatres. This concern to follow nature can be seen again in the Valley of the Kings (Biban el-Moluk) where the pyramid-shaped Theban summit guards the funerary syrinxes (narrow galleries cut in the rock) of the New Kingdom sovereigns; or again in the Necropolis of the Queens (Biban el-Harim) where the Grotto of the Great Goddess towers over the tombs of the Ramesside queens and princes.

The outlines and forms of drawings and statuary had to conform to rules laid down at the end of the Neolithic age. Craftsmen never really deviated from these magico-religious prescriptions until the disappearance of a purely autochthonic priestly and pharaonic dominance.

If one refers back to the earliest representations of human figures—those already being traced on the Naqada vases; or, a little later, in the Hierakonpolis paintings; or better still, carved on the ivory handle of a knife in Gebel el-Arak—one sees the emergence of the main lines of the first-known relief of the historic period, the palette of Narmer. Established and immutable rules were applied to drawing the image of a person or thing. The picture was not expected to reproduce the person as he appeared to the spectator, with all the distortion in perspective inherent in the angle of vision. The person had to be drawn—and so immortalized—as he really was and as completely as possible. Hence, in graphic art, the individual was represented with his face in profile, with an eye drawn in full, as if looking at you; the shoulders, which in profile would not have shown their full breadth, are also seen face-on and the pelvis is seen three-quarters view so that the very centre of procreation, although covered by a robe or loincloth *(pagne)*, remains free. In order to achieve this the leg of the (seated or standing) subject furthest from the viewer was always projected forward: in other words,

179

when the subject is facing right his left leg is forward, and vice versa. It was not until the dawn of the Saite period, when the country had more than 2500 years of history, that these conventions were first broken.

Once the sovereignty of the image was recognized, other rules followed to which the craftsman faithfully adhered in his service to the priesthood and the state. Whether the relief entrusted with the eternal form depicted the master of the land or the master of the tomb, it had to be a flawless synthesis of the subject at the height of his vigour. What was required was not a portrait representing a being at one fixed point in his life, but an epitome of the vibrant and ideal —therefore durable—personality. That, at least, is the message that most of the works have conveyed to us. Some representations of prominent individuals do not conform to this criterion: the masterly Old Kingdom portrait in the Boston Museum of the powerful Ankh-haf's time-worn face, or one of the statues from the second half of the 18th Dynasty, of Amenhotep, son of Hapu, an angular portrait of an old man (Cairo Museum), were certainly exceptional cases commissioned by a clergy still anxious to convey a religious idea. (Let us not forget that Amenhotep, son of Hapu, wisest of the wise, was endowed by God with 110 years of age, as was Joseph in the Bible.) Whatever the case, these statues still teach us lessons which the years have not blurred. Similarly, during the Middle Kingdom, the extreme realism of the anxious, sometimes even tragic, faces of the last 12th-Dynasty sovereigns expresses something more in the nature of a religious message than the exact look of the model. A relief or drawing also had to show the subject in a majestic pose to give the impression of immutable dignity, to be a suitable summary of his personality. A certain amount of freedom was, on the other hand, allowed—within the well-defined framework—for the conveying of movement and action. Scenes animated by ordinary folk, scenes of agriculture, workshops, feasts and war, could be employed to evoke the concepts to be attained: the anecdotal form was authorized for these compositions. So, too, the carved and painted registers that adorned the walls of temple courts or tomb chapels were illustrated with lively and sometimes even humorous episodes which gave them a special flavour. Only the walls of the sanctuaries and some of the funerary vaults escaped these fantasies. Here we return to serious representations of rites in which the dialogue with the divine images imposed the most austere dignity and total respect.

Such was also the case with divine, royal, princely and, later, townspeople's statues. The only permissible attitude was one of complete self-control, of absolute calm and an abstraction from any passing human feelings of joy or sorrow, for these were not appropriate to the perfect speechless dialogue with the unseen Eternal. The craftsmen (the best of them who filled the royal workshops were consummate artists) nearly always reached the desired goals, as we can still sense today when we look at the humblest funerary statuettes from modest tombs.

All these unquestioned prescriptions were imposed by priests who presided over the elaboration of forms. An inscription on the famous Palermo stone indicates that, during the first dynasties, decisions were made about what appearance to give to divine images. This could almost be said to prefigure the anxiety expressed, millennia later, by the Council of Trent which sought to save the threatened Catholic Church after the Reformation by imposing an iconography! Within this seeming monotony, however, was an internal evolution, so that masterpieces that were being continually produced during the impressive course of pharaonic history were marked by subtle variations of expression. In contrast to neighbouring countries with a different geography and without its rich soil, the 'Black Land', as its inhabitants called it (*Kemy* or *Kemet,* whence the name of the science of chemistry), was able to exploit, in addition to the Nile mud used in early pottery, a great variety of rock quarries placed under the absolute control of the pharaoh. The Egyptians obtained quartzite from Gebel Ahmar, limestone from Tura, nummulitic limestone from Hermopolis, ivory-coloured limestone from the west bank of Thebes, alabaster from Hatnub, schists and greywacke from the eastern wadis of Upper Egypt, sandstone from Gebel es-Silsileh and even diorite from western Nubia, not to mention breccia from the desert. Cornelian, desert agate, amethyst and feldspar from the south, turquoise from Sinai and garnet were soon used to decorate talismans and were inlaid in choice objects, divine and royal statues and temple sanctuaries.

Believing, as they did, that men were moulded from humus and straw, the Egyptians built all human dwelling-places, however palatial, out of unbaked clay bricks, with wood and stone added for door-frames and columns. The houses of eternity, on the other hand, temples and funerary complexes, were mostly built of quarried material. The dense and rare wood used in the manufacture of furniture came in the main from Africa, as did ostrich feathers, skins of certain kinds of cat and the gold which augmented the local resources of Upper Egypt. It was almost impossible to find silver locally, and so right up until the New Kingdom it was rarely used. It was imported indirectly from Anatolia and neighbouring regions, as was iron. Copper was extracted from ore found in Sinai. Probably introduced by metallurgists from the Caucasus, bronze appeared from the time of the Middle Kingdom on. Finally, the tall flagpoles erected in front of temples were brought from the Lebanon, rich in pine forests that were already famous in antiquity; while the magnificent deep-blue lapis lazuli so sought after by the pharaoh's workshops was supplied by caravans which brought the most precious varieties from far-off Bactria (Afghanistan).

The dwellers by the river, commonly called *Itraa* and *Hapi* when in flood (the name 'Nile', 'Neilos', was given to it by classical travellers because its letters were used to write '365 [days]'), had become fully sedentary in the Neolithic age. After a brilliant period, promising in its creativity, came a renewed wave of Semitic invasions. These consolidated once and for all the Hamitic-Semitic ethnic type whose genius suddenly became evident in the miracle of the 1st Dynasty. With the authority of his sceptre the legendary Menes—Narmer in the texts—instituted a strong, centralized government and took in hand the destiny of the country. This control was exercised, without exception, by all the pharaohs (the name comes from *per-aa,* the 'Great House') of the thirty dynasties recorded by Manetho, the historian of the later periods.

The first two dynasties are called Thinite because the city of This (near Abydos) was reckoned to be their capital, but about them little is yet known. The remains, however, suggest that here was already a civilization with a strong framework of institutions, with numerous scribes manipulating the hieroglyphic texts that appeared during the 1st Dynasty. One of the most notable figures of the 2nd Dynasty was the pharaoh Khasekhemui, who was called upon to defend his country against Libyan incursions. The first of the great historical periods in Egypt, called the Old Kingdom, began with the 3rd Dynasty. After Djoser, who initiated the stone architecture developed by the famous architect Imhotep and his immediate successors, the 4th Dynasty opened with the reigns of Sneferu, then Cheops, Chephren and Mycerinus, and also included the disputed reign of Dedefre. They established their capital at Memphis; to the west was their prestigious necropolis at Giza where, guarded by the famous sphinx, the three greatest pyramids in Egypt have been preserved beneath the sands. (The name 'sphinx' comes from the Egyptian *pa sechem ankh*, 'the image of life', while 'pyramid', from the Greek *pyramis,* meaning 'roll of bread', was a derisive term used for the funerary monuments by Greek mercenaries who had grasped neither their meaning nor their purpose.)

In this period of construction, when architects were achieving the same degree of control over massive stones that the pharaohs were gaining over an uncontested kingdom, civilization was already very highly developed. If one can believe the texts written slightly later, which describe events that took place during the 4th Dynasty, there were surgeons capable of teaching their disciples how to make a scientific diagnosis (Edwin Smith Papyrus). Morality and respect for humanity had meanwhile taken firm root. In one story, a magician was asked by Cheops to perform an experiment on a prisoner of war. 'No, my lord master,' replied the admirable old man, 'not upon the livestock of God.' And the pharaoh gave in: 'Bring me, then,' he said, 'a goose from the Nile' (Westcar Papyrus).

The earliest known Egyptian religious texts appeared on the walls of the last pyramid of the 5th Dynasty (that of Wenis). Their language reflects an archaism that goes back to the most obscure times. The texts contain the substance of everything that for millennia was to be recorded, illuminated, commented on, right up to the Ptolemaic period. The principal names of the divinities are cited; myths are provided for the mysteries of nature; the pharaoh is already truly the incarnate son of the force that governs the world, and after his earthly term he will rise towards that force and all those upon whom he has imposed just laws will benefit from the reverberations of this sublime destiny. Until the beginning of the New Kingdom, Egypt lived in virtual isolation, although it was in contact with neighbouring countries: expeditions were sent out towards the second cataract to seek the precious diorite, or to the Danga to bring back a 'dancing dwarf of the god' for the young king, or even to fetch back an eastern princess to share the master of Egypt's bed.

The 6th Dynasty ended with Egypt's longest reign, that of Pepi II, during which, despite the many monuments of grandeur it produced, the crown was weakened by the growing role of provincial lords. The Old Kingdom was finally destroyed by internal strife and an Asiatic invasion.

In the First Intermediate Period a kind of social revolution occurred which, in spite of its excesses, allowed the least favoured classes to acquire some rights. Then, the struggles between local governors and descendants of the monarchy ended in the rise to power of a southern prince called Mentuhotep. This was the start of the 11th Dynasty and the Middle Kingdom era. At first, the court was at Thebes, but from the 12th Dynasty its seat was in the Faiyum, a kind of oasis, close to the Nile, irrigated by the first canal parallel to the river, the long Bahr Yusuf that empties into Lake Karun. The Amenemhats and Sesostrises who followed were great kings concerned to expand the role of the administration and make it more flexible, and to open up more possibilities in agricultural life. Sesostris I was anxious to maintain peaceful relations with his neighbours and left a memorial that even the Ptolemies held in the highest regard, his notable foundation at Tod, south of Thebes. At the end of the 12th Dynasty Sesostris III had to wage war in Nubia, but his prestige was so great that he was deified in that far-off land, which he had completely pacified. In the following period it entered into an association with Egypt. On the eastern frontiers of the country, the pharaohs had had military citadels built like the ones used to defend the cataracts, and to the east of the Delta they formed the formidable 'Prince's Wall'. Here the Asiatic bedouins whom the Egyptians called the Hyksos were already infiltrating: when they eventually took over the Delta they were to govern as a ruling caste over a land in serious decline.

This Second Intermediate Period ended with the 17th Dynasty when the intruders were expelled, once again by southern princes, and the 18th Dynasty was founded, inaugurating the New Kingdom. With such turbulent neighbours, Egypt could no longer sit back and hope for peaceful relations. It had always been on good terms with Byblos, where there was even an Egyptian governor, but it was not so easy to restrain some of the smaller tribes without subjugating them. It was also necessary to re-establish the security of the caravan routes that passed along the coast or penetrated into the hinterland to reach the country of the Amorites. Amenophis and Tuthmosis were the first to shoulder this task, and so successful were they that when Princess Hatshepsut legally became pharaoh she could devote herself to reopening artists' workshops that had been abandoned since the troubled times, to rebuilding or restoring stricken sanctuaries, and even to undertaking the famous scientific and commercial expedition to Punt. Her nephew and successor, Tuthmosis III, gained glory for the Egyptian army in seventeen campaigns, pushing right up to the curve of the Euphrates. He brought peace and prosperity to the Black Land of Egypt that would benefit all his successors up to the end of the 18th Dynasty. Following the inexorable law of history, this period of luxury and euphoria distracted the rulers of the country from the more or less permanent threats to their frontiers. Meanwhile, however, Egyptian art, in the widest sense of that term, had gone through the familiar organic progression from primitivity and experimentation, through classicism and on to great refinement. Under Amenophis III it had reached the stage of mannerism. The pharaoh—Horus on earth, son of the sun-god Ra—succeeded the being who had rejoined Osiris slumbering in the entrails of the earth where he reigned over the transitory domain of the dead. Ra, the sun, was the vital force that gave life to all things, while Osiris, whose wound, inflicted by Seth, the spirit of evil, was hidden in great secrecy by his priests, was the energy that 'recharged his battery'. They were dual aspects of a single power.

But why continue to anthropomorphize these concepts and commit to legend things that men, in whom the priests had instilled a fear of Osiris, should have been able to perceive more naturally? This was what the great religious reformer, the pharaoh Amenophis IV–Akhenaten, must have had in mind when he ordered the suppression of all images that evoked the divine, except for the disc of the sun, Aten, to which he added rays ending in hands. He used the new dynamic forms that were suggesting themselves to artists to propound a monotheistic heresy.

However, within two decades of his death, the Amarna experiment ended. The young Tutankhamun, Akhenaten's son-in-law, went back to the worship of the hidden spirit, Amen, and the return to the old religion was accelerated under the iron rule of the reforming General Horemheb, who came to the throne soon afterwards.

Then came the 19th Dynasty, made illustrious by the Ramessides, the most glorious of whom, Rameses II, reigned for 67 years and was able to give Egypt a long period of respite by forming an opportune peace treaty with the Anatolian Hittites. Ramesside art retained all the technique acquired during the Amarna period, and as if obeying official dogma, gave expression on a grandiose scale to the universalism that Akhenaten had hoped would prevail. Rameses III was to achieve a great victory when he defeated a massive invasion of the Egyptian frontiers by the Sea Peoples. The New Kingdom ended around the year 1000 B.C. with the last of the Ramessides.

Next there was a Third Intermediate Period which lasted from the 21st to the end of the 24th Dynasty. Power was shared between the king-priests in the north, at Tanis, and the priest-kings in Thebes: the Psousennes and the Osorkhons, respectively. Libyans infiltrated into the country and the name Sheshonk is even recorded in the Bible (Shishak). Then princes from the Sudan, Piankhi, Shabaka and Taharqa, took possession of the throne in the 25th Dynasty, which ended tragically with the Assyrian invasion. Once again a native pharaoh reunited the country and established his capital at Sais on the Delta: this was the 26th Dynasty, the time of the Psamtiks. During the Saite period, also called the Neo-Memphite period, there was a revival of art which consciously looked back to the works of the past. But more recent attainments were too considerable to be ignored. Foreign influences could now, moreover, penetrate unhindered into an Egypt that was at first attracted to exotic fashions and then battered by various occupations. With the 30th Dynasty of the Nectanebos, the country again submitted to two waves of Persian domination. When Alexander reached Egypt (battle of Issus, 332) he was welcomed as a liberator. Merchants and administrators had come before him, however, and Greek scholars and philosophers had already arrived to imbibe the ancient wisdom of the sons of the Nile. The last

Egypt

Ptolemy (the 13th) and the 7th Cleopatra of the Egypt of Alexander's generals (the Ptolemies) were unable to hold out against Caesar. With the death of that courageous queen, the colonized country became the granary of the Roman world. Meanwhile, the last great priests still compelled the emperors to build the final pharaoh-style temples, their walls covered with heavy hieroglyphic inscriptions—repositories of the knowledge of a world condemned to obscurity.

This, then, was the awesome civilization of Egypt, spanning several millennia and epitomized by artistic creations that were faithful to laws dictated by a totally dominant religion. Only by systematically looking at numerous examples can one glimpse the constant but subtle evolution of this aesthetic expression and draw valid lessons from it. The method here has been to select and present such examples thematically. The first theme is architecture: architecture of the divine, of the dead, of civilians and of soldiers; for it is an excellent expression of a country's particular genius. Egyptian sculpture, studied next, was always an essential complement to it. Having isolated these themes, it becomes possible to highlight some of the most typical low reliefs and paintings. When one turns to the applied arts that metamorphosed and ennobled each moment of existence and escorted the deceased in their quest for eternity, one finds the same style as in monumental statuary, painting and animal art. In giving an account of some of them, the whole of their evolution can be sketched out.

Logically conceived, a handbook of forms cannot be illustrated by photographs, however accurate. Anyone not used to the archaeological analysis of a monument, of whatever kind, risks acquiring a faulty conception of it from a photograph. On the other hand, a drawing can convey the message of a design and the very style of a period by selecting significant lines and shapes. Because they avoid distorting detail and planes obscured by shadows, line drawings are particularly helpful in the study of architectural monuments or sculpture in the round. The lessons to be learnt are all the more profitable if the drawings are done by an archaeologist who is aware of the message to be conveyed.

CONCISE BIBLIOGRAPHY

ALDRED, C. *Middle Kingdom Art in Ancient Egypt.* London, 1950.
——————— *New Kingdom Art in Ancient Egypt during the Eighteenth Dynasty.* London, 1961.
——————— *Old Kingdom Art in Ancient Egypt.* London, 1949.
ANTHES, R. *Ägyptische Plastik in Meisterwerken.* Die Sammlung Parthenon. Stuttgart, 1954.
BADAWY, A. *Ancient Egyptian Architectural Design: A Study of the Harmonic System.* Berkeley and Los Angeles, 1965.
——————— *Le Dessin architectural chez les anciens Egyptiens. Etude comparative des représentations égyptiennes de constructions.* Cairo, 1948.
——————— *A History of Egyptian Architecture.* I. *From the Earliest Times to the End of the Old Kingdom.* Giza, 1954. II. *The First Intermediate Period, the Middle Kingdom, and the Second Intermediate Period.* Berkeley, Los Angeles and London, 1966.
——————— *A History of Egyptian Architecture: The Empire (The New Kingdom).* Berkeley and Los Angeles, 1968.
——————— 'La Maison mitoyenne de plan uniforme dans l'Egypte pharaonique' in *Bulletin of the Faculty of Arts, Cairo University,* XVI, 2. Cairo, 1953.
BARGUET, P. 'Le temple d'Amon-Ré à Karnak. Essai d'exégèse' in *Recherches d'archéologie, de philologie et d'histoire,* XXI. Cairo, 1962.
CENIVAL, J.L. de. *Egypte, époque pharaonique.* Architecture Universelle. Fribourg, 1964.
CLARKE, S. 'Amarna Reliefs' in *Ancient Art.* The Norbert Schimmel Collection. Mainz, 1974.
DAUMAS, F. 'La Civilisation de l'Egypte pharaonique', in *Les Grandes Civilisations.* Paris, 1965.
DAVIES, NINA M. DE GARIS. *Ancient Egyptian Paintings.* Chicago, 1936.
DESROCHES-NOBLECOURT, C. *Le Style égyptien.* Paris, 1946.
——————— *Vie et mort d'un pharaon, Toutankhamon.* Paris, 1963; 2nd ed., 1976.
——————— and BOURGET, P. du. 'L'Art égyptien' in *Les Neuf Muses.* Paris, 1962.
——————— *et al. Catalogue de l'exposition 'Ramsès le Grand'.* Paris, 1976.
——————— *et al. Catalogue de l'exposition 'Toutankhamon et son époque'.* Paris, 1967.
EVERS, H.G. *Staat aus dem Stein, Denkmäler, Geschichte und Bedeutung der ägyptischen Plastik während des Mittleren Reiches.* 2 vols. Munich, 1929.
FECHHEIMER, H. 'Die Plastik der Agypter'. Vol. 1 in *Kunst des Ostens.* Berlin, 1920.
GIEDION, S. *The Eternal Present: The Beginning of Architecture.* Bollingen Series, XXXV, 6, 11. Washington, D.C., 1957.
HAYES, W.C. *Most Ancient Egypt.* Chicago, 1965.
——————— *The Scepter of Egypt: A Background for the Study of Egyptian Antiquities in the Metropolitan Museum of Art.* I. *From the Earliest Times to the End of the Middle Kingdom,* 1953. II. *The Hyksos Period and the New Kingdom,* 1959. Cambridge, Mass.
HORNEMANN, B. *Types of Ancient Egyptian Statuary.* 7 vols. Copenhagen, 1951–1969.
IVERSEN, E. *Canon and Proportion in Egyptian Art.* London, 1955.
JEQUIER, G. *L'Architecture et la décoration dans l'ancienne Egypte.* I. *Les Temples memphites et thébains des origines à la XVIIIème dynastie,* 1920. II. *Les Temples ramessides et saïtes de la XIXème à la XXXème dynastie,* 1922. Paris.

Egypt

—————— *Manuel d'archéologie égyptienne.* Paris, 1924.

KLEBS, L. *Die Reliefs und Malereien des Neuen Reiches (XVIII.–XX. Dynastie, ca. 1580–1100 v. Chr.). Material zur ägyptischen Kulturgeschichte.* Part I.*Szenen aus dem Leben des Volkes.* Vol. 9 in *Abhandlungen der Akademie der Wissenschaften zu Heidelberg.* Heidelberg, 1934.

LANGE, K., and HIRMER, M. *Egypt, Architecture, Sculpture and Painting.* London and New York, 1968.

LAUFFRAY, J. *Karnak d'Egypte, domaine du divin.* Paris, 1979.

—————— 'Le secteur nord-est du temple jubilaire de Thoutmosis III à Karnak. Etat des lieux et commentaire architectural' in *Kêmi,* 19. Paris, 1969.

LEGRAIN, G. *Statues et statuettes de rois et de particuliers.* Catalogue général des antiquités égyptiennes du Musée du Caire. 3 vols. Cairo, 1906–1914.

LHOTE, A. *Les Chefs-d'œuvre de la peinture égyptienne* (photos by Hassia; pref. by J. Vandier). Arts du Monde. Paris, 1954.

MÜLLER, H.W. *Altägyptische Malerei. Von der Vorgeschichte bis zum Ende des Neuen Reiches.* Meisterwerke Ausseuropäischer Malerei. Berlin, 1959.

NIMS, C.F. *Thebes of the Pharaohs.* London, 1965.

PERROT, G., and CHIPIEZ, C. *Histoire de l'art dans l'antiquité.* 1. *Egypte.* Paris, 1882.

PETRIE, W.M.F. *The Pyramids and Temples of Gizeh.* 2nd ed. London, 1883.

PRISSE D'AVENNES, E. *Histoire de l'art égyptien d'après les monuments depuis les temps les plus reculés jusqu'à la domination romaine.* I. *Architecture.* Paris, 1878.

RICKE, H. *Der Grundriss des Amarnawohnhauses.* Deutsche Orient-Gesellschaft. Leipzig, 1932.

SCHÄFER, H. *Von ägyptischer Kunst. Eine Grundlage.* Wiesbaden, 1963.

SMITH, E.B. *Egyptian Architecture as a Cultural Expression.* New York, 1938.

SMITH, W.S. *The Art and Architecture of Ancient Egypt.* The Pelican History of Art. 2nd ed. Harmondsworth, 1965.

—————— *A History of Egyptian Sculpture and Painting in the Old Kingdom.* Boston, 1946; 2nd ed., 1949.

—————— *Interconnections in the Ancient Near East: A Study of the Relationships between the Arts of Egypt, the Aegean and Western Asia.* New Haven and London, 1965.

STEINDORFF, G., and WOLF, W. *Die thebanische Gräberwelt.* Vol. 4 in *Leipziger Ägyptologische Studien.* Glückstadt, 1936.

VANDERSLEYEN, C. *Das alte Ägypten.* Vol. 15 in *Propyläen Kunstgeschichte.* Berlin, 1975.

VANDIER, J. *Manuel d'archéologie égyptienne.* I. *Les Epoques de formation* (1. *La Préhistoire;* 2. *Les trois premières dynasties*), 1952. II. *Les Grandes Epoques* (1. *L'Architecture funéraire;* 2. *L'Architecture religieuse et civile*), 1954 and 1955. III. *Les Grandes Epoques, La statuaire,* 1952 and 1958, 2 vols. IV. and V. *Bas-reliefs et peintures, Scènes de la vie quotidienne,* 1964 and 1969. Paris.

WOLF, W. *Le Monde des Egyptiens.* Grandes Civilisations de l'Antiquité. Paris, 1955.

WRESZINSKI, W. *Atlas zur altägyptischen Kulturgeschichte.* Vols. 1–2. Leipzig, 1915, 1923.

YOYOTTE, J. *Les Trésors des pharaons.* Geneva, 1968.

Encyclopédie photographique de l'art. Les Antiquités egyptiennes du Musée du Louvre. Paris, 1936.

Encyclopédie photographique de l'art. Le Musée du Caire. Paris, 1949.

Recommended as a recent collection of studies on ancient Egyptian art are the three volumes of L'Univers des Formes *L'Egypte des pharaons,* published by Gallimard, Paris: 1. *Le Temps des pyramides,* 1978, 2. *L'Empire des conquérants,* 1979, and 3. *L'Egypte du crépuscule,* 1980.

MAJOR MUSEUMS

Austria
Kunsthistorisches Museum, Ägyptisch-Orientalische Sammlungen, Vienna

Belgium
Musées Royaux d'Art et d'Histoire, Brussels

Denmark
Ny Carlsberg Glyptotek, Copenhagen

Egypt
Museum of Pharaonic Art, Cairo
Museum of Ancient Egyptian Art, Luxor

France
Musée du Louvre, Paris
Musée Borély, Marseilles
Musée Calvet, Avignon
Musée des Beaux Arts, Grenoble

Germany, East
Staatliche Museen, East Berlin

Germany, West
Ägyptisches Museum der Staatlichen Museen, West Berlin
Staatliche Sammlung Ägyptischer Kunst, Munich

Great Britain
British Museum, London
Ashmolean Museum, Oxford
Fitzwilliam Museum, Cambridge
University College, Petrie Museum, London

Italy
Soprintendenza per le Antichità Egizie, Turin

Netherlands
Rijksmuseum, Leiden

U.S.A.
Metropolitan Museum of Art, New York
Brooklyn Museum, New York
Museum of Fine Arts, Boston
Field Museum of Natural History, Chicago
Cleveland Museum of Art, Cleveland

U.S.S.R.
Hermitage, Leningrad
Pushkin Museum of Fine Arts, Moscow

PRINCIPAL ARCHAEOLOGICAL SITES
IN EGYPT

1 Alexandria
2 Sais
3 Tanis
4 El-Kantara
5 El-Arish
6 Gaza
7 Qantir (Pi-Ramses)
8 Bubastis
9 Athribis
10 Merimda
11 Abu Rowash
12 El-Qatta
13 Heliopolis
14 Cairo
15 Giza
16 Memphis
17 Lisht
18 Tarkhan
19 El-Girza
20 Meidum
21 Kasr el-Sagha
22 Medinet el-Faiyum
23 Mit Faras

24 Hawara
25 Illahun
26 Kahun
27 Heracleopolis
28 Beni Hasan
29 Speos Artemidos
30 Bersha
31 Amarna (Akhetaten)
32 Hermopolis
33 Tuna el-Gebel
    (Tomb of Petosiris)
34 Meir
35 Asyut
36 Badari
37 Qaw el-Kebir
38 Reqaqna
39 Beit-Khallaf
40 This (?)
41 Abydos
42 El-Amra
43 Gebel el-Arak
44 Dendera
45 Koptos
46 Nagada

47 Thebes
48 Karnak
49 Luxor
50 Esna
51 El-Kab
52 Hierakonpolis
53 Edfu
54 Kom Ombo
55 Aswan
56 Abu Gurob (Abusir)
57 Ma'adi
58 Mit Rahina
59 Saqqara
60 Dahshur
61 Deir el-Bahri
62 Deir el-Medina
63 Ramesseum
64 Qurna
65 Madamud
66 Medinet Habu
67 Malkata
68 Armant (Erment)
69 Tod

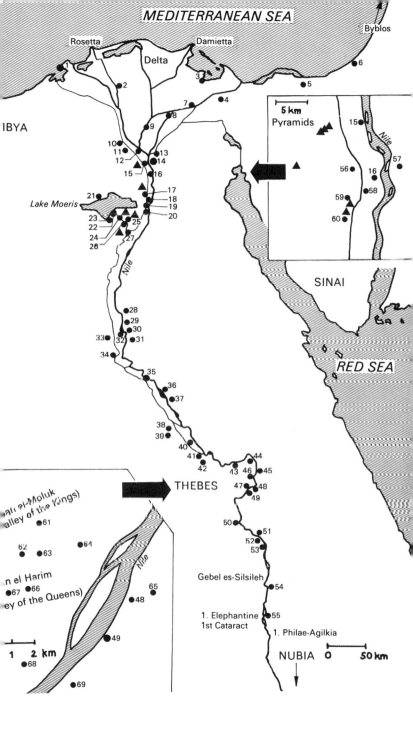

MEDITERRANEAN SEA

Byblos

Rosetta   Damietta

Delta

●1
●2
●3
●5
●6

LIBYA

●7
●8
●9

5 km
Pyramids

▲▲
●15

●1
●10
●11 ●13
●12 ●14
▲
●15 ●16
▲

▲   ●56
●16   ●57
●59   ●58
▲
●60

Lake Moeris
●21
▲
●17
●18
●19
●20
●23 ▽▽▽
●22 ▽▽●25
●24 ▲▲
●26 ●27

Nile

SINAI

RED SEA

●28
●29
●30
33● ●31
32●
34●

●35

●36
●37

●38
●30
●40
●41
●42
●44
●43 ●46 ●45
●47 ●48
●49

ari el-Moluk
alley of the Kings)

●61
THEBES

62● ●64
●63

n el Harim
●66
67●
ey of the Queens)
●65
●48

●50
●51
●52
●53

Gebel es-Silsileh   ●54

1. Elephantine   ●55
1st Cataract
1. Philae-Agilkia

NUBIA   0   50 km

1   2 km

●49

●68
●69

189

CHRONOLOGICAL TABLE

*c.*3000 B.C.	Beginning of history. Unification of Egypt. Use of writing	
2955–2635	*Thinite period* = Dynasties 1–2	
2635–2155	OLD KINGDOM = Dynasties 3–6 Period of the great pyramids (Cheops, Chephren, Mycerinus)	
2155–2060	*First Intermediate Period* = Dynasties 7–11 Troubled period	
2060–1785	MIDDLE KINGDOM = Dynasties 11–12 Reigns of Mentuhotep, Amenemhat, Sesostris	
1785–1554	*Second Intermediate Period* = Dynasties 13–17 Disorder. Foreign invasion by the Hyksos	
1554–1080	NEW KINGDOM = Dynasties 18–20	

	1554–1305	18th Dynasty Reigns of the Tuthmosides and Amenophides. Religious reform of Amenophis IV–Akhenaten. Tutankhamun restores the cult of Amen
	1305–1196	19th Dynasty Rameses I (1305–1303) Seti I (1303–1290) Rameses II (1290–1224) Merneptah (1224–1214) Amenmeses (1214–1210) Seti II (1210–1204) Siptah and Tausert (1204–1196)
	1196–1080	20th Dynasty Sety-nekht and the last Ramessides

1080–332	LATE PERIOD = Dynasties 21–31	

	1080–715	*Third Intermediate Period* = Dynasties 21–24
	1080–946	21st Dynasty Joint reigns of the kings of Tanis and the high priests at Thebes Psousennes I (1054–1004) Sa-amen (979–960)
	946–332	22nd–31st Dynasties Period of foreign invasions: Libyan, Ethiopian, Persian Saite renaissance = 26th Dynasty (664–525)

332	Conquest of Egypt by Alexander the Great	

THE OLD KINGDOM

Even before the dawn of their historical period—the time, that is, when writing appeared and a centralizing power coordinated essential tasks—the Egyptians had created an art style. Evidence of this comes from the Neolithic site at Gerza (hence the Gerzean period), where animal and human figurines that were discovered are proof of an uncommon ability to observe, understand and synthesize. An entire bestiary was chipped from soft stone and sometimes even modelled in clay. At first one can often make out what looks like the head of a ram—an amulet no doubt—which has allowed itself to be put under the protection of the leader of the herd. But one also comes across images of hippopotamuses, tortoises, cattle, frogs, birds and, above all, monkeys—solitary monkeys in the most astonishing poses, but also monkeys depicted in pairs, or a mother with a baby monkey on her lap seeking protection. Earthenware vases (at the beginning undecorated but in shapes that were to be repeated for centuries) copied precious vessels cut from the hardest stone and polished with infinite care: breccia, diorite and granite were used, and later alabaster. To begin with, the surfaces of the beautiful ovoid pots and tall goblets were coloured red and glazed. The tops were black, discoloured because for firing they were turned on their necks: the haematite in the glaze then turned very dark. When the funerary concepts that were developing began to spread, decorations in the form of outline drawings were often traced on the sides of votive vases; these depicted the local flora and fauna, or scenes of what were probably funeral processions set in the Nile countryside, or again, hunting scenes destined to adorn the chieftains' vaults—traces of which have been preserved for us on the walls of a tomb at Hierakonpolis. These thread-like beings, reminding us of hieroglyphics, were also moulded in clay and varnished red, or even carved from bone or ivory. There are silhouettes of a weeping woman, or of a 'mourner', or again of a mother and child, but more often than not it is the 'official' image of the man or the woman that is featured. Early on, the forms were still clumsily—or rather primitively—rendered, but soon the artists gained control over their material, so that the naked or cloaked statuettes with remarkably elaborate hair-styles that came at the end of the prehistoric period indicate an art that is already blossoming.

The Nile people had long been working small slates of schist into geometric shapes: squares, rhomboids, rectangles and even circles. Animal silhouettes, face to face, were soon added as decoration; then the background on both sides was filled with magical pictures of men and animals. A masterpiece, the most complete example of this type—and the latest in time—is the famous palette of King Narmer (Cairo). At the top of both sides are the outlines of two cow's-heads. In the centre of the reverse side is the cupule that adorns all palettes decorated with historical or legendary designs. There is a picture, too, of the first king of Egypt, the pharaoh revealed in his majestic and official role. Also illustrated are people of foreign ethnic types, and the vanquished citadels fortified with 'redented' walls (walls constructed with projecting spurs), that were to inspire Egyptian architecture. And there are the hieroglyphics.

From this time onwards, statuary developed with great vigour. Stone monuments were undoubtedly harder to shape than those cut from soft ivory. But the lion about to spring, the kneeling man or seated woman, their limbs still held stiffly, were carved making use of lines of force—conforming to essential laws that governed the creation of these 'presentation' portraits, destined for eternity. After the 2nd Dynasty and the impressive images of the pharaoh Khasekhemui, came the Old Kingdom and the 3rd Dynasty founded by the pharaoh Djoser, whose statue is the most beautiful example of Egyptian monumental court statuary. The archaic block seat (for more than 3000 years it was the ceremonial throne of the pharaohs and divine images), the sovereign's pose facing the eternal domain, legs together, forearms resting on thighs or crossed over chest (according to the statue's intended purpose, ritual or official), head perfectly straight—everything obeyed the famous 'frontality' law.

Meanwhile, architecture reached a turning point: builders began to use unbaked clay bricks instead of *pisé* (rammed clay). The round hut thus became a dwelling with right-angled walls. The El Amra model shows this Neolithic version of a shape which continued throughout the whole of the pharaonic period, with the desirable additions of a terraced roof, high windows and a door topped by a 'roller blind'. The chapels and sanctuaries built of domestic wood—palm, sycamore, acacia, willow—were of relatively modest dimensions. But in the 3rd Dynasty the architect Imhotep made general use of stone (it had appeared regularly in sepulchres from the time of the 1st Dynasty) and, on the desert plateau of Saqqara, he translated the traditional slight buildings into magnificent and magnified monuments of limestone. The old brick and wood forms were copied, just as the funerary chattels of the first kings were reproduced in enduring materials—with votive baskets carved in soft schist and gold being fashioned into mollusc-shaped boxes. The dominating idea behind these metamorphoses was always the same: to render imperishable everything that had to enter eternity, the monument, the funerary chattels, the statue or relief representing in 'majesty' candidates for eternal blessedness.

A style developed, then, within a definitive framework, for statues whether of sovereigns, on the one hand, or humble mortals, on the other. The archaism of a Sepa or a Neset is easily detected because there is still a certain stiffness about the limbs, a difficulty in disengaging neck from shoulders and, of course, the impossibility of rendering fully in stone the forward-stretching arm holding the staff and the other arm along the side of the body, holding a sceptre; the accessories are 'patched' onto the body, in a technique derived from, and more successful in, wooden statuary.

By the time the 4th Dynasty had abandoned light buildings for a monumental style and had begun to handle massive stones with virtuosity, Egypt had once and for all fixed the mode of its divine and funerary architecture: it was not to be transitory as were the simple dwellings of mortals. Processions would then come from the Nile, land at the 'access' temples and enter the ascending corridor that led to the Upper Chapel that was attached to the pyramid, or to whichever buildings were designed for the celebration of the divine cult and the periodic renewal of the royal energies. Different kinds of stone corresponded to different elements of the sacred buildings. The top of the immense stepped ('ascensional') tomb of the master of the land, presenting the most perfect geometrical shape, was constructed in stages. The vaults of great lords were topped by the huge trapeziums called by the excavators *mastabas* (an Arabic word meaning 'bench'). Reliefs were concerned with 'presentation' portraits of those to whom the buildings were dedicated and depicted their subjects seated or standing in the serene attitude that was intended to express the whole person as alive on earth. Only decorative scenes of magical intent were filled with profane and unknown characters, or animals. A picture showing the sovereign smiting his country's enemies is an exception to this rule, as is a portrayal of the master of the tomb maintaining order at his level as he destroys marsh creatures or the harmful hippopotamus. The only other movement permitted on the royal reliefs was the ritual jubilee race.

But statuary was never able to render such activity. In the 4th Dynasty a harmony of line was achieved and the technique of the sculptor—who, like the painter, was still anonymous—reached its peak. Perhaps the forms were slightly less elegant than they were to become in the 5th Dynasty but still they had a majesty, a vigour, a plenitude that have never been equalled. One is confronted by a gallery of portraits which, in spite of deliberate idealization, are all extraordinarily different from one another while still retaining an admirable serenity. One wanders in a world of statues, statues of groups, of triads, of seated men and standing women (the reverse is rare), of men in scribal poses, of seated couples (less slender in the 4th than in the 5th Dynasty), and of compositions into which children were introduced.

By studying drawings of these sculptures, one can discern the nature and evolution of their themes—their details, costumes, wigs, poses, in short all the variety in uniformity that is so characteristic of Egyptian art in all its periods.

By the end of the Old Kingdom, in the 6th Dynasty, faces were becoming less expressive, statuary less powerful, proportions less attended to. The copper statues (e.g., the statue of Pepi I) first appearing now show the progress that was being made in metalwork, which had already produced masterpieces in gold, such as the falcon's head at Hierakonpolis.

The style of painting followed that of the plastic arts which, like graphic art, were never more than complementary to architecture. Colours were less varied and at times painted decorations virtually became coloured drawings, demonstrating the fact that this decoration was fundamentally an enlargement of hieroglyphic shapes.

Finally, towards the end of this majestic period, there often appeared in funerary vaults groups composed of one or more anonymous figurines depicting the crafts which prepared the provisions and furnishings needed by the deceased on his final journey. Mostly carved in limestone, often painted, they illustrate an artistry freed from the magico-religious restraints imposed in an austere representation of a synthesis of the human character.

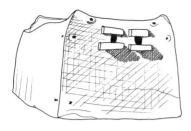

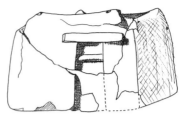

1
Model of a house, terracotta, L.
45 cm., W. 27.5 cm., H. 20 cm., end of
protodynastic period, El Amra, B.M.

2
Another view of No. 1

3
Amulet: bovine head, ivory, H.
3.5 cm., prehistoric period, St. Mus.,
W. Berlin

4
Frog, ivory, H. 2.9 cm., protohistoric,
Naqada (?), St. Mus., E. Berlin

5
Hippopotamus, clay, H. 13.7 cm., predynastic, Mus. of Fine Arts, Boston

6
Tortoise, terracotta, L. 14 cm., predynastic, Dendera, Ashmolean Mus.

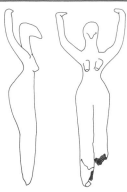

7
Female figurine: profile and front view, terracotta, H. 19.5 cm., prehistoric, Mus. of Fine Arts, Boston

8
Female figurine: front view and profile, painted terracotta, H. 22.9 cm., Metropolitan Mus.

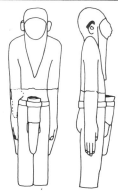

9
Female figurine, unbaked clay, H. 35.4 cm., predynastic, Royal Ontario Mus., Toronto

10
Bearded man, black basalt, H. 40 cm., protodynastic period, Ashmolean Mus.

11
Squatting man, terracotta, H. 7 cm., predynastic period, N.Y. Memorial Art Gall., Rochester

12
Front view of No. 11

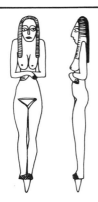

13
Female figurine, ivory, H. 10.5 cm.,
Naqada II period, predynastic, B. M.

14
Female figurine (?), ivory, H. 17.9 cm.,
protodynastic, Hierakonpolis, Ashmolean Mus.

15
Female figurine: front view, ivory, H.
13.5 cm., protodynastic, Louvre

16
Back view of No. 15

17
Female figurine, ivory, H. 16 cm.,
protodynastic, Hierakonpolis, Ashmolean Mus.

18
Back view of No. 17

19
Woman carrying a child in her arms, ivory, H. 7.4 cm., beginning of historic period, St. Mus., E. Berlin

20
A child with his finger to his mouth, chrysocolla, H. 3.3 cm., protodynastic, Hierakonpolis, Ashmolean Mus.

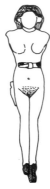

21
Female figurine: front view, ivory, H. 12.5 cm., protodynastic, Louvre

22
Back view of No. 21

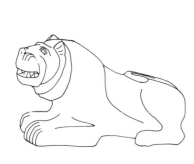

23
Lion, granite, L. 31.5 cm., 1st Dynasty, St. Mus., E. Berlin

24
Seated monkey, alabaster, H. 53 cm., 1st Dynasty, Saqqara, St. Mus., E. Berlin

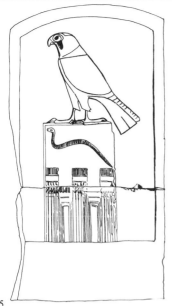

25
The stele of the serpent king, limestone, H. 1.45 m., 1st Dynasty, Abydos, Louvre

26
Ruins of the redented tomb of Horus Djet, 1st Dynasty, Saqqara

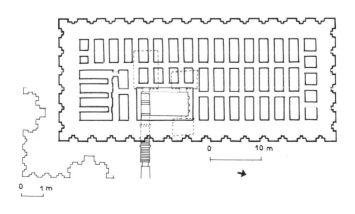

27   Redented tomb of Horus Den: plan, 1st Dynasty, Saqqara (the arrow indicates north)

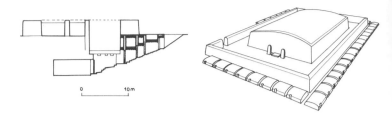

28
Redented tomb of Horus Den: cross-section showing descending passage and crypt, 1st Dynasty, Saqqara

29
Cenotaph of Queen Merneith: reconstruction, 1st Dynasty, Abydos

30   Tomb attributed to Merneith: reconstruction, 1st Dynasty, Saqqara

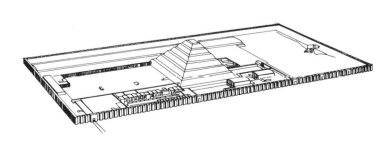

31   Funerary complex of King Djoser: reconstruction, 3rd Dynasty, Saqqara

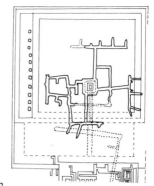

32
Funerary complex of King Djoser: reconstruction of the entrance façade, 3rd Dynasty, Saqqara

33
Stepped pyramid of King Djoser: plan of the subterranean galleries, 3rd Dynasty, Saqqara

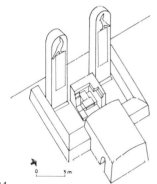

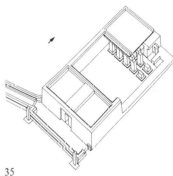

34
Upper Temple in the funerary complex of King Sneferu: reconstruction, 4th Dynasty, Dahshur

35
Valley Temple of the rhomboid pyramid: reconstruction, 4th Dynasty, Dahshur

36
Truncated pyramid at Maidum, 4th Dynasty

37
Rhomboid pyramid, 4th Dynasty, Dahshur

38   Pyramids of Giza, 4th Dynasty

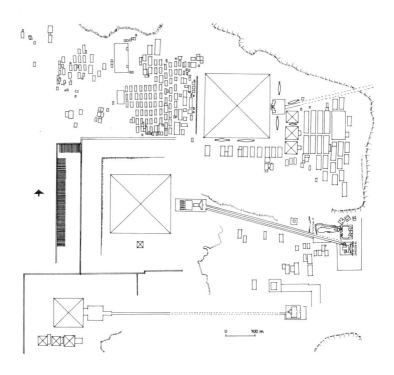

39   Pyramid complex at Giza: plan, 4th Dynasty

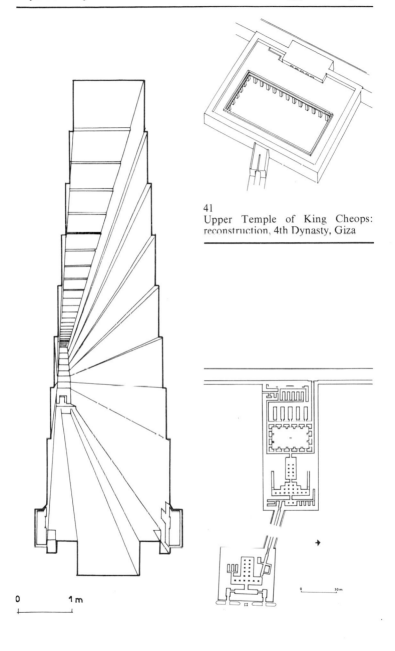

41
Upper Temple of King Cheops:
reconstruction, 4th Dynasty, Giza

0   1 m

40
Pyramid of King Cheops: perspective
on the Grand Gallery, 4th Dynasty,
Giza

42
Valley Temple and Upper Temple of
Chephren: plan, 4th Dynasty, Giza

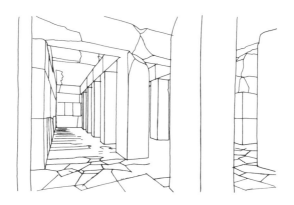

43   T-shaped hall in the Valley Temple of King Chephren, 4th Dynasty, Giza

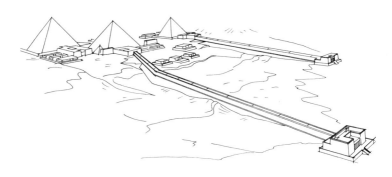

44   General view of the Abusir funerary complexes: reconstruction, 5th
Dynasty

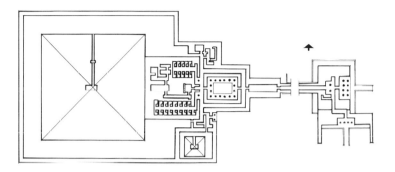

45   Funerary complex of King Sahure: plan (landing-stages cut short), 5th
Dynasty, Abusir

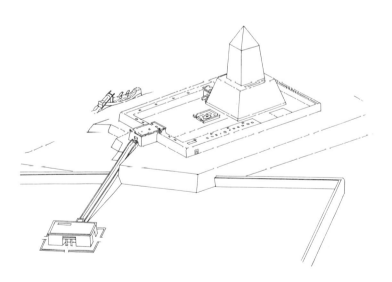

46   Sun temple of Niuserre: reconstruction, 5th Dynasty, Abu Gurob

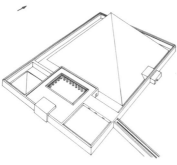

47
Pyramid and Upper Temple of Userkaf: reconstruction, 5th Dynasty, Saqqara

48
Funerary complex of Pepi II: reconstruction, 6th Dynasty, South Saqqara

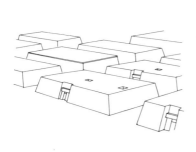

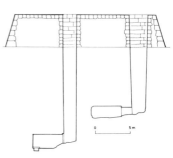

49
A group of mastabas in pyramid complex, 4th Dynasty, Giza

50
Mastaba: section, 4th Dynasty, Giza

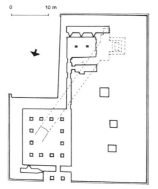

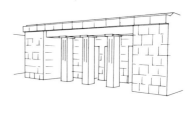

51
Mastaba of Ti: plan, 5th Dynasty, Saqqara

52
Porticoed façade of the mastaba of Mereruka: reconstruction, 5th Dynasty, Giza

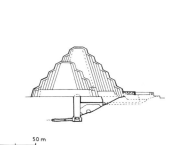

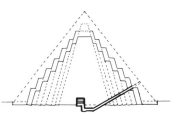

0 ____ 50 m

53
Stepped pyramid of Djoser: section, 3rd Dynasty, Saqqara

54
Pyramid of Sneferu: section, 4th Dynasty, Maidum

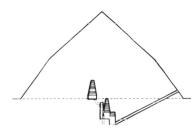

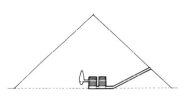

55
Rhomboid pyramid: section, 4th Dynasty, Dahshur

56
True pyramid of Sneferu: section, 4th Dynasty, Dahshur

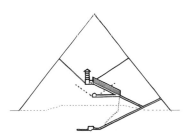

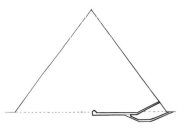

57
Perfect pyramid of Cheops: section, 4th Dynasty, Giza

58
Chephren pyramid: section, 4th Dynasty, Giza

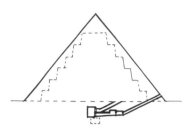

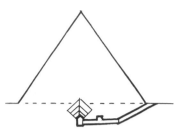

59
Pyramid of Mycerinus: section, 4th Dynasty, Giza

60
Pyramid of Userkaf: section, 5th Dynasty, Saqqara

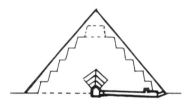

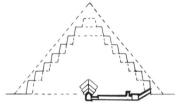

61
Pyramid of Sahure: section, 5th Dynasty, Abusir

62
Pyramid of Neferirkare: section, 5th Dynasty, Abusir

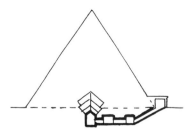

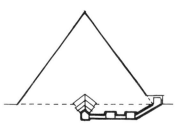

63
Pyramid of Wenis: section, 5th Dynasty, Saqqara

64
Pyramid of Teti: section, 6th Dynasty, Saqqara

66
King Khasekhemui, schist, H. 56 cm.,
2nd Dynasty, Kom el-Ahmar, Cairo
Mus.

65
Palette of King Narmer, schist, H.
64 cm., 1st Dynasty, Hierakonpolis,
Cairo Mus.

67
King Djoser, limestone, H. 1.44 m.,
3rd Dynasty, Saqqara, Cairo Mus.

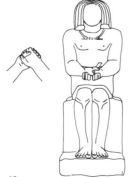

68
Statue of Nezem-ankh, diorite, H.
63 cm.,   3rd   Dynasty,   unknown,
Louvre

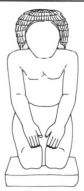

69
Statue of Hetepdief, speckled granite,
H. 40 cm., 3rd Dynasty, Mit Rahina,
Cairo Mus.

70
Statue of Sepa (front view), limestone,
H. 1.66 m., 3rd Dynasty, unknown,   71
Louvre   Back view of No. 70

72
Statue of Neset (front view), limestone, H. 1.52 m., 3rd Dynasty,   73
unknown, Louvre   Back view of No. 72

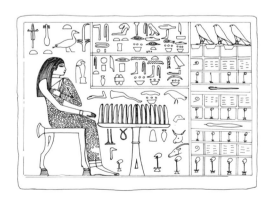

74   Slab-stele of Nefert-yabet, painted limestone, H. 37.5 cm., 4th Dynasty,
     western Cheops cemetery, Giza, Louvre

75   King Chephren, diorite, H. 1.68 m., 4th Dynasty, Giza, Cairo

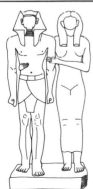

76
Mycerinus and Queen Khamerer-
nebti, schist, H. 1.45 m., 4th Dynasty,
Giza, Mus. of Fine Arts, Boston

77
Triad of Mycerinus, Hathor and Dios-
polis Parva goddess, schist, H. 96 cm.,
4th Dynasty, Giza, Cairo Mus.

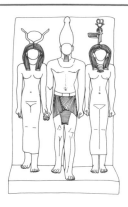

78
Front view of No. 102

79
Ka-aper, known as 'Sheikh el Beled', wood, H. 1.10 m., end of 4th Dynasty, Saqqara, Cairo Mus.

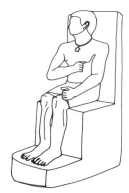

80
Princess Nofret, limestone, H. 1.18 m., 4th Dynasty, Maidum, Cairo Mus.

81
Prince Rahotep, limestone, H. 1.20 m., 4th Dynasty, Maidum, Cairo Mus.

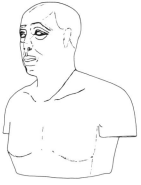

82
Head of a man, limestone, original life-size, 4th Dynasty, Giza, Cairo Mus.

83
Bust of Ankh-haf, stuccoed, painted limestone, H. 58 cm., 4th Dynasty, Giza, Mus. of Fine Arts, Boston

84   The 'Maidum geese': fragment from a bird-trapping scene, painting on *muna*, 4th Dynasty, mastaba of Atet at Maidum, Cairo Mus

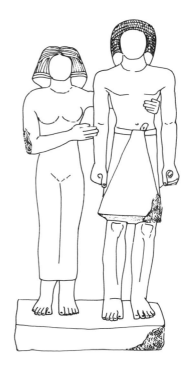

85–86
Memphite official and his wife, wood H. 69 cm., 4th Dynasty, Louvre

87
Imysetkai and Khuitbaiwenu (?), limestone, H. 57 cm., 4th Dynasty, Giza, Cairo Mus.

88
Djoser-senedj and Nefertka, granite,
H. 42 cm., 4th Dynasty, St. Mus., E.
Berlin

89
King Menkau-hor seated, alabaster,
H. 47.5 cm., 5th Dynasty, Karnak,
Cairo Mus.

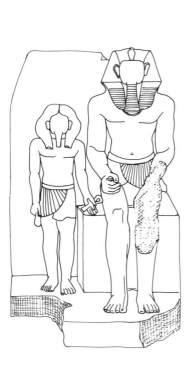

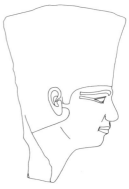

91
Royal head: Userkaf, schist, life-size,
5th Dynasty, Abusir, Cairo Mus.

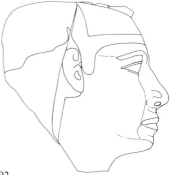

90
King Sahure and the Koptos genius,
diorite, H. 63.5 cm., 5th Dynasty, Saqqara, Metropolitan Mus.

92
King Userkaf: colossal head, granite,
H. 67 cm., 5th Dynasty, Saqqara,
Cairo Mus.

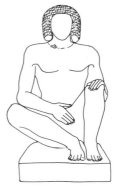

93
Statue of Ti, limestone, H. 1.995 m.,
5th Dynasty, Saqqara, Cairo Mus.

94
Ne-ankh-re, limestone, H. 64.5 cm.,
5th Dynasty, Giza, Cairo Mus.

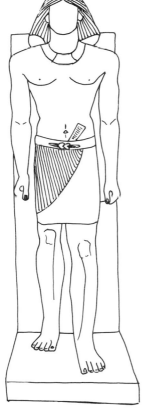

95
Statue of Ranofer, limestone, H.
1.80 m., 5th Dynasty, Saqqara, Cairo
Mus.

96
Statue of Ranofer (wigless), limestone, H. 1.85 m., 5th Dynasty, Saqqara, Cairo Mus.

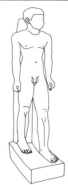

97
Statue of a woman, standing, alabaster, H. 50 cm., 5th Dynasty, Saqqara, Cairo Mus.

98
Thenti naked and standing, limestone, H. 59 cm., 5th Dynasty, Giza, Cairo Mus.

99
Seated man, granite, H. 67.5 cm., 5th Dynasty, Saqqara, Cairo Mus.

100
The dwarf Khnumhotep, limestone, H. 46 cm., 5th Dynasty, Saqqara, Cairo Mus.

101
Portrait of Ranofer, limestone, 5th Dynasty, Saqqara, Cairo Mus.

102
Bust of Werkhuu, limestone, H. 35 cm., 6th Dynasty, Giza (?), Cairo Mus.

103
The scribe Dersenedj, speckled granite, H. 68 cm., 4th Dynasty, Giza, St. Mus., E. Berlin

104
The scribe Iku, limestone, H. 24.5 cm., 4th Dynasty, Giza

105
The scribe Setymu, limestone, H. 25 cm., 4th Dynasty, Cairo Mus.

106
The 'Cairo scribe', limestone, H. 51 cm., 5th Dynasty, Saqqara, Cairo Mus.

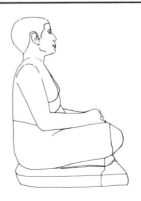

107
The 'Louvre scribe', painted limestone, H. 53 cm., 5th Dynasty, Saqqara, Louvre

108
Profile of No. 107

109
Back view of No. 107

110
The scribe Ptahshepses, limestone, H. 42 cm., 5th Dynasty, Saqqara, Cairo Mus.

111
The scribe Ptahshepses, limestone, H. 32.5 cm., end of 5th Dynasty, Giza, Hildesheim

112
The scribe Ptahshepses, black granite, H. 29.5 cm., 4th Dynasty, Leiden Mus.

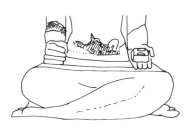

113
Attitude of the scribe Khnum-baf, granite, H. 36.3 cm., 5th Dynasty, Giza, Mus. of Fine Arts, Boston

114
Position of hands of No. 113

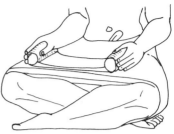

115
Scribal attitude, grey granite, H. 47.5 cm., 5th Dynasty, Saqqara, Cairo Mus.

116
Attitude of the scribe Maa-nefer, granite, H. 47 cm., 5th Dynasty, Saqqara, Cairo Mus.

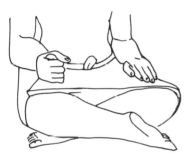

117
Scribal attitude, black granite, H. 37 cm., 5th Dynasty, Cairo Mus.

118
Scribal attitude, grey granite, H. 47.5 cm., 5th Dynasty, Saqqara, Cairo Mus.

119
Scribal attitude, limestone, H. 40.5 cm., 5th Dynasty, St. Mus., W. Berlin

120
Scribal attitude, alabaster, H. 33 cm., 5th Dynasty, Saqqara, Cairo Mus.

121
Ka-em-ked kneeling, limestone, H.
43 cm., 5th Dynasty, Saqqara, Cairo
Mus.

122
The dwarf Seneb with his wife and
children, limestone, H. 34 cm., end of
5th Dynasty, Giza, Cairo Mus.

123
Ptah-khenu and his wife, limestone,
H. 70.1 cm., 5th Dynasty, Giza, Mus.
of Fine Arts, Boston

124
Priest of Neith, with the goddess, pink
granite, H. 52 cm., 5th Dynasty, Saqqara, Cairo Mus.

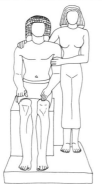

125
Ankhti-nefer and his wife, limestone,
H. 45 cm., 5th Dynasty, Saqqara,
Cairo Mus.

126
Couple seated on the ground: back
view, pink granite, H. 52.5 cm., 5th
Dynasty, Giza, Cairo Mus.

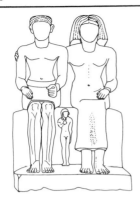

127
Seated couple with son, limestone, H.
75 cm., 5th Dynasty, Louvre

128
Iruka-ptah with his wife and son,
limestone, H. 73.5 cm., 5th Dynasty,
Saqqara, Brooklyn Mus.

129
Khentetka, surnamed Khent, with his
son, Redju, limestone, H. 54 cm., 5th
Dynasty, Giza, Vienna Mus.

130
Sekhemka seated, with his wife and
son standing, limestone, H. 68 cm., 5th
Dynasty, Giza, Louvre

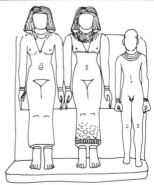

131
Nikaure with wife and child, standing,
limestone, H. 57.5 cm., 5th Dynasty,
Brooklyn Mus.

132
Wives and child, standing, limestone,
H. 69.7 cm., 5th Dynasty, Giza (?),
Leiden

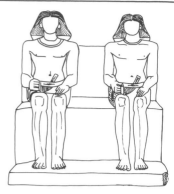

133
Ankh and his son, standing, lime-
stone, H. 72 cm., 5th Dynasty, Cairo
Mus.

134
'Pseudo-group' of Itisen, limestone,
H. 54 cm., 5th Dynasty, Louvre

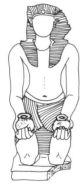

135
King Pepi I making the wine offering,
green schist, H. 15.2 cm., 6th Dynasty,
Saqqara, Brooklyn Mus.

136
King Pepi I in walking attitude,
copper, H. 1.77 m., 6th Dynasty,
Hierakonpolis, Cairo Mus.

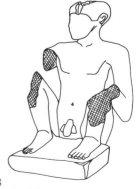

137
King Pepi I during his Jubilee, alabaster, H. 26.5 cm., 6th Dynasty, Saqqara, Brooklyn Mus.

138
King Pepi I squatting (as sun-child),
alabaster, H. 16 cm., 6th Dynasty,
Saqqara, Cairo Mus.

139   Low relief from the mastaba of Ti: transporting a funerary statue in the
      southern *naos*, limestone, 5th Dynasty, Saqqara

140
Relief from the mastaba of Ti: transporting another funerary statue, limestone, 5th Dynasty, Saqqara

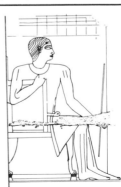

141
Detail of a relief from the mastaba of
Akhtihetep, limestone, 5th Dynasty,
Saqqara, Louvre

142
Bearer of offerings: low relief from the
tomb of Ti, limestone, 5th Dynasty,
Saqqara

143
Another bearer of offerings, as No.
142

144   A boat in the papyrus marshes: low relief from the tomb of Ti, painted
limestone, 5th Dynasty, Saqqara

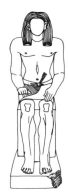

145
Iteti, seated, limestone, H. 92 cm., 6th
Dynasty, Saqqara, Cairo Mus.

146
Couple standing, limestone, H. 68 cm.,
6th Dynasty, Giza, Cairo Mus.

147
Man in walking posture, wood, H.
34 cm., 6th Dynasty, Saqqara, Cairo
Mus.

148
Tchau seated, schist, H. 34.5 cm., 6th
Dynasty, Saqqara, Cairo Mus.

149
Meryre-hashtef naked, standing,
wood, H. 74 cm., 6th Dynasty, Sed-
ment, Cairo Mus.

150
Nawepkau and his wife, limestone, H.
52.4 cm., end of 5th–beginning of 6th
Dynasty, Oriental Inst., Chicago

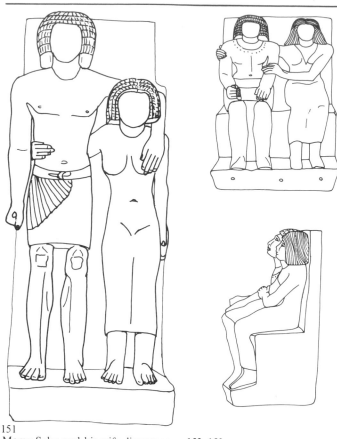

151
Memy-Sabu and his wife, limestone,
H. 61 cm., 5th–6th Dynasty, Giza,
Metropolitan Mus.

152–153
Seated couple, limestone, H. 39.5 cm.,
end of Old Kingdom, Edfu, Louvre

154   Painting: transporting livestock, 5th Dynasty, tomb of Kaiemankh, Giza

THE MIDDLE KINGDOM

During the interval that separated the Old from the Middle Kingdom (First Intermediate Period) the Egyptians made widespread funerary use of the 'models' portraying everyday life that had begun to appear towards the end of the Old Kingdom. Provincial tombs have yielded charming pieces, sometimes rudimentary and carved in quite unpretentious wood but imbued with life: processions of servants, herds returning, granaries crowded with porters and scribes checking the arrival of the grain, fishing boats or skiffs for pilgrimages decorated with the sacred eye *udjat*, and so on. The masterpiece of this genre is without doubt the famous 'Trough Bearer' in the Louvre. Graceful, elongated figures can be seen, too, in tomb wall-paintings of the period. The artists in the capital had been replaced by provincial workers without a workshop background whose brushes were inspired by a vitality that showed promise in spite of occasional clumsiness.

When the Mentuhoteps founded the 11th Dynasty, the new capital-city of Thebes created its own style of statuary. The crudeness of the new southern art has been much discussed, in such examples as the statue of Mentuhotep (from Bab el-Hosan), or Kawit's relief (Deir el-Bahri), or the private statues exhumed in the locality of the first cataract of the Nile. The architecture of the Middle Kingdom, with the capital re-established in the north in the Faiyum from the 12th Dynasty on, has largely disappeared. Pyramids were less opulently constructed than in the 4th Dynasty but must still have been impressive, for though made of unbaked clay bricks, they were dressed with limestone slabs and attracted grave robbers in very ancient times. Traces of royal funerary complexes bear witness to their grandeur, and the numerous labyrinthine chapels were worthy of a Sesostris or an Amenemhat. One need only contemplate the ruins of the temple and tomb of the great Mentuhotep at Deir el-Bahri to be convinced of their past splendour. The temple backed on to a rocky amphitheatre and must have been crowned with a pyramidal cap-stone. An ambulatory at the base had a ceiling supported by square pillars which imparted a unique lightness to the building.

Few traces have come down to us of the temples of the period, because they were built on sacred places and so were often swallowed up by later buildings, or else taken apart for use in the monuments of the dynasties that followed. There have been found, for instance, in the third pylon of Karnak, all the elements required for the complete reconstruction in fine sculptured limestone of a little chapel for the sacred barque. In it one can see the prototype of the peripteral building (with a row of columns on all sides) that was so characteristic of ancient Egypt. On top was a roof-terrace bordered by the famous cavetto cornice which imitated the ribs of a palm leaf. Another plant-form element is in the torus-moulding decorated with a sculpted band, framing each side of the building and simulating the joined branches of primitive architecture. The square pillars are engaged at their bases into a low, barrelled wall which forms part of the raised base of the building. A stepped ramp on either side allowed entrance and exit. Other ruins of temple-chapels contain remains of bundle columns, which had already been recorded in the Old Kingdom. Indeed, from this time architectural supports followed an appropriate course and took the form of square pillars or bundle columns with lotiform capitals (mainly for the princely hypogea) or closed papyriform capitals. A column was sometimes topped with the open umbel of a papyrus flower head; the papyrus always had a triangular section on the shaft. The idea of the 'Proto-Doric' column dates from the royal monuments of Saqqara: during the Middle Kingdom it became a convention. In this same period there appeared, in its classic aspect, the 'Osiride' pillar, decorated, as its name indicates, by a statue of the king in the guise of the god Osiris wrapped in his cloak. But the royal head did not, as in the caryatids, support anything: the entablature was held up by the pillars themselves, embellished with the projecting Osirian image. The Hathoric pillar, on the other hand, was topped by the human head of the goddess Hathor, with cow's ears. In use from the Old Kingdom on were dactyliform and palmate capitals. Great monolithic stone 'needles' were substituted for the massive obelisks of the 5th Dynasty, built up in several layers.

From traces that have been found of dwellings it is clear that their basic design had been worked out in the Old Kingdom and subsequently improved. One can get an idea of the great rural residences from ruins of the vast complex of 'Kahun', a settlement inhabited by the people who built the El-Lahun pyramid. In the heart of the annexes and shops the lord's quarters can be recognized, composed of the three fundamental, classic areas common to all accommodation in all periods: forecourt, reception rooms and rooms designed for private and family use. Often there was a kind of patio ornamented with delicate bundle columns opening onto a sunken garden bordered with sycamores. The houses of ordinary people were constructed in a more confined space and looked like one- or two-storeyed towers, pierced by windows with little bars and always with flat, terraced roofs surrounded by low walls.

The military fortresses that had already existed in the Old Kingdom became more important in the Middle Kingdom: they can be seen in mural pictures (at Beni Hasan, for example) with their crenellated walls. Their remains found under the sands of Nubia, and even beyond the second cataract in modern Sudan, have allowed the reconstruction of remarkable fortified works. There were small garrison towns with temples, defended by thick walls of mud brick, with glacis (sloping banks), bastions with loopholes, curtain-walls—in short, a prototype of the mediaeval European fortress.

The royal statuary of the 12th Dynasty, which was mirrored by low reliefs, rapidly evolved towards a new style expressed by two main schools and best detected in the treatment of facial features—the body continued to be rendered with extreme care following long-established models. The southern school is characterized by the sculpture of realistic faces, stern to the point of being tragic. The school of the north is said to have been inspired by Old Kingdom models. But this does not completely explain the phenomenon. It is certain that the ravaged face of an Amenemhat III or a Sesostris III corresponded as much to the physical types of those sovereigns as the southern sculptors would have portrayed them. There is evidence to suggest that, to ensure a funerary image of the sovereign that 'worked', it was necessary to commemorate the fulfilment by this divine figure (now more nearly human than in the Old Kingdom, thanks to the evolution of religious concepts) of *two* cycles: his 'solar cycle', radiating with youth, and his 'Osirian cycle', only reached by old age. Thus the effigies of youth and those of great maturity were both translated by genius into stone.

Hallmarks of the Middle Kingdom can also be seen in a certain evolution in dress (for example, a longer *pagne* or the projection of the 'apron' at the front) and by the poses and sex of the statues (statues of queens, seated, wearing the voluted Hathoric wig). At the end of the 12th Dynasty the severity of the royal features was even more accentuated on the so-called Hyksos monuments: sphinxes, statues, bearers of offerings. The 13th Dynasty was characterized by a return to more insipid faces, the appearance of some royal colossi and also by a fondness for the 'pseudo-group'—two images of the same person set side by side.

The evolution of religious ideas and above all the diffusion throughout the whole country of the Osirian cult gave a very special stamp to all the private statuary. In particular, the effigies of men and women seemed to be much closer to their models. A breath of realism animates the female images, wrapped, as they were, so closely in sheath-like clothes that they seem still naked: a certain sensuality underlines their anatomy. The men, dressed in longer *pagnes* made of several pieces of cloth that came up under the armpits and fell over the ankles, were always given features inspired by those of their sovereign. The popularity of pilgrimages to Abydos, the holy city of the dead god, stimulated the manufacture of portable funerary statuettes which were deposited there. And the fact that now the whole population had access to the Osirian destiny meant that instead of there being funerary portraits of privileged couples only, there were statues of real family groups in which the ancestors, parents and children were placed together on the same base (or socle). The funerary stele, too, now grouped likenesses of all the members of the family circle.

The beauty of the female face is sometimes very striking, so reminiscent is it of the European ideal. There was now more variety of attitudes, but always within specified conventions. Often the body was draped in a pilgrim's cloak which covered the arms and legs. The block-statue of a squatting or crouching man, with only the head, hands and feet emerging from his cloak, and the 'pseudo-group' were introduced into the repertoire. Images of men cast in scribal poses, on the other hand, temporarily disappeared. The anecdotal form continued to characterize graphic art; and in tomb paintings at, for example, El-Bersha and Beni Hasan, are preserved scenes of princesses wearing pendants and floral diadems similar to those which have been found in tombs, or processions of foreigners coming to pay a visit to the pharaoh's governors. Here the artists faithfully pictured Semite women dressed in robes whose shape and details were quite different from Egyptian fashions.

Pottery workshops produced many beautiful wares, and their glazed figurines in brilliant turquoise are among the most successful and original creations of Egyptian industry.

1
Model of a female brewer, limestone,
H. 26.7 cm., 5th Dynasty, Giza, Cairo
Mus.

2
Model of a female brewer, limestone,
H. 32 cm., 5th–6th Dynasty, Giza,
Oriental Inst., Chicago

3
Model of a butcher, limestone, H.
37 cm., 5th–6th Dynasty, Giza, Oriental Inst., Chicago

4
Model of a baker, painted limestone,
H. 26.5 cm., 5th Dynasty, Giza, Hil-
desheim

5
Model of a potter, limestone, H.
14 cm., 5th–6th Dynasty, Giza, Oriental Inst., Chicago

6
Nursing mother having her hair
dressed, limestone, H. 7.2 cm., 12th
Dynasty, Lisht, Metropolitan Mus.

7
Woman bearing a trough, polychrome wood, H. 1.04 m., 11th–12th Dynasty, Asyut, Louvre

8
Man carrying a calf, painted wood, H. 35.5 cm., 1st Intermediate Period, Louvre

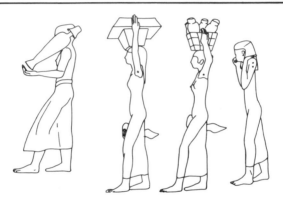

9   Offering-bearers, polychrome wood, H. (left to right) 31.5, 39, 39, 32 cm., Middle Kingdom, tomb of Djehuty-nakht, El-Bersha, Mus. of Fine Arts, Boston

10
Nursing woman, limestone, H. 10.5 cm., 5th–6th Dynasty, Giza, Metropolitan Mus.

11
Wrestlers (?), limestone, H. 9.8 cm., Middle Kingdom, Arab el-Bourg near Asyut, Mus. Royaux, Brussels

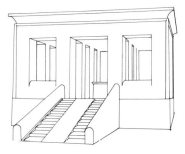

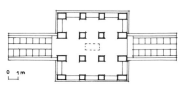

12
Barque shrine, the so-called White Chapel of Sesostris I, limestone, 12th Dynasty, Karnak

13
White Chapel of Sesostris I: plan, 12th Dynasty, Karnak

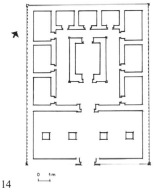

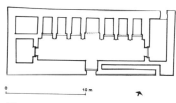

14
Temple of Sesostris I: reconstruction of the plan (two of the four pillars are problematic), 12th Dynasty, Tod

15
Temple at Qasr el-Sagha: plan, Middle Kingdom

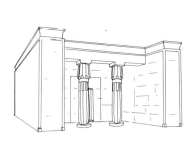

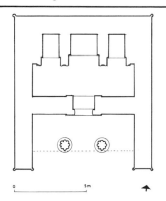

16
Temple at Medinet Ma'adi: reconstruction of the façade, Middle Kingdom

17
Temple at Medinet Ma'adi: plan, Middle Kingdom

233

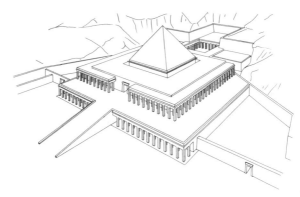

18   Funerary temple of Mentuhotep: reconstruction, 11th Dynasty, Deir el-
Bahri (the small pyramid is disputed)

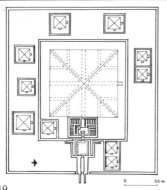

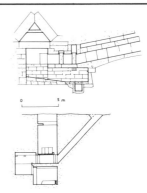

19
Funerary complex of Sesostris I and
members of the royal family: plan,
12th Dynasty, Lisht

20
Pyramid of Amenemhat II: crypt, 12th
Dynasty, Dahshur. Mastaba of Impy:
infrastructure, 12th Dynasty, Lahun

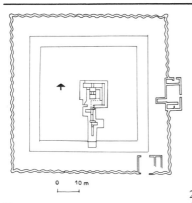

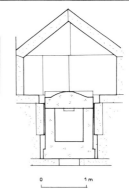

21
South pyramid at Mazghuna: plan,
Middle Kingdom

22
Civil, or private, tomb no. 306: section
of the funerary chamber, Middle
Kingdom, El-Riqqa

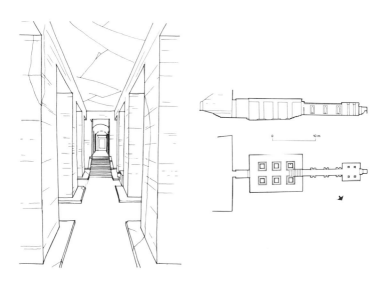

23
Rock tomb of the nomarch Sirenput II, contemporary of Amenemhat II: interior, 12th Dynasty, Aswan

24
Tomb of the nomarch Sirenput II: section and plan, 12th Dynasty, Aswan

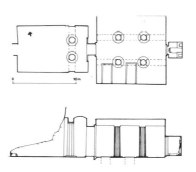

25–26   Tomb of Amenemhat: section and plan, 12th Dynasty, Beni Hasan

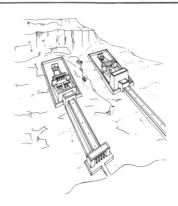

27   Funerary complex of Wahka I and Ibu: reconstruction, 12th Dynasty, Qaw el-Kebir

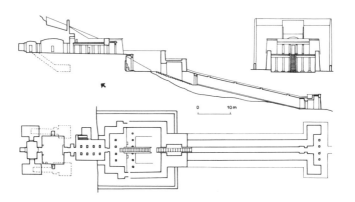

28   Tomb of Wahka I: sections and plan, 12th Dynasty, Qaw el-Kebir

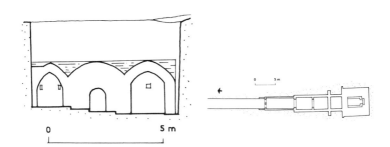

29
Tomb no. 1: section, Middle Kingdom, Qatta

30
Tomb no. 2: plan, Middle Kingdom, Qatta

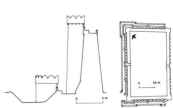

31
Painting of the attack on a fortress, 12th Dynasty, tomb no. 2 at Beni Hasan

32
Fortress of Sesostris I: reconstructed plan and section, 12th Dynasty, Aniba

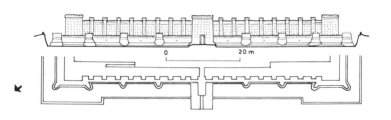

33 Fortress seen from the western side: reconstructed plan and elevation, 12th Dynasty, Buhen

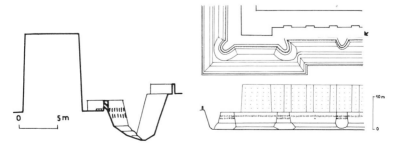

34
Details of the bastions, 12th Dynasty, Buhen

35
Details of the fortress, 12th Dynasty, Buhen

237

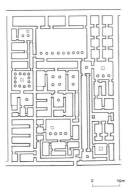

36
Plan of a large house, Middle Kingdom, Kahun

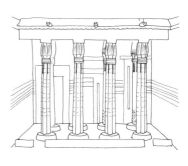

37
Model, portico with bundle lotiform columns, wood, 11th Dynasty, tomb, Deir el-Bahri, Metropolitan Mus.

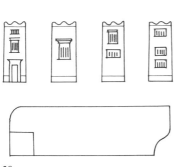

38
Model of the house of Amenemhat: plan and elevation, Middle Kingdom, El-Bersha

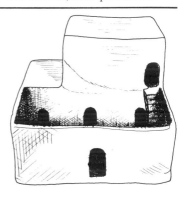

39
Model of a house, terracotta, Middle Kingdom, Louvre

40   Painted representation of granaries in the tomb of Antefoker, vizier to Sesostris I, 12th Dynasty, western Thebes

41
Seated statue of King Mentuhotep the
Great, sandstone, H. 2.08 m., 11th
Dynasty, Deir el-Bahri, Cairo Mus.

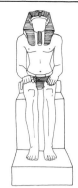

42
King Sesostris I, seated, wearing the
nemes, limestone, H. 1.94 m., 12th
Dynasty, Lisht, Cairo Mus.

43
King Sesostris I standing, wearing the
white crown, wood, H. 56 cm., 12th
Dynasty, Lisht, Cairo Mus.

44
Queen Nofret, Sesostris II's wife,
seated, grey granite, H. 1.55 m., 12th
Dynasty, Tanis, Cairo Mus.

45
Osiride pillar of Sesostris I as king of
the South, limestone, H. 1.89 m., 12th
Dynasty, Lisht, Cairo Mus.

46
Osiride pillar of Sesostris I as king of
the North, limestone, H. 1.83 m., 12th
Dynasty, Lisht, Cairo Mus.

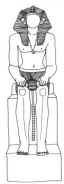

47
King Amenemhat III, wearing the *nemes,* yellow limestone, H. 1.60 m., 12th Dynasty, Hawara, Cairo Mus.

48
King Amenemhat III, standing, black granite, H. 2 m., 12th Dynasty, Memphis, St. Mus., E. Berlin.

49
King Amenemhat III, standing (short *pagne* and *nemes*), granite, H. 1.10 m., 12th Dynasty, Karnak, Cairo Mus.

50
King Sesostris III, kneeling and offering wine, sandstone, H. 52 cm., 12th Dynasty, Karnak, Cairo Mus.

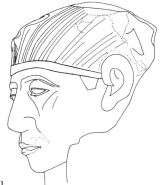

51
Head of Amenemhat III in profile, obsidian, H. 10.2 cm., 12th Dynasty, Gulbenkian Foundation, Lisbon

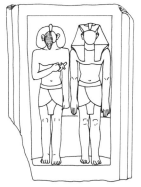

52
Naos of Amenemhat III, pink granite, H. 2.15 m., 12th Dynasty, Hawara, Cairo Mus.

53
King Amenemhat III as a sphinx, grey granite, L. 2.20 m., 12th Dynasty, Tanis, Cairo Mus.

54
Amenemhat III (?), black granite, H. 1 m., Middle Kingdom (?), Mit Faras, Cairo Mus.

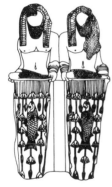

55
Geniuses of the Inundation, black granite, H. 1.60 m., Middle Kingdom, Tanis, Cairo Mus.

56
Side view of No. 55

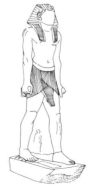

57
Naos of King Neferhetep I, limestone, H. 1 m., 13th Dynasty, Karnak, Cairo Mus.

58
King Sekhem Wadj-khau-re-Sebekemsaf, pink granite, H. 1.47 m., 13th Dynasty, Abydos, Cairo Mus.

59
High dignitary, bronze, H. 28 cm.,
Middle Kingdom, Dahshur, Louvre

60
Unknown man, standing, wood, H.
37.8 cm., 12th Dynasty, St. Mus., W.
Berlin

61
Man standing, wood, H. 27 cm.,
Middle Kingdom, Cairo Mus.

62
The priest Amenemhat Ankh, sand-
stone, H. 72 cm., 12th Dynasty,
Louvre

63
The official Antef, limestone, H.
37 cm., Middle Kingdom, St. Mus., W.
Berlin

64
The lady Iymeret neb-es (with detach-
able wig), wood, H. 48 cm., 12th
Dynasty, Leiden

65
Statuette of the lady Anuket, alabaster (wooden base), H. 18 cm., Middle Kingdom, Elephantine, Cairo Mus.

66
Headless female statuette; back and front, grey ivory, H. 18.5 cm., Middle Kingdom, Louvre

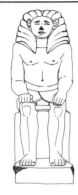

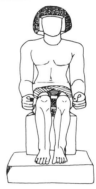

67
Seated man, limestone, H. 47 cm., Middle Kingdom, Leiden

68
The nobleman Mentuhotep, seated, limestone, H. 27 cm., 11th Dynasty, Dendera, Cairo Mus.

69
Dignitary in the attitude of a worshipper, granite, H. 46 cm., 12th Dynasty, Kiman Faris, Cairo Mus.

70
Statuette of a man resting, bronze, H. 51.3 cm., 12th Dynasty, Metropolitan Mus.

71
The vizier (?) Hemet-Tcha (?), granite, H. 1.15 m., 12th Dynasty, Karnak, Cairo Mus.

72
The lady Sennui: detail, granite, t. H. 1.72 m., Middle Kingdom, Sudan, Mus. of Fine Arts, Boston

73
Kemehu squatting, hard stone, dark maroon, H. 19 cm., Middle Kingdom, Abydos, Cairo Mus.

74
Kheti squatting, wrapped in his cloak, granite, H. 20.5 cm., Middle Kingdom, Abydos, Cairo Mus.

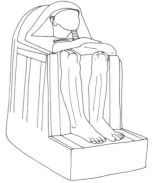

75
'Block-statue' of Senusret-seneb-ef-ni, quartzite, H. 68.3 cm., 12th Dynasty, Brooklyn Mus.

76
Hetep in her sedan chair, limestone, H. 1.10 m., Middle Kingdom, Saqqara, Cairo Mus.

77
High-relief stele for the persons of the couple, limestone, H. 48 cm., 1st Intermediate Period, Leiden

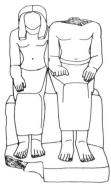

78
Seated couple, red sandstone, H. 20 cm., Middle Kingdom, temple of Pepi II at Saqqara, Cairo Mus.

79
Couple standing, steatite, H. 17.5 cm., 12th Dynasty, Kom ol Hiam, Cairo Mus.

80
A couple holding hands, black granite, H. 12.6 cm., 12th Dynasty, Metropolitan Mus.

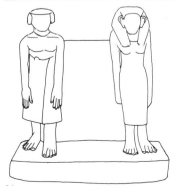

81
A couple with the figures well separated, serpentine, H. 16.5 cm., 12th Dynasty, Metropolitan Mus.

82
Deceased flanked by wife and son, black stone, H. 20 cm., Middle Kingdom, Thebes, St. Mus., W. Berlin

245

83
Block-statues, with female figure, red sandstone, H. 25 cm., Middle Kingdom, Kom el-Shatain, Cairo Mus.

84
Sehetepibre-ankh-Nedjem and his son, red sandstone, H. 83 cm., 12th Dynasty, Memphis, Louvre

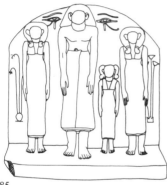

85
High-relief stele: Wah-hotep and his family, dark grey granite, H. 31.5 cm., 12th Dynasty, Meir, Cairo Mus.

86
Group of Betcha and his family, limestone, H. 47.5 cm., 1st Intermediate Period, Abydos (?), Louvre

87
Sebekhotep with female relatives, granite, H. 34 cm., W. 32 cm., 13th Dynasty, Kiman Faris, Cairo Mus.

88
High-relief stele: Senpu and his family, limestone, H. 24 cm., offering table in alabaster, 12th Dynasty, Louvre

89
Relief: King Mentuhotep the Great,
limestone, 11th Dynasty, Tod, Louvre

90
Painting: daughter of Djehuty-Hetep
(detail), painted *pisé*, H. 80 cm., 12th
Dynasty, El-Bersha, Cairo Mus.

91   Detail of carved coffin from sarcophagus of Kawit, wife of King Mentuhotep, limestone with traces of polychrome, 11th Dynasty, Deir el-Bahri, Cairo
Mus.

92
Relief, detail: Ptah and Sesostris I,
limestone, 12th Dynasty, Karnak,
Cairo Mus.

93
Detail (as No. 92): Horus and Sesostris I

94   Wall painting: Hyksos noblewomen, 11th Dynasty, rock tomb of Khnumhetep, Beni Hasan

95   Wall painting: Hyksos chiefs on a peaceful visit, 11th Dynasty, rock tomb
of Khnumhetep, Beni Hasan

96   Wall painting: scene showing acrobatics, 11th Dynasty, rock tomb no. 15
of Prince Baket, Beni Hasan

THE NEW KINGDOM

With the New Kingdom and the 18th Dynasty, Thebes, the capital, became one of the centres of the civilized world. This was the time when the royal funerary temple was dissociated from the tomb. Sanctuaries were erected beyond the farmland areas, in the dried-out wadis on the right bank; rock vaults hid actual underground apartments which were still topped by the great natural pyramid formed by the mountain peak. The original plans followed a curved line, then they formed a right-angle and finally, around the Amarnian period, like a ray of sun piercing straight through the rock, came the 'syrinx' distribution of rooms in the royal vaults, so-called because it reminded ancient Greek visitors of a flute. The private hypogea always had a rock-chapel on top shaped like a cross, capped with a small pyramid and sometimes decorated with columns.

The most prestigious of this period's royal funerary temples, 'Temples of Millions of Years', is the one constructed by Senmut for the queen, Hatshepsut. Near Mentuhotep's monument, at the base of the semicircle formed by the mountains at Deir el-Bahri, is a veritable 'funerary Versailles' which seems to rise up to vie with the mountain. Central ramps connect three successive terraces which are bordered with square pillars and Osiride pillars. The funerary chapels of the queen and the first two Tuthmosides were on the top level of this huge building called the 'Sublime of the Sublimes'.

Still on the left bank, the remains of the great foundation of Amenophis III help us to imagine the splendour and importance of these buildings erected just before the Amarnian period. It was at this time that the first colossi (monoliths 20 metres high) were raised up in front of religious buildings.

Over on the right bank, at Luxor, this same Amenophis III had had his temple built, famous for its court surrounded by bundle columns with closed lotiform capitals. The whole of the hypostyle hall was decorated with similar columns. In front of the court was a majestic colonnade of open papyrus-flower capitals forming a sort of triumphal way (which, under Rameses II, ultimately led into the centre of the hypostyle). Rameses II added a forecourt and a large two-towered pylon in front of the Luxor colonnade.

The pattern of the classic temple, as seen in the Rameses complexes on the left bank, does not yet appear to have been definitive in the 18th Dynasty. At Karnak, city of the god Amen, each sovereign was anxious to enlarge, complete, innovate, to leave his mark in the heart of this great machine for renewing the cosmic forces. In front of the third pylon, constructed by Amenophis III, a vast colonnade had been erected, as at Luxor. Horemheb, Rameses I, Seti I and Rameses II gradually flanked it with 122 columns with papyrus-bud capitals, each of them a single shaft and shorter than those in the original colonnade, so that the tops of the central columns could be joined by high stone windows with small grilles, forming a clerestory. This was the basilica style, under a terraced roof, that our cathedrals have inherited.

The temples dedicated by Amenophis IV to the solar disc (eye), Aten, were all built open to the sky. Those at Amarna are gigantic, furnished with at least one altar for each day of the year, and with exceptionally ornate pylons in front of them with five flagpoles per tower. It was not until the 19th Dynasty and the Ramesseum erected by Rameses II in Western Thebes (and copied by Rameses III at Medinet Habu) that one comes across a temple with all the features that were to continue right up until the Late Period: obelisks and colossi in front of the high trapezoid towers of the pylons (each embellished with one to four flag-poles), two courts (for the jubilee foundations), then a hypostyle hall (basilical) and finally the third part which consisted of the annexes which preceded and sur-rounded the sanctuary or Holy of Holies. Round about were arranged outbuild-ings, storehouses, offices, workshops, cow-sheds and even a small palace for the sovereign's ritual sojourn.

Tuthmosis III had a special predilection for peripteral temples, built for the sacred barques. The Nubian cenotaphs and rock-temples, on the other hand, were mainly in vogue under Seti I and Rameses II.

To judge from the wall decorations and pavements painted with bucolic scenes that were found in the ruins of Amenophis III's palace at Malkata (on the left bank of Thebes) and in the ones at el-Amarna, or those of Seti and the Rameseses at Pi-Ramses on the Delta (modern Qantir), the official royal palaces—which were as a rule built on the river's right (eastern) bank—must have been sumptu-ous. They contained a room for the throne and for festivities, private apartments, the house of the Great Royal Wife, dwellings reserved for the Second Wives and the royal children: they were almost little towns themselves. The plan, however, conformed to the same law which governed the arrangement of areas in temple or tomb: forecourt (court, antechamber, hall); reception (hypostyle hall, large audience chambers, main parts of the funerary chapel); and finally the Holy of Holies in the temple, private apartments in the residence (provided with lavator-ies) and in the tomb, the vault.

The ruins of Tell el-Amarna (ancient Akhetaton) contain remarkable remains of vast houses arranged in flower gardens with rectangular ornamental lakes. The presence of offices and outhouses—servants' dwellings, kitchens, silos, ken-nels, cow-sheds, stables, bakers' and butchers' shops, weaving workshops—made each domain into a small private economy. In the city the *loggia* was replaced by one solid storey with high, barred windows. Painted decorations on the walls of private funerary chapels sometimes carried pictures of the master's dwelling-place. By good fortune a drawing showing a cross-section of the house of Djehuty-Hetep at Thebes has been preserved. In the half-basement the spin-ning workshops can be seen; the raised ground floor contains the master's apart-ments and reception chamber; a wide stair leads to the half-terraced first floor; and there can even be seen, under lean-to roofs, the bakery, the kitchens and an airy place for drying pieces of meat.

Fortified buildings of the past were strengthened and new citadels built. The need to do this was not felt so much in Nubia, although the cataracts still had to be defended. Garrisons were posted at the entrances to goldmines and at the arrival points for caravans. The marches along the Libyan frontier were vigor-ously fortified by the Ramessides. From the start of the 18th Dynasty, all the defences on Egypt's Asian side, which protected the wells and coastal route to Ugarit (Ras Shamra), were put in good order. Fortified towns on the Orontes such as Kadesh and, beyond that, Dapur (the architecture of which had been influenced by the building art of the Amorites and even the Hittites) provided new models for the military architects.

At the beginning of the 18th Dynasty, the Theban workshops, weakened by the long Hyksos occupation, drew all their inspiration from models of the earlier kingdom. Not until the peaceful reign of Hatshepsut did artists regain their momentum. Wars of liberation and closer contact with Asian lands had provided patterns of ostentation and luxury for emulation by the rich and powerful. The return of the good life and the opulence ensured by Tuthmosis III's conquests directly affected all the arts that had evolved alongside architecture. Suppleness, elegance and charm suffused the reliefs, statuary and all the creations of the artisan-artists and gave them increasing vitality.

The grace and beauty of Hatshepsut's royal face seemed to be communicated to all 18th-Dynasty statues. Even effigies of pharaohs with powerful musculature came under this influence. Wigs changed with successive fashions. From the charming youthful figure of Amenophis II to the almond-eyed Amenophis III, official statuary was matched by more informal portraits of the sovereigns in their rich and dressy court clothes. Reliefs and paintings, noble stone statuary, smaller works of precious wood sometimes plated with gold leaf, all rendered images of the most beautiful men and women in the world. The heights of sweetness and refinement seemed to have been reached. Kneeling worshippers holding before them a *naos* or a stele, block-statues of high tax officials from whose laps the little heads of princesses peep, distinguished couples with pleated robes and ornamented wigs: it was all a feast for the eyes.

And then suddenly Amenophis IV–Akhenaten decided to instruct new workers himself, to encourage them to become revolutionaries and to return as closely as possible to pure realism, thereby abandoning the original religious message. Pushing expressionism to the extreme, he even urged them to exaggerate certain lines in order to draw attention to the most characteristic and salient features. Discarding some (but not all) of the official principles of figuration, he decided to represent the royal couple—and the children who guaranteed their fertility— joined physically, embracing, intertwining, holding hands, with the folds of the 'wet' drapery usually clinging to the sensual body of the queen. Reliefs and paintings expressed a realism, movement, quivering life that animated all the walls. Colours were rendered in half-shades that had never been used before. After this 'Amarna' experiment, despite all efforts to revive a classicism that had disappeared, artistic productions would never be the same again. Certainly Rameses II had copies made of the colossi that Amenophis III had, by force, made fashionable, but statuary had been permanently affected by a spirit unknown under the last Tuthmosides. A portrait was even sculpted of the great Rameses in the long pleated robe of contemporary dress, the uraeus on his forehead as prominent as under Akhenaten, head bent slightly to one side.

The statuary of private persons, with its themes continuously evolving, presented its subjects decked out in sumptuous costumes, the locks of the ladies' wigs falling onto their breasts. These faces of perfect beauty still bore a look of metaphysical contemplation (statues of the vizier Pa Ramessu or of Bakenkhonsu). Often the deceased, with or without a child, was portrayed flanked by his mother and his wife. Pharaoh appeared in majesty, in the circle of divinities who, seated at his sides, put their arms around his waist or shoulders. From the Amarnian period on, the squatting-scribe theme showed the writer bent over his work, absorbed in his task under the benevolent eye of the cynocephalic Thoth. Similarly, the kneeling figure of the king was represented as under the tutelage of the divinity, which looked down on his image from behind. Sovereign and civilian, equally, could be portrayed as ensign-bearers. And there were also the graceful compositions of Rameses as an athlete, on his knees pushing an offering.

From the time that the horse was introduced into Egypt, irrepressible movement enlivened all compositions (the large works, and even the miniatures)—thus making a break with the perpetual decoration in registers—led by the majestic pharaoh, driving his chariot.

In reliefs and paintings realistic expression replaced conventional gestures. For proof of this one need only compare, for example, the same scene of wailing women before, during and after the Amarnian period.

And yet many problems are still to be resolved. Why, for instance, in pictures of couples, is the woman sometimes placed to the right of the man and sometimes to his left? This occurred in every period.

But of one thing one can be sure: the New Kingdom, which drew to a close with the last Ramessides, in spite of a rather overloaded, impersonal classicism was the period when the taste for the precious and the pursuit of beauty were taken to such a degree that in certain pieces (e. g., the little gazelle in the Metropolitan Museum, New York), perhaps for the first time in Egypt, it is possible to detect the notion of the art-object as a source of pleasure.

EGYPT AND THE EXTENT OF ITS INFLUENCE UNDER THE NEW KINGDOM

1	Carchemish	10	Qantir (Pi-Ramses)
2	Mari	11	Memphis
3	Kadesh	12	Lisht
4	Byblos	13	Faiyum
5	Tyre	14	Tell el-Amarna (Akhetaten)
6	Megiddo	15	This (?)
7	Gaza	16	Thebes
8	El-Arish	17	Napata
9	Petra	18	Khartoum

HITTITE EMPIRE

MITANNIAN
EMPIRE

CRETE

CYPRUS

Orontes

TO ASSYRIA

Tigris

MEDITERRANEAN SEA

RETENU

SYRIAN DESERT

Euphrates

BYA

ARABIAN DESERT

SINAI

Bahriya Oasis

Dakhla Oasis

Kharga Oasis

1st CATARACT

WAWAT

2nd CATARACT

Selima Oasis

Nile

3rd CATARACT

KUSH

NUBIA

RED SEA

4th CATARACT

5th CATARACT

100 200 300 400 km

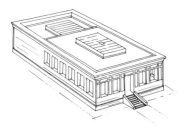

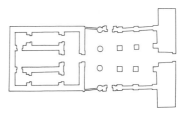

1
Reconstruction of the small Tuthmoside temple at Medinet Habu, beginning of 18th Dynasty, Thebes

Chapel at Amada: plan, 18th Dynasty, Nubia

3
Façade of the temple of Amen-Re: two obelisks in front of the pylon and the colossi, 19th Dynasty, Luxor

4
Temple of Khonsu: antique drawing of façade of the second pylon, temple of Amen-Re, 20th Dynasty, Karnak

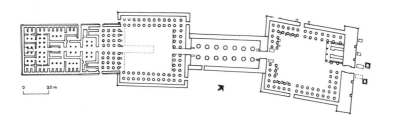

5   Temple of Luxor: plan, 18th and 19th Dynasties

6   Hypostyle hall of Amenophis III, 18th Dynasty, Temple of Luxor

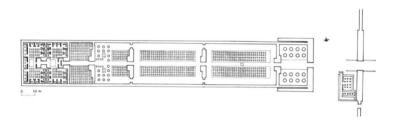

7   Great temple of Aten at Tell el-Amarna, the Per Hai: plan, end of 18th
Dynasty

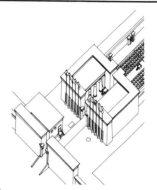

8
Great temple at Tell el-Amarna, the
Gem-Aten: plan, end of 18th Dynasty

9
Entrance of the Per Hai: reconstruction, axonometric perspective, end of
18th Dynasty, Tell el-Amarna

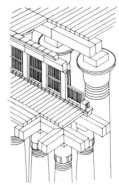

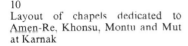

10
Layout of chapels dedicated to Amen-Re, Khonsu, Montu and Mut at Karnak

11
Temple of Amen-Re, reconstruction, ceiling and 'clerestory' of hypostyle hall at Karnak, 19th Dynasty

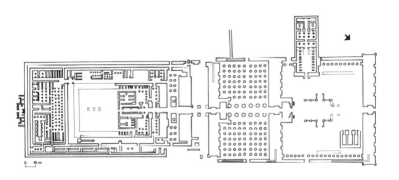

12   Great Temple of Amen at Karnak: plan

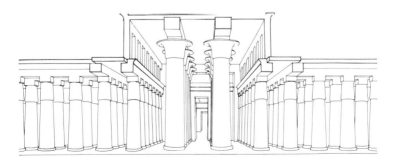

13   Hypostyle hall at Karnak (after Perrot and Chipiez), New Kingdom

14
Façade of the Great Temple of
Rameses II at Abu Simbel, 19th
Dynasty

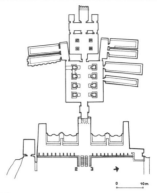

15
Great Temple of Rameses II at Abu
Simbel: plan, 19th Dynasty

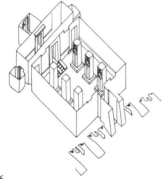

16
Small Temple of Queen Nefertari at
Abu Simbel: axonometric section,
19th Dynasty

17
Small Temple of Queen Nefertari at
Abu Simbel: façade, 19th Dynasty

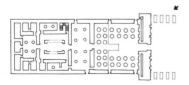

18
Temple of Khonsu at Karnak: plan,
20th Dynasty

19
Temple of Khonsu at Karnak: axonometric reconstruction, 20th Dynasty

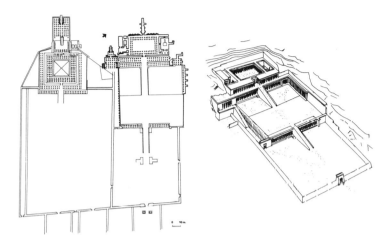

20
Temple of Mentuhotep I–III and
temple of Hatshepsut: plans, 11th and
18th Dynasties, Deir el-Bahri

21
Temple of Hatshepsut: reconstruction, 18th Dynasty, Deir el-Bahri

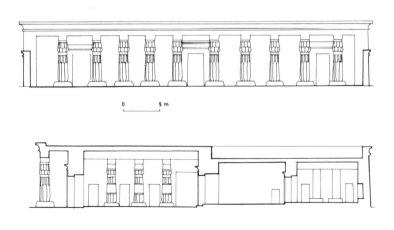

22   Temple of Seti I: façade and longitudinal section, 19th Dynasty, Qurna

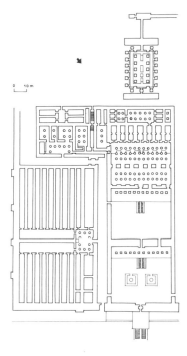

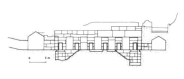

24
Cenotaph in the temple of Seti I, Osireion: longitudinal section of the infrastructure, 19th Dynasty, Abydos

23
Temple of Seti I and Osireion: plan, 19th Dynasty, Abydos

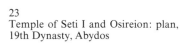

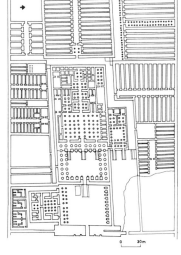

25
Temple of Seti I: median longitudinal section, 19th Dynasty, Abydos

26
Jubilee temple, the Ramesseum, small temple of Tuy and annexes: plan, 19th Dynasty, western Thebes

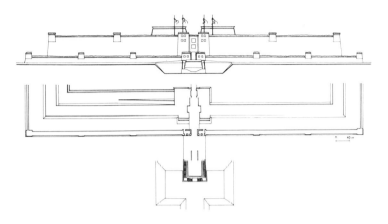

27   Enceinte of the jubilee temple of Rameses III: elevation and plan of the entrance with the landing stage, 20th Dynasty, Medinet Habu, Thebes

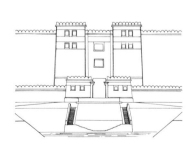

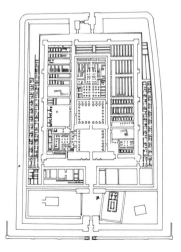

28
Temple at Medinet Habu: landing-stage and monumental gate, 20th Dynasty, Thebes

29
Jubilee temple of Rameses III: plan of the *temenos,* 20th Dynasty, Medinet Habu, Thebes

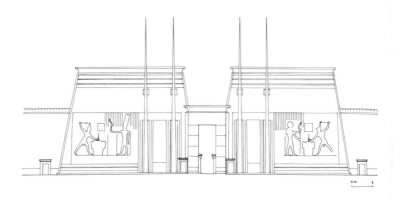

30   Temple at Medinet Habu: façade, 20th Dynasty, Thebes

31   Temple at Medinet Habu: longitudinal section, 20th Dynasty, Thebes

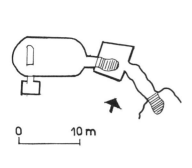

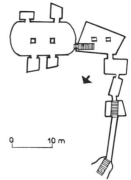

32
Plan of the tomb of Tuthmosis I, 18th Dynasty, western Thebes, Valley of the Kings

33
Plan of the tomb of Tuthmosis III, 18th Dynasty, western Thebes, Valley of the Kings

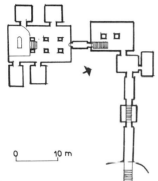

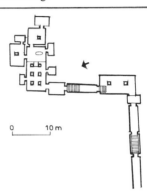

34
Plan of the tomb of Amenophis II, 18th Dynasty, western Thebes, Valley of the Kings

35
Plan of the tomb of Amenophis III, 18th Dynasty, western Thebes, Valley of the Kings

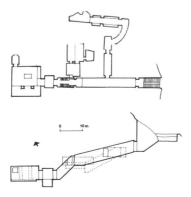

36–37   Plan and section of the royal tomb, Tell el-Amarna: Dar el-Melek, 18th Dynasty

38
Plan of the tomb of Horemheb, 18th Dynasty, western Thebes, Valley of the Kings

39
Plan of the tomb of Seti I, 19th Dynasty, western Thebes, Valley of the Kings

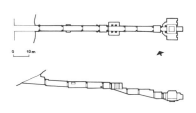

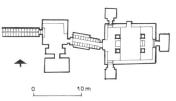

40
Plan and section of the tomb of Rameses VI, 20th Dynasty, western Thebes, Valley of the Kings

41
Plan of the tomb of Nefertari, 19th Dynasty, western Thebes, Valley of the Queens

42
Inner chapel representing the ancient sanctuary of the South, 18th Dynasty, tomb of Tutankhamun, Cairo Mus.

43
Second and third chapel (ancient sanctuary of the North), 18th Dynasty, tomb of Tutankhamun, Cairo Mus.

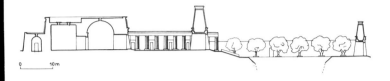

44 Funerary temple of Amenhotep, son of Hapu, divinized royal architect, reconstructed section, 18th Dynasty, western Thebes

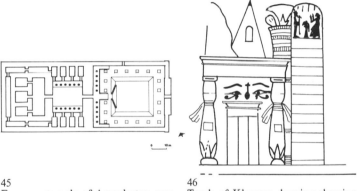

45
Funerary temple of Amenhotep, son of Hapu: reconstructed plan, 18th Dynasty, western Thebes

46
Tomb of Khonsu: drawing showing the façade of a civil or private funerary chapel, 19th Dynasty, western Thebes

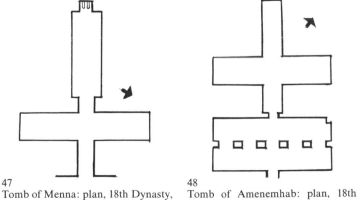

47
Tomb of Menna: plan, 18th Dynasty, Sheikh Abd el-Qurna, no. 69, western Thebes

48
Tomb of Amenemhab: plan, 18th Dynasty, Sheikh Abd el-Qurna, no. 85, western Thebes

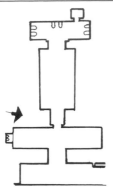

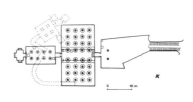

49
Tomb of Khaemhat: plan, 18th Dynasty, Sheikh Abd el-Qurna, no. 57, western Thebes

50
Tomb of Ramose: plan, 19th Dynasty, Sheikh Abd el-Qurna, no. 55, western Thebes

51   Restored chapel in the tomb of Ramose: section, 19th Dynasty, Sheikh Abd el-Qurna, no. 55, western Thebes

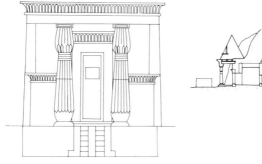

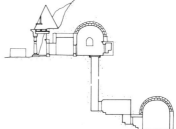

52
Tomb of Ipuy: wall painting depicting a peripteral kiosk, 19th Dynasty, Deir el-Medina, western Thebes

53
Artisan's tomb, *hemi-speos* type: longitudinal section, New Kingdom, Deir el-Medina, western Thebes

54   Tomb of Djehuty Hetep: ancient drawing of a section of a town house, 18th
      Dynasty, Sheikh Abd el-Qurna, no. 80, western Thebes

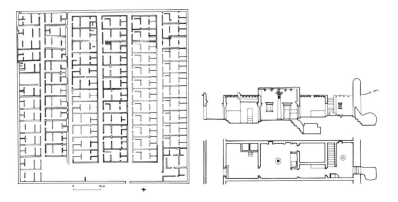

55
Eastern artisans' village: plan, 18th
Dynasty, Tell el-Amarna

56
Worker's house: section and plan,
New Kingdom, Deir el-Medina

57
Model of a citizen's house, New Kingdom, Louvre

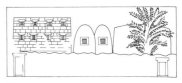

58
Estate of Ineny, New Kingdom, Sheikh Abd el-Qurna, no. 81, western Thebes

59
Tomb of Nebamon: drawing of his house, New Kingdom, Sheikh Abd el-Qurna, no. 90, western Thebes

60
Fortress with bastions: axonometric section in perspective, 12th (?) and 18th Dynasties, west Semna

61
Drawing of the fortress at Kadesh, temple of Rameses II, 19th Dynasty, Abu Simbel

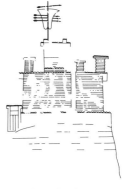

62
Hypostyle hall in the Ramesseum: drawing of the fortress of Dapur, 19th Dynasty, western Thebes

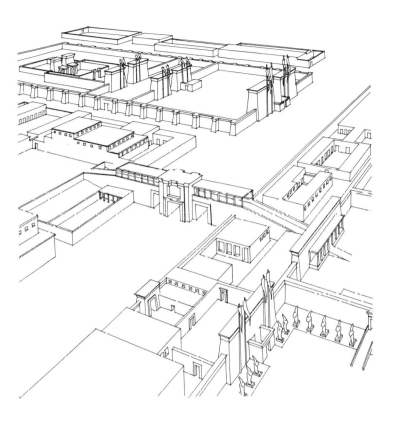

63   Perspective reconstruction of the central quarter of the city of Akhetaten (temples and palace), 18th Dynasty, Tell el-Amarna

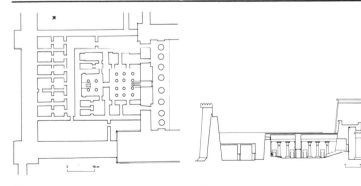

64
Palace annex of Rameses III: plan, 20th Dynasty, Medinet Habu, western Thebes

65
First palace of Rameses III: longitudinal section, restored, 20th Dynasty, Medinet Habu, western Thebes

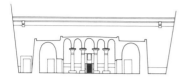

66
First palace of Rameses III: restored transverse section, 20th Dynasty, Medinet Habu, western Thebes

67
Reconstructed house: north–south axial section (V 37-1), 18th Dynasty, Tell el-Amarna

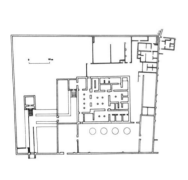

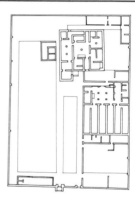

68
House of an eminent person (T. 36.II): plan, 18th Dynasty, Tell el-Amarna

69
House and offices of the tax-collector: plan, 18th Dynasty, Tell el-Amarna

70   Commercial quarter of the city of Akhetaten: perspective reconstruction, 18th Dynasty, Tell el-Amarna

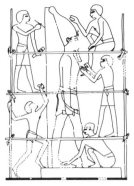

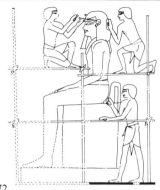

71

Painting: artisans working on a royal statue, 18th Dynasty, from tomb of Rekh-mi-re in western Thebes

72

Painting: another scene from tomb of Rekh-mi-re in western Thebes (see No. 71)

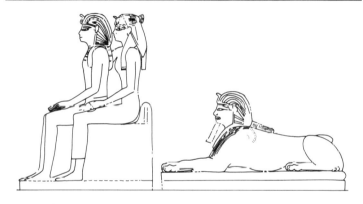

73   Painting: statues of royal couple and of King Thutmosis III as a sphinx, 18th Dynasty, tomb of Rekh-mi-re in western Thebes

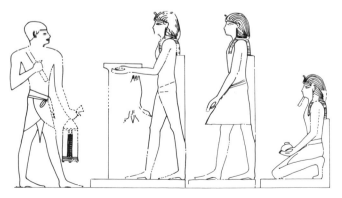

74   Painting: finished royal statues being inspected by the vizier's scribe, 18th Dynasty, tomb of Rekh-mi-re in western Thebes

75
Queen Tetisheri, mother of Amosis, painted limestone, H. 37 cm., 18th Dynasty, Dar Abul'Naga, B.M.

76
Statue of Queen Hatshepsut, seated, black granite, H. 1.50 m., 18th Dynasty, Deir el-Bahri

77
Mut-Nofret, mother of King Tuthmosis II, sandstone, H. 1.65 m., 18th Dynasty, Qurna, Cairo Mus.

78
Isis, mother of Tuthmosis III, black granite, H. 98 cm., Karnak, Cairo Mus.

79
Queen Hatshepsut offering wine, pink granite, H. 2.80 m., 18th Dynasty, Deir el-Bahri, Metropolitan Mus.

80
King Tuthmosis III, limestone, H. 27.5 cm., 18th Dynasty, temple of Deir el-Medina, Cairo Mus.

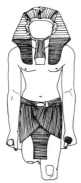

81
King Tuthmosis III, standing, schist, H. 89cm., 18th Dynasty, Karnak, Cairo Mus.

82
King Tuthmosis III as a sphinx, grey granite, L. 63 cm., 18th Dynasty, Karnak, Cairo Mus.

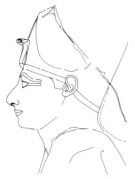

83
King Tuthmosis III; profile, grey-green schist, H. 2 m., 18th Dynasty, Karnak, Cairo Mus.

84
King Amenophis II, kneeling, grey granite, H. 1.21 m., 18th Dynasty, Karnak, Cairo Mus.

85
King Amenophis II, standing, pink granite, H. 1.44 m., 18th Dynasty, Karnak, Cairo Mus.

86
Headless statue of King Amenophis II, grey granite, H. 63cm., 18th Dynasty, Karnak, Cairo Mus.

87
King Tuthmosis IV and his mother, seated, black granite, H. 1.10 m., 18th Dynasty, Karnak, Cairo Mus.

88
King Amenophis III, Tiy and their daughters, limestone, H. 70 cm., 18th Dynasty, western Thebes, Cairo Mus.

89
Relief: King Amenophis III, limestone, nearly life-size, 18th Dynasty, western Thebes, St. Mus., E. Berlin

90
Relief: Queen Tiy, limestone, H. 42 cm., 18th Dynasty, western Thebes, Mus. Royaux, Brussels

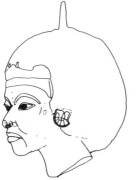

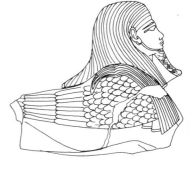

91
Head of Queen Tiy, boxwood and other materials, H. 10.7 cm., 18th Dynasty, Faiyum, St. Mus., W. Berlin

92
Amenophis III as sphinx, blue glazed composition, H. 29.5 cm., L. 28 cm., 18th Dynasty, Karnak, Cairo Mus.

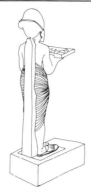

93
King Amenophis III, maroon schist, H, 23 cm., 18th Dynasty, Metropolitan Mus.

94
King Amenophis IV: back view, yellow limestone, H. 37 cm., 18th Dynasty, Tell el-Amarna, Cairo Mus.

95
Colossus of King Amenophis IV, sandstone, H. 4 m., 18th Dynasty, Karnak, Cairo Mus.

96
Colossus of King Amenophis IV, sandstone, H. 2.95 m., 18th Dynasty, Karnak, Cairo Mus.

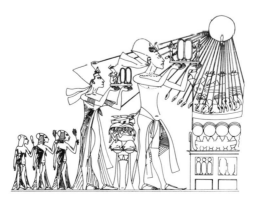

97   Low relief: Amenophis IV–Akhenaten, Nefertiti and three princesses making offerings to the sun, 18th Dynasty, tomb of Apy, Tell el-Amarna

98
Unfinished statuette: Akhenaten and
daughter, limestone, H. 42 cm., 18th
Dynasty, Cairo Mus.

99
Torso of Queen Nefertiti, red quartzite, H. 30 cm., 18th Dynasty, Louvre

100
Amarnian relief: Nefertiti consecrat-
ing offerings, sandstone, H. 21.5 cm,
W. 26.3 cm., 18th Dynasty, priv. coll.

101
Group of Akhenaten and Nefertiti,
polychrome limestone, H. 22.5 cm.,
18th Dynasty, Tell el-Amarna, Louvre

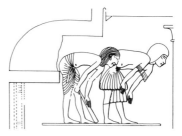

102
Wall painting: two daughters of King
Akhenaten, 18th Dynasty, palace at
el-Amarna, Ashmolean Mus.

103
Drawing of the positioning of a sculpture: palace personnel, 18th Dynasty,
tomb of Ramose, western Thebes

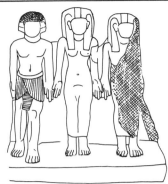

104
The lady Ahmes, Sen[i] and Wadjet, limestone, H. 16.2 cm., 17th–18th Dynasty, Asasif, Metropolitan Mus.

105
Archaistic male statue, wood, H. 17.8 cm., New Kingdom, Louvre

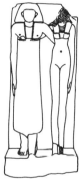

106
The vizier Userman and his wife, black granite, H. 88 cm., 18th Dynasty, Karnak, Cairo Mus.

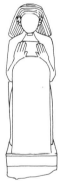

107
Amenemhat holding a stele, sandstone, H. 45 cm., 18th Dynasty, Asasif, western Thebes, Cairo Mus.

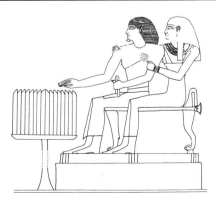

108   The master of the tomb and his wife before the offering table, tomb of Pu-yem-re, 18th Dynasty, Sheikh Abd el-Qurna, western Thebes

109   Painting: the vizier and his wife receiving *sistra* and *menats* from their daughters, 18th Dynasty, tomb of Rekh-mi-re, Sheikh Abd el-Qurna, no. 100, western Thebes

110
Wall painting: guests and servants at the funeral banquet, 18th Dynasty, tomb of Rekh-mi-re, as no. 109

111
Setau on his knees, holding a crypto-gram, limestone, H. 26.7 cm., 18th Dynasty, Louvre

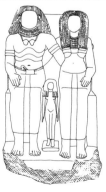

112
Unknown family trio, limestone, H. 46 cm., 18th Dynasty, Leiden

113
Sennefer and Sene[t]nai with their daughter, black granite, H. 1.20 m., 18th Dynasty, Karnak, Cairo Mus.

114
Block-statue of Amenemhat, black granite, H. 80 cm., 18th Dynasty, temple of Mut at Karnak, Cairo Mus.

115
Man standing, wood, H. 18.4 cm., 18th Dynasty, Meermanno Westreenianum Mus., The Hague

116
The lady Nai, wood, H. 26.4 cm., 18th Dynasty, Louvre

117
Statuette of an official, wood, H. 43 cm., 18th Dynasty, Thebes, St. Mus., W. Berlin

118
Painting: banquet scene, 18th Dynasty, tomb of Rekh-mi-re, western Thebes

119
Fragmented wall painting: banquet scene (music and dancing), 18th Dynasty, western Thebes, B.M.

120
Nubian tribute-bearer with a monkey on a lead, 18th Dynasty, tomb of Rekh-mi-re, no. 100, western Thebes

121
Wall painting: harvesting, 18th Dynasty, tomb of Menna, no. 69, western Thebes

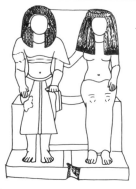

122
Tchai and Naia, seated, limestone, H. 90 cm., 18th–19th Dynasty, Saqqara, Cairo Mus.

123
Iny and Tentimentet, seated, limestone, H. 29 cm., 18th Dynasty, Qurna, Cairo Mus.

124
Young naked girl holding a cat to her breast, wood, H. 14.3 cm., New Kingdom, B.M.

125
Young naked girl holding a cat to her breast, wood, H. 10.5 cm., New Kingdom, Louvre

126
The parents of Ramose: the royal favourite, Mai, and his wife Wel, 18th Dynasty, western Thebes

127
Statuette of Tchai, ebony, H. 40 cm., 18th Dynasty, Saqqara, Cairo Mus.

128
The lady Tui, wood, H. 33.2 cm., 18th Dynasty, Thebes (?), Louvre

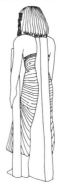

129
Amennakt as ensign-bearer: back view, wood, H. 60 cm., 18th Dynasty, St. Mus., E. Berlin

130
Amennakt as ensign-bearer (as No. 129): front view

131
Amenhotep, son of Hapu, black granite, H. 1.28 m., 18th Dynasty, Karnak, Cairo Mus.

132   Fragmented painting: hunting scene, 18th Dynasty, tomb of Nebamon (?), Sheikh Abd el-Qurna, no. 90, western Thebes, B.M.

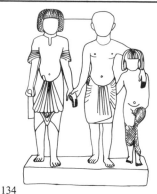

133
Statuette of a priest (?), wood, H. 25.5 cm., New Kingdom, St. Mus., E. Berlin

134
Amarnian civil group, limestone, H. 17.5 cm., 18th Dynasty, Tell el-Amarna (?), Metropolitan Mus.

135
Amarnian official, limestone, H. 18 cm., 18th Dynasty, Tell el-Amarna, Cairo Mus.

136
Scribe with cynocephalic Thoth, steatite, H. 14 cm., 18th Dynasty, Tell el-Amarna, Cairo Mus.

137
Monumental statue of Maya, limestone, H. 2.16 m., 18th Dynasty, Saqqâra (?), Leiden

138
Ptah-mai and his family, limestone, H. 95 cm., 18th Dynasty, Memphis, St. Mus., E. Berlin

139
A noble and his wife, steatite, H. 15.9 cm., 19th Dynasty, Metropolitan Mus.

140
Horemheb as a scribe, grey granite, H. 1.17 m., 18th Dynasty, Memphis, Metropolitan Mus.

141
Osirian triad framing King Horemheb, black granite, H. 1.42 m., 18th Dynasty, Abydos, Cairo Mus.

142
Painting: wailing women, 18th Dynasty, tomb of Ramose, Sheikh Abd el-Qurna, no. 55, western Thebes

143   Relief: wailing women (detail), limestone, end of 18th Dynasty, tomb of
Horemheb, Saqqara, Louvre

144   Wall painting: scene of wailing women on the roof of the deceased's
barque, 19th Dynasty, tomb of Nebamon and Ipuky, no. 181 at Khokha, western
Thebes

145   Relief: King Rameses and his heir the prince capturing a wild bull, 19th
Dynasty, temple of King Seti I at Abydos

146
Rameses II seated (detail), black granite, t. H. 1.94 m., 19th Dynasty, Karnak, Turin

147
Ostracon: two royal heads, limestone with ochre drawing, H. 12.4 cm., New Kingdom, Deir el-Medina, Cairo

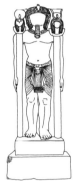

148
King Rameses II as ensign-bearer, pink granite, H. 2.62 m., 19th Dynasty, Armant, Cairo Mus.

149
Rameses II and seated god, pink granite, H. 1.68 m., 19th Dynasty, Memphis, Cairo Mus.

150
Rameses II, kneeling, protected by the god Amen, schist, H. 55 cm., 19th Dynasty, Karnak, Cairo Mus.

151
Rameses II passing over the sacred tree, schist, H. 27 cm., L. 76 cm., 19th Dynasty, Karnak, Cairo Mus.

152
Bust of a wife of Rameses, poly-
chrome limestone, H. 77 cm., 19th
Dynasty, western Thebes, Cairo Mus.

153
King Merneptah as ensign-bearer,
pink granite, H. 1.96 m., 19th Dynasty,
Cairo Mus.

154
King Merneptah threatening an
enemy prisoner, pink granite, H.
1.65 m., 19th Dynasty, Cairo Mus.

155
King Seti II as ensign-bearer, pink
sandstone, H. 2.90 m., 19th Dynasty,
Karnak, Cairo Mus.

156
Ostracon: dancing-girl, painted lime-
stone, H. 10.5 cm., L. 16.8 cm., New
Kingdom, western Thebes, Turin

157
Painting: blind harpist singing, 19th
Dynasty, tomb of Nakht, Sheikh Abd
el-Qurna, no. 52, western Thebes

158
Irnakhtamen (?) and his wife Wiay, red sandstone, H. 45 cm., New Kingdom, Leiden

159
The intendant of finances, Maya, and his wife Merit, limestone, H. 1.58 m., 18th Dynasty, Saqqara, Leiden

160
The scribe In ger iautef, seated, holding a divine image, limestone, H. 1.28 m., 19th Dynasty, Leiden

161
Bearer of ram-headed ensign, wood, H. 42.5 cm., 19th Dynasty, Deir el-Medina (?), Louvre

162
The vizier Paser kneeling and presenting a shrine, grey granite, H. 1.10 m., 19th Dynasty, Karnak, Cairo Mus.

163
The intendant Hapy, pink sandstone, H. 70 cm., 19th–20th Dynasty, Karnak, Cairo Mus.

164
Mahuhi presenting the *naos* of Amen, schist, H. 38.6 cm., New Kingdom, Karnak, Cairo Mus.

165
The royal scribe Ramessenakht with Thoth, grey granite, H. 80 cm., 20th Dynasty, Karnak, Cairo Mus.

166
Block-statue of Piai, limestone, H. 84 cm., 19th Dynasty, Cairo Mus.

167
Block-statue of Khai presenting the *naos* of Horus, limestone, H. 1.10 m., 19th Dynasty, Saqqara, Cairo Mus.

168
Statuette: gazelle, ivory, H. 11.5 cm., end of 18th Dynasty, western Thebes, Metropolitan Mus.

169
Statue of cynocephalous Thoth, sandstone, H. 92 cm., 19th Dynasty, Abu Simbel, Cairo Mus.

THE LATE PERIOD

After the collapse of the New Kingdom, spiritual and temporal power was divided between the kings of Tanis in the Delta region and the priest-kings of Aten and the 'Divine Votaresses' at Thebes. The new sovereigns in the northern capital, with reduced resources, transported and re-erected a number of elements from the architectural monuments that the Ramessides had built at Qantir (Pi-Ramses). The Libyan kings at Thebes, on the other hand, had walls and gates built with hardly any changes to inherited forms. Small chapels were also constructed in honour of the Divine Votaresses.

Things changed again when, in the 25th Dynasty, Taharqa ruled all of Egypt. He was concerned to embellish the works of his predecessors and at Karnak, for example, had several colonnades erected which served as propylaea before the temples. The majestic column with open papyrus capital in front of the second pylon bears witness to this 'Ethiopian' king's fidelity to the most classic autochthonous architecture.

During the Saite renaissance, sanctuaries were undoubtedly erected according to the ancient rules; the Great Neith temple at Sais must have deserved the reputation given it by Greek travellers. In the Delta, however, irrigation of cultivable land has meant that the monuments have mostly disappeared. A few indigenous buildings survive in Upper Egypt—such as the shrine of the barque of Achoris and Neferites at Karnak; the Tuthmoside temple at Medinet Habu, enlarged by the Ethiopians and then by the Graeco-Romans; the great Ptolemaic and Roman temples of Upper Egypt and Nubia. These examples illustrate how, up to the very end, the architects were true to the law 'created by Imhotep'. The most powerful invaders, however dominant over a conquered Egypt, could only rule the land of the Nile if they were prepared to carry on ancient traditions. Of course, some inevitable innovations had been accepted: there were 'composite' capitals with several tiers of plant corolla between which there sometimes appeared flower buds, bunches of dates, lotus bouquets and so on.

Beyond the first court of the temples, the façade of the hypostyle was in some cases composed of bahut walls with engaged columns. A long ambulatory was laid out between the temple proper and its encircling wall and a nilometer was sometimes set into this mysterious promenade. Architectural decoration remained faithful to tradition, being distinctive only with respect to its execution and in the exaggeration of certain lines. One original creation should be mentioned: the double temple at Kom Ombo with twin plans dedicated to the two forms of the divinity, Sebek and Horus. Finally, an evolution in the Hathoric capital had appeared: from the Saite period on, four heads of the goddess were presented, one on each of its sides, instead of only two as in classic times.

The most poetic sanctuary of this period is without question the prestigious complex on the island of Philae. The architectural overseers took care to integrate the sacred buildings into the landscape of the holy island: nature itself became part of the architectural symbolism. Most of the buildings were set up on the western side of the island, which on the new site still roughly resembles the shape of a bird with its head turned towards Nubia. This is the reason that the axis of the main buildings follows the curve of the shoreline. There was one innovation: a magnificent double colonnade (each of its capitals unlike the others), which led—and still leads—to the great pylon of Isis. To the west of the court is the *mammisi* (birth-place of the young god) which is typical of the period and ornamented, of course, with Hathoric capitals.

In the great Graeco-Roman temples, as in the classic 'Millions of Years' temples, each part was on a different level, with the heights of the terrace-ceilings decreasing with each level (probably a reminder of Senmut's innovation at Deir el-Bahri).

If the sepulchres of the Tanis monarchs, with their modest proportions, no longer bore any relation to the sumptuous Theban hypogea, the vaults of the Saite nobles (such as that of Petamenopet on the left bank at Thebes) could be veritable underground labyrinths. The lords in the north, at Saqqara for instance, had had vast shafts dug deep beneath the sands of the Old Kingdom necropolises and at the bottom vaults had been skilfully built with very elaborate anti-intrusion devices. Replacing the funerary chapel at the top was a small cuboid building with solid walls and a sculpted frieze decoration on the outside. Remains of these friezes have given us refined samples of extremely original reliefs which took up the ancient themes of musical, rural and poetic scenes.

In Middle Egypt the famous Petosiris, who at the dawn of Alexander's conquest was High Priest of Thoth at Hermopolis, was considered worthy of a quasi-royal burial. His funerary chapel still took the form of a small temple (with 'horned' altar) but the pastel reliefs on the inside walls were executed in a mixture of Egyptian and Greek styles that was to prove abortive. (The same phenomenon occurred in statuary: Alexander Aigos in the Cairo Museum was portrayed with a Macedonian head on a purely pharaonic body.)

Statuary throughout the whole of the Third Intermediate Period (21st–25th Dynasty) continued the forms of the later Ramesside era with hardly any changes. The statuette of Osorkhon III on his knees, pushing in front of him an image of the sacred barque, was really a copy—in a fairly impersonal style—of analogous works from Rameses II's time.

The block-statues of a crouching figure in a jubilee mantle, holding out a divine figurine, bear, thanks mainly to this detail, the hallmark of their time, as do the effigies that are decorated with carved or engraved divine processions. Once more the *pagnes* were shown in their archaic form, hair-styles were shorter and bodies detailed but lacking in vigour. The great innovation of this period was without doubt the art of the bronze-worker. One of the masterpieces is the statuette of the Divine Votaress Karomama inlaid with gold, silver and electrum. In the 25th Dynasty the 'Ethiopians' injected new spirit into the plastic arts, which were threatening to become totally insipid. Now once more powerful portraits appeared, such as the bust of Montuemhat at Cairo. Graceful yet realistic low reliefs heralded an art which was to flower again in the Delta workshops during the Saite period. With the Delta productions proportions were changing and a slightly academic charm crept in. Through many dynasties the human canon had not changed. The height of the subject, from the sole of the feet to the point where the wig reached the forehead, had to be divided into 18 squares. In the 26th Dynasty these proportions were modified and, for sculpture in the round or low relief, were increased to between 21 and 21¼ squares.

There was a love of fine materials (especially hard, polished stones); a taste for the typical portraits of old, bald-headed men with very 'intellectualized' faces that were more synthetic than ever; echoes of Old Kingdom poses in the scribes and crouching men; a return to portraying subjects in the Middle Kingdom's long *pagne* or the very short one of the time of the pyramids: and everything was treated with an elegant detachment. Meanwhile the bronze-workers enlarged their field of production. With the near-disappearance of the funerary chapels so common in the past, production of the stone votive statues and statuettes slowed down. The insecurity of the times changed customs and practices. The master of the tomb, lord of his serdab, his tranquil impunity translated into stone by an image he believed inviolable, had been replaced by a small, portable bronze figurine of a worshipper. This figure was represented in every attitude of prayer, rite or ecstasy and fixed to a large socle or base, face to face with an evocation of his god often portrayed with a paredrus on either side. There are masses of these statuettes, the individual constituents usually separated, and even sometimes broken off from their socles, that have come down to us from the sanctuaries. Up until the beginning of the Ptolemaic period they had a soberly elegant quality and were remarkably well finished. Then with the last Nectanebos, the bodies began to take on an exaggerated roundness, to the point of looking bloated, and faces lost expression.

Real masterpieces of animal art were produced during the Late Period by artisans who catered for the taste of a whole population turning to the tangible and familiar hypostases of the forces that surrounded them.

Until the end of the 30th Dynasty low reliefs had been charming and original, perhaps a little too rounded, touched by Persian and then Greek influence; but now they took the same path as sculpture. Plastic art produced compositions that were puffed out to an exaggerated rotundity. The garments on the pharaohs and priests were unbelievably overdone, so that their outlines on the walls of the last temples of Roman Egypt were thick and awkward.

The taste of a person of any property tended towards objects fashioned in workshops under foreign influence, such as the famous Hellenistic pottery factories in Mit Rahina. Ladies' ornaments were inspired by delicate Greek jewellery and then by the Roman compositions that had been dedicated for a time to Cleopatra's 'Snakes'.

The art of the architect and sculptor died out in Egypt with the last pharaonic sanctuary. In Meroe, however, far beyond Napata in the Sudan, a degenerate form continued, gradually distorting the image of both pharaoh and his world, and changing it into something essentially African.

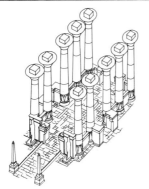

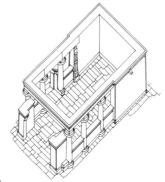

1
Temple of Amen-Re, first court, Taharqa's colonnade: reconstruction, 25th Dynasty, Karnak

2
Temple of Amen-Re: chapel of Achoris: reconstruction, 29th Dynasty, Karnak

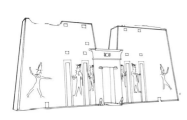

3
Temple of Horus: main façade, Ptolemaic period, Edfu

4
Temple of Horus: view onto the pronaos, Ptolemaic period, Edfu

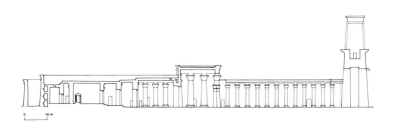

5   Temple of Horus: longitudinal section, Ptolemaic period, Edfu

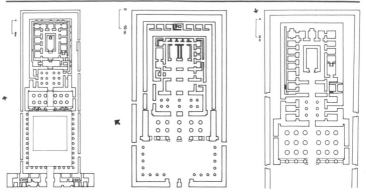

6–7–8   Left: temple of Horus: plan, Ptolemaic period, Edfu. Centre: double temple of the Elder Horus and of Sebek: plan, Ptolemaic period, Kom Ombo. Right: temple of Hathor: plan, Ptolemaic period, Dendera

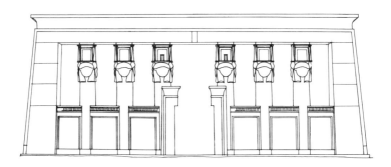

9   Temple of Hathor: façade of the pronaos, Ptolemaic period, Dendera

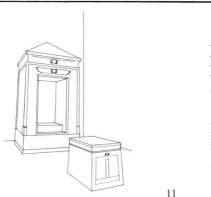

10
Temple of Horus: monolithic *naos* and socle of the sacred barque, granite, Ptolemaic period, Edfu

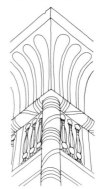

11
Temple of Hathor: façade of the pronaos: detail of the crown, Ptolemaic period, Dendera

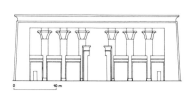

12
Temple of Khnum: façade of the
pronaos, Roman period, Esna

13
Island of Philae: general plan

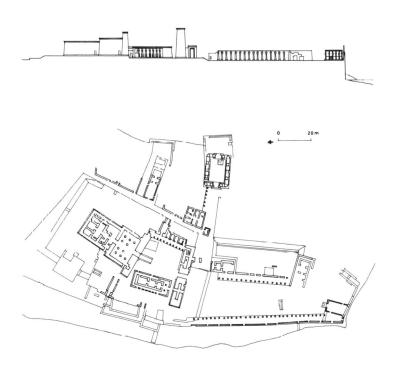

14   Island of Philae: plan and elevation of the temples, Graeco-Roman period

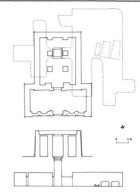

15
Kiosk of Trajan: elevation, oman period, island of Philae

16
Tomb of Petosiris: plan and section, beginning of Ptolemaic period, Tuna el-Gebel

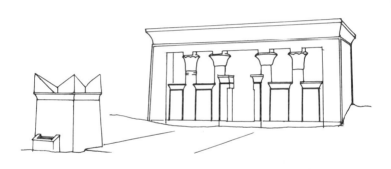

17   Tomb of Petosiris, beginning of Ptolemaic period, Tuna el-Gebel

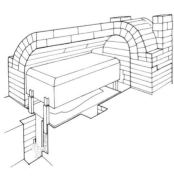

18
Tomb of Neferibre-Sa-Neith: section of the vault, Saite period, 26th Dynasty, Saqqara

19
Model of a citizen's house, limestone, Graeco-Roman period, Cairo Mus.

20
King Osorkhon III, limestone, H.
18 cm., 23rd Dynasty, Karnak, Cairo
Mus.

21
The divine votaress Karomama,
bronze inlaid with gold and silver, H.
59 cm., 22nd Dynasty, Thebes, Louvre.

22
Nespawety-tawy with flower of re-
birth, granite, H. 52.2 cm., 21st–22nd
Dynasty, Karnak, Cairo Mus.

23
Nakhtef muti, presenting the divine
image of Ptah, limestone, H. 42 cm.,
22nd Dynasty, Karnak, Cairo Mus.

24
Block-statue of the high priest Hor,
black granite, H. 69.5 cm., 22nd
Dynasty, Karnak, Cairo Mus.

25
Block-statue of the high priest Hor
protected by divine forms (No. 24):
profile

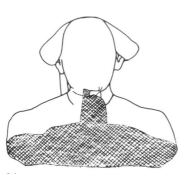

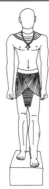

26
Fragmented statue of Montuemhat, black granite, H. 50 cm., 25th Dynasty, Karnak, Cairo Mus.

27
Prince Harmakhis, standing, red sandstone, H. 66 cm., 25th Dynasty, Karnak, Cairo Mus.

28
Queen Amenirdis, alabaster (granite base), H. 1.70 m., 25th Dynasty, Karnak, Cairo Mus.

29
The divine votaress Ankhnes-nefer-ib-re, greenish basalt, H. 71 cm., 26th Dynasty, Karnak, Cairo Mus.

30
The vizier Monthuemhat in jubilee mantle, granite, H. 47.5 cm., 25th Dynasty, Karnak, St. Mus., E. Berlin

31
Iuef-aau presenting a statuette of a seated Osiris, schist, H. 36 cm., Late Period, Karnak, Cairo Mus.

32   Relief: grape picking, limestone, H. 35.5 cm., 25th Dynasty, Sais, Louvre

33
Petamenophis as a scribe, pink sandstone, H. 75.5 cm., 26th Dynasty, Karnak, Cairo Mus.

34
Horbes, presenting the image of Osiris, basalt, H. 61.5 cm., 26th Dynasty, Karnak, Metropolitan Mus.

35
High official, presenting the image of Osiris, basalt, H. 44 cm., 26th Dynasty, Metropolitan Mus.

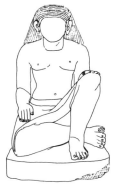

36
Padi-amen-Nebnesuttawy in an attitude of repose, limestone, H. 74 cm., Late Period, Karnak, Cairo Mus.

37
Head of an old man (the 'green head'), green schist, H. 21 cm., 26th Dynasty, Memphis, St. Mus., W. Berlin

38
Block-statue of a high official wearing a *bat* pendant, limestone, H. 17.5 cm., Late Period, Cairo Mus.

39
Statue of the priest Amosis, black granite, H. 98 cm., Late Period, Karnak, Cairo Mus.

40
Psamtek-Saneith with image of Osiris, greenish schist, H. 44 cm., Late Period, Mit Rahina, Cairo Mus.

41
King Aspalta, granite, H. 3.32 m., Late Period, Napata, Mus. of Fine Arts, Boston

42
Alexander Aigos, pink granite, H. 2 m., beginning of Ptolemaic period, Karnak, Cairo Mus.

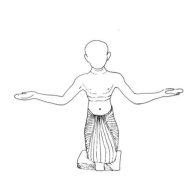

43
Priest kneeling in prayer, bronze, H. 8.5 cm., 26th Dynasty, Louvre

44
Priest carrying the animal image of Thoth, bronze, H. 5.6 cm., 26th Dynasty, Mus. Royaux, Brussels

45
Priest making a libation with a *situla*, bronze, H. 6,4 cm., Late Period, Anvers, old butcher's shop

46
Worshipper dressed in Macedonian costume, bronze, H. 14.5 cm., Late Period, Louvre

47
Priest (?) illustrating a ritual dance step, bronze, H. 6.7 cm., Late Period, Louvre

48
Statuette of Imhotep, revered and deified architect, bronze, H. 11 cm., Late Period, Hildesheim

49   Low relief: banquet scene, limestone, 26th Dynasty, tomb of Nefer-Seshem-Psamtek, Alexandria

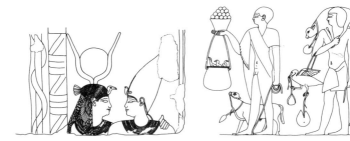

50
Low relief: Nectanebo II and Isis, painted limestone, 30th Dynasty, serapeum at Memphis, Louvre

51
Low relief: the offering-bearers of the deceased Horhotep, limestone, H. 30 cm., Late Period, Buto, Cairo Mus.

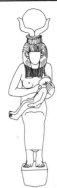

52
Isis suckling the sun-child, Horus, bronze, H. 42 cm., Late Period, Hildesheim

53
Divine image of a seated Osiris, bronze, traces of gold, H. 23.7 cm., Late Period, Hildesheim

54
Divine image of Harpocrates, bronze, H. 24 cm., Late Period, Hildesheim

55
Hor-sematawy, sun emerging from the lotus, bronze, H. 19.6 cm., Late Period, Hildesheim

56
Divine image of Khonsu, bronze, H. 11.9 cm., Late Period, Hildesheim

57
Divine image of Nefertum, bronze, H. 20.2 cm., Late Period, Hildesheim

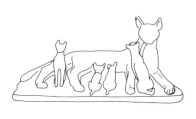

58
Worshipper with Neith and sun-child Horus, bronze, H. 14.5 cm., Late Period, Walters Art Gall., Baltimore

59
Cat of Bastet with her kittens, bronze, L. 12.7 cm., Late Period, St. Mus., W. Berlin

60
Divine image of Bastet with aegis and basket, bronze, H. 11.6 cm., Late Period, Hildesheim

61
Priest wearing the mask of Horus and making a gesture of purification, bronze, H. 95 cm., Late Period, Louvre

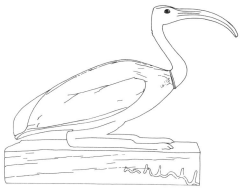

62 Funerary statuette of an ibis, bronze and stuccoed wood, Late Period, Tuna el-Gebel (?), Louvre

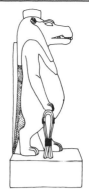

63
Divine image of Anubis, bronze, H. 20.7 cm., Late Period, Walters Art Gall., Baltimore

64
Animal image of the divine Thueris, green schist, H. 96 cm., 26th Dynasty, Karnak, Cairo Mus.

65
Divine image of Khnum, bronze, H. 12.6 cm., Late Period, Hildesheim

66
Divine image of Sebek, bronze, H. 23 cm., Late Period, Kestner Mus., Hanover

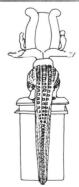

67
Divine image of Wadjet, bronze, H. 21 cm., Late Period, Hildesheim

68
The crocodile of Sebek: back view, bronze, H. 12.2 cm., Ptolemaic period, B.M.

69
Walking lion (marble base), bronze, H.
15.6 cm., Late Period, Leontopolis, St.
Mus., W. Berlin

70
Mouse, bronze, H. 3 cm., Late Period,
Louvre

71
Female figurine in the pose of a queen,
limestone, H. 48 cm., Ptolemaic period,
Karnak, Cairo Mus.

72
Relief: pharaoh as ensign-bearer,
Roman period, temple of Dendera

73   Relief: return from the temple terrace: the queen playing *sistra* and the king
sprinkling incense on the tabernacle which is carried by priests, Roman period,
temple of Dendera

PRINCIPAL ARCHITECTURAL SUPPORTS
THROUGHOUT PHARAONIC HISTORY

LOTIFORM COLUMNS

Old Kingdom   Old Kingdom

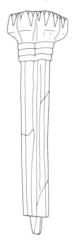   

1
Small ivory column, 1st Dynasty, Hel-
wan

2
Mastaba of Ptahshepses, 5th Dynasty,
Abusir

LOTIFORM COLUMNS

Middle Kingdom   New Kingdom

5
Reconstruction of a column, 12th
Dynasty, El-Lahun

6
Column drum, Tell el-Amarna (Maru
Aten), 18th Dynasty

LOTIFORM COLUMNS

Old Kingdom   Middle Kingdom

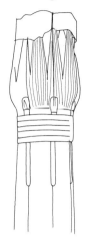

3
Mastaba of Ptahshepses, 5th Dynasty,
Abusir: detail of the capital

4
Tomb of Khety, 12th Dynasty, Beni
Hasan

LOTIFORM COLUMNS

Late Period

7
Capital from the palace of Apries,
26th Dynasty (?), Memphis

OPEN PAPYRIFORM COLUMNS

Old Kingdom   New Kingdom

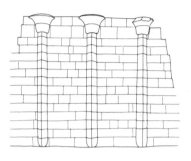

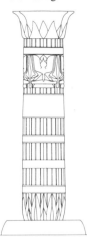

8
Engaged column in the North Building (Saqqara), 3rd Dynasty, funeral
complex of King Djoser

9
Reconstruction of a column from the
palace at Tell el-Amarna, 18th
Dynasty

OPEN PAPYRIFORM COLUMNS

COMPOSITE COLUMNS

Late Period   Ptolemaic Period

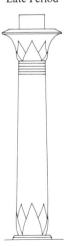

12
Column in the Taharqa kiosk, first
court of the Amen-Re temple, Karnak, 25th Dynasty

13
Model of a column, limestone, Louvre

OPEN PAPYRIFORM COLUMNS

New Kingdom   New Kingdom

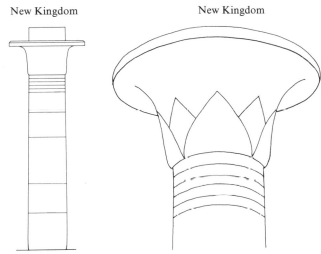

10
Column in the central nave of the
hypostyle hall of the Amen-Re temple
at Karnak, 19th Dynasty

11
Detail of the capital (No. 10)

COMPOSITE
COLUMNS

Ptolemaic Period

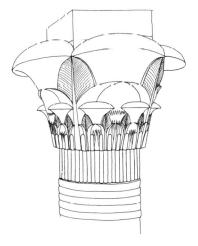

14
Detail of a capital in the pronaos of the
temple of Horus at Edfu

CLOSED PAPYRIFORM COLUMNS

Old Kingdom   Old Kingdom

15
High temple of Niuserre, 5th Dynasty,
Abusir

16
Funerary complex of Sahure, 5th
Dynasty, Abusir: detail of the capital

CLOSED PAPYRIFORM COLUMNS

New Kingdom   New Kingdom

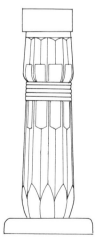

19
Column from the time of Amenophis
IV, 18th Dynasty, Tell el-Amarna

20
Column from the time of Seti I, 19th
Dynasty

CLOSED PAPYRIFORM COLUMNS

Middle Kingdom   New Kingdom

17
Limestone column, Madamud, Louvre

18
Column from the time of Amenophis III, 18th Dynasty, Luxor

CLOSED PAPYRIFORM COLUMNS

New Kingdom

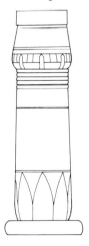

21
Column from the time of Rameses III, 20th Dynasty

PROTO-DORIC COLUMNS

Old Kingdom

Middle Kingdom

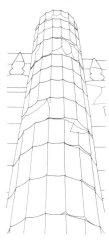

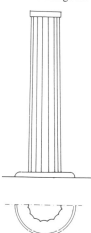

22
Engaged column in the façade of the South Building, Saqqara: funerary complex of King Djoser, 3rd Dynasty

23
Rock-tomb, 12th Dynasty, Beni Hasan

HATHORIC COLUMNS

Middle Kingdom

New Kingdom

26
Sandstone capital from Bubastis, Mus. of Fine Arts, Boston

27
Chapel of Hathor, temple of Queen Hatshepsut at Deir el-Bahri, 18th Dynasty

PROTO-DORIC COLUMNS

New Kingdom

New Kingdom

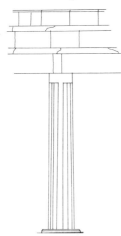

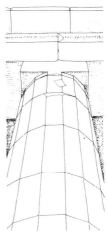

24
Column and entablature in the chapel
of the god Anubis, Deir el-Bahri,
temple of Hatshepsut, 18th Dynasty

25
Detail of part of the so-called Proto-
Doric colonnade, Deir el-Bahri,
temple of Hatshepsut, 18th Dynasty

HATHORIC COLUMNS

New Kingdom

Graeco-Roman Period

28
Pillar in the rock-temple of Nefertari
at Abu Simbel, 19th Dynasty

29
Kiosk of Kertasi: detail of a capital

PALMIFORM COLUMNS

Old Kingdom

Old Kingdom

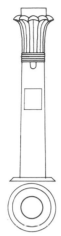

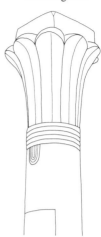

30
High temple of Sahure, 5th Dynasty,
Abusir

31
Detail of a capital from the funerary
complex of Sahure, granite, 5th
Dynasty, Abusir, Cairo Mus.

OTHER TYPES OF
COLUMNS AND PILLARS

New Kingdom

New Kingdom

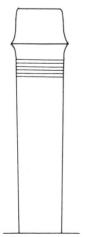

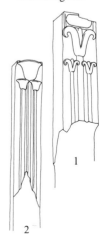

34
Tent-peg shaped column, festival hall
of Tuthmosis III, 18th Dynasty,
temple of Amen-Re at Karnak

35
Pillars symbolizing Upper (1) and
Lower (2) Egypt, great temple of
Amen-Re, Karnak, 18th Dynasty

PALMIFORM COLUMNS

Middle Kingdom

Roman Period

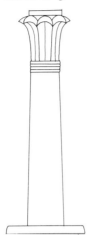

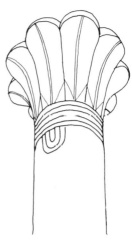

32
Tomb of Prince Djehuty-Hetep, 12th
Dynasty, El-Bersha

33
Temple of Khnum at Esna: detail of a
capital in the pronaos

OTHER TYPES OF
COLUMNS AND PILLARS

Middle Kingdom

New Kingdom

36
'Osiride' pillar of Sesostris I as king of
the south (white crown), limestone. H.
1.89 m. 12th Dyn., Lisht, Cairo Mus.

37
'Osiride' pillar, rock-temple of
Rameses II, Abu Simbel, 19th
Dynasty

Greece

by Alain Pasquier
Curator, Department of Greek and Roman Antiquities,
Louvre

Drawings by Christiane Simon

GREECE

The history of the art of Hellas, or Greece, begins long before the 1st millennium B.C. To this early period the generic term 'pre-Hellenic' has been applied. It was not until the end of the 2nd millennium that the last Indo-European migration —that of the Dorians—finally completed the complex process of the settlement of Greece. Before the arrival of the Dorians, the inhabitants of the Mediterranean peninsula which makes up the south-eastern part of the continent of Europe, and of the small islands scattered like seeds over the Aegean Sea, had already created—and abandoned—many art forms and styles.

Even before the coming of the first Indo-Europeans, there were people building, sculpting and decorating at the end of the Neolithic Age (4500–3200). The vases they shaped were embellished with a surprisingly rich repertoire of carved or painted motifs. Traces of such activity have been found in Macedonia, Boeotia, Attica and the Peloponnese. But it is above all on Thessalian soil that they are in evidence. This region's geographical position gave it a privileged relationship with Anatolia, whose own Neolithic civilization contributed a great deal to Neolithic Greece. Here was the first evidence of the links between Greece and the East that in good times and bad never ceased to fertilize her art.

A bronze metallurgy, probably brought to the area through contact with the East, appeared gradually during the 4th millennium; but not until the end of this millennium can one talk about the advent of the Bronze Age. Historians subdivide the Bronze Age into three periods: Early Bronze Age (3200–2100), Middle Bronze Age (2100–1580) and Late Bronze Age (1580–1150).

The Early Bronze Age saw a spectacular upsurge of art on the islands, first of all in the Cyclades whose position at the heart of the trading routes between Greece and Asia Minor was crucial. These tiny 'stepping-stones' went through a period of intense artistic activity (Early Cycladic) of which their marble idols offer the most notable evidence. But at nearly the same time another island of more imposing proportions was at the dawn of a brilliant era. Early Bronze Age (Early Minoan) Crete was producing works by the end of the 3rd millennium which, in quality of inspiration and technique, were a prelude to the masterpieces achieved in the 2nd millennium. Stone, clay, ivory and especially gold took on rich and varied shapes far superior to those fashioned in continental Greece during the same period (Early Helladic).

The Middle Bronze Age was the golden age of Minoan Crete (Middle Minoan). Sumptuous palaces were built in different parts of the island, in the middle of important urban centres. The way they were decorated and the luxurious objects found in them give us a measure of the extraordinary development of this Cretan civilization. The princely dwelling-places in Knossos, Phaistos and Mallia were astonishing both for their general arrangement and for the care taken by their architects to respond to the daily needs of palace life. Pottery and goldwork

321

achieved a level of perfection. There was a triumph of fantasy in all areas of art, a freedom of inspiration, a *joie de vivre* and a delight at participating in nature's miracles.

Those first palaces were destroyed by a disaster, perhaps an earthquake, but were soon rebuilt in a new phase which lasted until the beginning of the Late Bronze Age and in a form which carried the Minoan 'style' to a climax. Enlivening the walls of the labyrinth in the palace of Knossos were frescoes of colourful scenes, paintings which demonstrate a penchant for the observation of natural spectacles. The same predilection is evident in the decoration of objects.

Frescoes are currently being discovered in excavations at Akrotiri on Thera where rich citizens lived in private houses each of which had at least one room decorated with paintings of a startling freshness. In these can be seen an even keener sensitivity to natural forms, an unparalleled delicacy of feeling for nature. The savage destruction caused by a volcanic eruption, probably around 1500, interrupted the life of this community. Perhaps it can be related to the destruction of the second-phase Cretan palaces, although it is likely that that occurred later. Everything in this sphere is uncertain.

What we do know is that in the 16th century B.C. a new power arrived on the Aegean scene, this time in mainland Greece, though the Middle Helladic Age (2000–1580) gave no hint of its coming ascendancy. The cradle of this civilization was the Argolid, in the north-eastern Peloponnese, and its main centre was the acropolis of Mycenae. There, native tradition mixed with Cretan influences. By the 15th century, the period of the destruction of the second Cretan palaces, the balance of power tipped in favour of the Mycenaean rulers. Although the Mycenaeans were steeped in Minoan culture, their way of life in the last phase of the Late Bronze Age (1400–1150) marked a clear departure from that of their predecessors. Here was a strongly hierarchical, warlike, expansionist society, as can be seen in the Homeric poems with their ample references to the Mycenaean world. Fortresses (Mycenae, Tiryns, Pylos among them) replaced palaces, even if with interior decorations that still copied the Knossos frescoes. Mycenaean civilization spread all over the Mediterranean world from Syracuse to Cyprus, and established what amounted to sovereign states, on Rhodes for example. The decipherment of the Linear B script, preserved above all on numerous archival tablets, has proved that the Mycenaeans spoke Greek. Little by little their art moved away from its dependence on Minoan models, as can be seen in their deliberately abstract and more rigidly organized pottery decoration. Architecture became simpler and more massive. The tholos (circular) tombs constituted a new form. Goldwork (jewellery, arms, vases) again became a favourite discipline. The products of Mycenaean art were widely exported.

After many vicissitudes the Mycenaean empire collapsed around 1150, at a time of general confusion. The migrations of the 'Sea Peoples' threw the whole of the Mediterranean world into turmoil—the Hittite empire, Syria and Palestine right up to the Egyptian borders—and devastated Greece from Thessaly to the southern Peloponnese.

Were the Dorians, the last peoples to settle Greece, among the devastators? Or did they penetrate—gradually—into a world already in decay? One thing is certain: their settlement coincided with a period of inertia and cultural poverty (the Greek 'Dark Ages') that was to be succeeded by a cultural and social renaissance. Greek art seems to have risen from the ashes at the turn of the 2nd and 1st millennia. This was the so-called Geometric Age which came after a short preparatory Proto-Geometric period (1025–900) in which one can, with difficulty, discern transitional elements related to the end of the Mycenaean period. The Geometric era stretched over nearly two centuries (900–725) and is characterized by artistic productions whose patterns are based on geometric shapes. And so abstraction reigned, imposing its rigorous canon even on the human form. The many painted vases and bronze or terracotta figurines that survive bear witness to the trend. Architecture, however, remained rudimentary. A phenomenon of the utmost importance in the history of Hellenism became apparent during the Geometric period: it was the birth of the city, the coming into being of a new political entity which would endure until the arrival of the Romans, and even beyond, as the focus of Greek civilization. Such organization into small autonomous communities, stimulated as much by historical as by geographical factors, was to have its effect on artistic productions too. From the Geometric period on, diverse art centres developed and the workshop tradition perpetuated their individual characteristics down through the generations. Different ideas of beauty were evident in painted vases and figurines, depending on whether the artist worked in Athens (which was then taking on great importance), Thebes or Corinth.

Around the end of the 8th century the Geometric style weakened in all the schools. Human and animal figures were introduced more and more as a reaction against the prescribed forms. Contact with oriental decorations had never been entirely lost, and now it was available to provide a source of pleasing ornamental or representational motifs which were to carry the Greek artists towards a new phase in their history.

At the end of the 8th century there was an enthusiasm for hybrid monsters—sphinxes and griffins, chimaeras and centaurs—and a burgeoning of ornaments of plant origin such as the lotus bud, the tree of life and the palmette. This signalled the beginning of the Orientalizing period (725–620), the culmination of all the influences coming in from the East. All the centres of creativity were affected, but each assimilated the new forms in its own particular way, merging its traditional genius with the imported styles. The Greeks, while yielding to the temptations of the East, never gave in to slavish imitation.

The confrontation with exotic decorative forms led to a joyous creative exuberance and its field of action was considerably enlarged by 'colonization'. Since the 8th century Greeks had, in fact, been impelled by economic difficulties to leave their cities of origin to found colonies along the seaboards of the Mediterranean and Black Sea. From southern Italy and Sicily across Cyrene to the Hellespont new cities sprang up. At first subservient to their mother cities or 'metropolises', the colonies eventually developed an autonomous existence, their freedom being reflected in the productions of their artists' workshops.

Cities like Corinth, geographically privileged crossroads regions, grew rich from trading in art-objects such as painted vases: their small clay flasks flooded the markets of the Mediterranean world. It was the Corinthian artists who invented the black-figure style in pottery—consisting of painted silhouettes with incised details against a light background. This technique was to enjoy an immense vogue. Athens was more reserved in its techniques but with much experimentation was acquiring skills that, some generations later, were to help it gain and maintain its dominance. The Cyclades abounded in workshops and their products were widely exported. Marble was beginning to be sculpted there. The most Orientalizing objects of all were fashioned in Rhodes and on the Greek coast of Asia Minor—jewels and vases on which rows of animals repeated the 'wild goat' motif a thousand times over. Finally Crete, on the route to the Orient, played an important role: a genuine renaissance flowered there during the 7th century. 'Daedalic' sculpture moved decisively away from Geometric fantasies, and the Cretans led this movement.

The end of the 7th and beginning of the 6th century saw a rise to prominence of styles that were eventually to define the look of Greek Archaism. First there was a standardization in architectural structures and differentiation between the Doric and Ionic orders. Two major motifs of Greek sculpture also came to the fore, indeed were enthroned: the kouros and the kore. Then, in addition the Corinthian black-figure technique spread into nearly all the pottery workshops, where it was to reign supreme for a century. The Orientalizing style survived into the 7th century, but decoration was beginning to abandon demons and oriental ornaments to make more room for the human figure in the depiction of the myths and exploits of gods and heroes.

After an early period (620–580) during which the new forms took root and asserted themselves in the network of art centres from Asiatic Greece to southern Italy and Sicily in the west, there came a whole series of masterpieces which celebrated the maturity of Archaism (580–530). Sculptors worked feverishly, driven by a competitive spirit to surpass each other in invention and execution. The Ionian influence, ornamental and graceful, inspired smiling faces, while drapery cascaded down in endlessly repeated folds. Architects vied with one another: at Samos and Ephesus there arose sumptuous Ionian buildings. In Greece proper and western Greece Doric edifices, less grandiose in tone, sprang up in great diversity. The major sanctuaries at Delphi and Olympia were filled with small buildings—the Treasuries—which showed piety as well as pride. Fanned by commercial zeal, a bitter struggle developed between the different pottery workshops. Among all these factories, Corinth and Athens opposed each other without respite until the eventual victory of the latter towards the middle of the 6th century, when it established its supremacy with products ranging from the solemnity of the master painter Exekias to the miniatures of the 'minor masters'. At Corinth, as in many other cities, the bronzesmiths worked indefatigably at creating anything from totally utilitarian items to the most precious ex-votos. Towards the end of the Archaic period this creative exuberance subsided somewhat, but not to the extent of impoverishing the art centres. The graceful procession of marble korai in the Acropolis Museum is evidence that political upheavals (in Athens democracy replaced the tyranny of the Pisistratids) and mounting dangers from abroad (Persian threats were becoming more menacing) did not have a paralysing effect on the sculptors. But the faces they carved became graver as they drew nearer to the decisive confrontation of the Persian wars. The art of vase-painting in Athens reached its apogee at the end of the 6th century with a new technique which reversed the existing technique: figures were no longer black but red, and the light silhouette standing out against a dark background gave scope for a greater freedom of expression, for a more analytical approach paying more attention to the value of details. On Aegina, an island near Attica, a temple was dedicated to Athena: this miracle of harmonious design, summarizing the successes of Archaism, proved to be its last architectural statement.

The transition from Archaic to Classical art is exemplified in the two pediments of the Aegina temple. The figures on the west pediment, still bearing the graceful ornaments of the past, are juxtaposed in a sort of ballet in which each participant is isolated in his own activity. The east side, executed fifteen years later, depicts a real battle and a unifying spirit pervades the movement of the whole composition. The ground had been laid for the birth of new values and forms.

The Classical Age (480–330) lasted a century and a half. But it would be wrong to think of it as a static period. The Severe style was the first to evolve. After the trials of war, Hellenism had emerged victorious, and had encouraged more austere artistic forms which were thought of as a return to reality. Poses were released from convention, athletes were portrayed accomplishing specific feats; as these were easier to translate into bronze, that metal came into greater use. Faces no longer smiled mechanically but expressed a range of emotions. After the studied variations of Archaic drapery, one is impressed by the very simplicity of pre-Classical representations of fabric and the feeling of volume given to materials. The pediments of the temple of Zeus at Olympia show the changes most clearly, although these trends are just as much in evidence in western Greece as on the coast of Asia Minor, and are as apparent in the most celebrated examples of great statuary as in the humblest clay figurines. The architects, whether in Olympia or in western Greece, where they were very active, drew upon the experiments of the past to form a clear monumental language linking geometric forms to mathematical calculations.

The great period of Classicism was the thirty years between 450 and 420. Athenian artistic pre-eminence, prepared for by the city's dominant role in the struggles against the Persian invaders and reinforced by its imperialist policies in the Aegean world (the Delian League), was confirmed in almost all areas of creative activity. Pericles placed Phidias in charge of a great architectural project which was to have a lasting effect on the future of Greek art in particular, and on Western art in general. The concepts behind the monuments covering the soil of Attica and the rock of the Acropolis in particular reveal a desire to apply genuine architectural plans. The planners went so far as to modify the axis of the Propylaea on the Acropolis in order to set off the Parthenon more gloriously: an audacious act which was perhaps the sign of a truly democratic spirit. The buildings of this period, with their commingling of the Orders, demonstrate a masterly resolution of the delicate problem of the liberation of interior space: the statue of a standing Athena in the cella of the Parthenon was much more at home than was the seated Zeus in the temple at Olympia. Building finesse can be seen particularly in several carefully judged optical corrections.

Everything was subordinate to *nous*, to reason. Such criteria governed the sculpture of Pericles' generation. Less enamoured of truth than their predecessors of the Severe period, masters like Polykleitos or Phidias created human figures which exalted self-control, calm strength, serenity. These artists applied complex calculations of proportions to their figures. The perfect architecture of the human body immortalized an ideal of Beauty which, for a time, was thought to be the end of the journey, the crowning of all past endeavours.

This equilibrium was both strong, for it haunts our aesthetic senses still, and fragile, since it was the accomplishment of one brief generation. It is preserved in perpetuity in the Parthenon sculptures in which men and gods share the same faith, the faith in reason. No sculptor since then has been able to take up his chisel, nor any painter his brush, free from an awareness of the Panathenaic procession. And such a concentration of the vital forces of Greek art could not fail to bring in its wake certain modifications in the creative canon. Distinctions between schools, a principal motivation in Archaic art, gradually diminished. The objective from then on was to reproduce well-known types. This can be particularly felt in the declining number of examples, and impoverished inspiration, of the small bronze models. The same loss of vitality can be seen in painted-vase production, in spite of a remarkable series of funeral lekythoi; their technique of a white ground covered after firing with decorations in varied colours offered a far more interesting range of pictorial effects. But whether the subjects were terracotta figurines or in painted decoration, the same desire could everywhere be seen to create serene and balanced forms and perfect faces that gaze into eternity.

It was at this point that the whole edifice was toppled by the Peloponnesian war and the deaths of Pericles and Phidias. A new period had commenced and from 420 to 390 new values predominated. The vehicle was still Classical but the contents were altogether different. The return of aristocrats to the government of Athens led to a restoration of the Ionic style in architecture—richer, more ornate, more attentive to detail, as in the past. A similar evolution can be seen in sculpture where the mannered arrangement of 'wet' draperies revealed bodies in much less serene postures. The upheavals of war provided new inspiration: instead of the masculine ideal of the triumphant young athlete, one comes across works in which artists have discreetly shown their sensitivity to considerations that had previously been scorned—a concern for the individual, and for women and children. Vases painted in Athens were covered with gynaeceum scenes in which draperies billow in great agitation. Many scenes present Aphrodite and the infant Eros. From now on a kind of melancholy throws a chaste shadow over faces that have lost their certainty. The age of questioning has arrived, the age of Socrates.

This lack of equilibrium, or destabilization, to use the fashionable term, was to be conveyed in all 4th-century creations (390–320), up to the campaigns of Alexander. Architects took a fuller interest in daily life, in men's dwellings and leisure activities. Encounters at Xanthos and Halicarnassus with the barbarian world of the Anatolian princes prompted architects to adapt Greek styles to unknown concepts, and that laid the ground for the syncretism of the Hellenistic period. Sculpture abandoned the serene Periclean mode: Skopas carved tormented faces which jut out from the stone, their pathetic stares questioning the heavens; Praxiteles expressed anxiety by means of the ambiguous gender of his listless bodies, and by the tender melancholy that softened the faces of his gods. In a new development that was a far cry from the idealism of high Classicism, the art of portraiture indicated an interest that centred on the individual, as we have seen, on the human face as the expression of a unique soul. That was how the last major figure of the 4th century, Lysippos, active throughout the transition to Hellenistic art, set the youthful features of Alexander in bronze. And if Lysippos reverted to compositions with Polykleitan athletes, his athletes are not frozen in accordance with absolute laws, but are tortuous bodies whose limbs take possession of space, our own space. In the field of painted pottery, it was no longer Athens that was the great centre of production. Italy had become the most abundant creator of new wares in various regional workshops which had fairly quickly shrugged off Attic influences. Athens did, however, see a revival of the craft as a result of orders from barbarian princes in the Crimean region, whose tastes had some influence on the imagery used. But there too, side by side with exotic conflicts between Arimaspi and griffins, religious disquiet crept into the Dionysiac and Eleusinian scenes. It was the last flickering flame of an art whose light had been cast especially brilliantly over Greek soil.

The victory of the Macedonian state over the Greek city-states, epitomized by that of Philip II over Demosthenes, and the formidable exploits of Alexander who carried Hellenistic values to the borders of Afghanistan, were to have a dramatic effect on artistic creativity in Greece. Art centres multiplied and mingled Greek traditions with barbarian influences in varying proportions. Many different currents ebbed and flowed through these three centuries of history (330–30 B.C.). It is best to look at them as a single meandering stream. Architecture did not neglect the lessons of the past and continued to use the old formulas in the Ionic and Doric styles. But the new Corinthian order with its acanthus capitals came increasingly into vogue. The constantly growing desire for richer decoration at the heart of monumental complexes drew builders towards the production of an ostentatious architecture in which each element awaited the application of a motif. The functional aspect of a structure took second place to ornamental effect. Consequently greater and greater liberties were taken with the traditional rules for the use of the Orders. The most striking innovation was conceiving a building no longer as a simple unit but as many monuments woven together on a different and vaster scale. Urban planning, which was very popular at the time, demonstrated this leaning towards architectural composition, as did the policies of the Hellenistic monarchs who were eager to enhance their prestige by the creation of more and more luxurious complexes. Pergamon is without doubt the most famous example, and its great Altar to Zeus is a summary of all the characteristics of Hellenism.

Its carved decorations, which treat the traditional subject of the struggles between gods and giants, form a magisterial frieze where the most diverse styles intermingle in a torrent of images. Here new accents in sculptural art can be perceived, even if in actual fact it was a matter of certain 4th-century tendencies being carried to their limits. The realism of some of the anatomy—which can indeed have a clinical feel—illustrates the Hellenistic artist's interest in observation. The Hellenistic period was the golden age of portraiture, ranging from the 'academic' face of Menander to the mask inspired by Homer, and including the soberly realistic countenance of a philosopher here and a monarch there. Realism came in time to be overtaken by baroque impulses, so that tragedy was expressed by excess, by an appeal at once to terror and to pity: it featured tortured forms in which humans could give the impression of being menaced by suffering or bestiality. But in the Pergamon sculptures we also find an echo of one permanent feature of the Hellenistic period: the recurrence of past forms. The Hellenistic masters claimed the Classical heritage as theirs. Is this not clearly to be seen in the face of the Venus de Milo? 'Alexandrian' art could be looked on as a means of perpetuating the aesthetic language of Praxiteles. He was probably the inspiration for the taste for fluidity in female or infantile forms, for the slightly affected gallantry of some of the subjects. The return to the past can be even more radical: if the last Hellenistic century saw the rebirth of the mid-5th-century athletic ideal, it also left us works which aimed at reviving the Archaic style. Such was the abundance of styles adopted in the last period of Greek art. The same inspiration and talent were to nourish Hellenistic painting, though regrettably we can only catch a glimpse of it by way of the Roman copyists and mosaicists. For in the Hellenistic period vase-painting finally ceased to count. The few extant series suffice to show an unmistakable decadence in the art. Mural painting, on the other hand, was to flower thanks to a new interest in the interior decoration of private houses. The Roman villas of Herculaneum and Pompeii give an idea of the goals sought by the Hellenistic masters, many of whose names have come down to us, though their works have not. They strove to conquer space by giving a suggestion of depth and using the principles of perspective: light and shadow played a role here. New elements also appeared that were unfamiliar in Greek art: painted scenes were framed by architectural elements, or by a natural background with the colours of true landscape, at times minutely accurate, and at times imaginary and depicted with excessive artifice. That, then, was the final flourish in the dazzling evolution of Greek art. The first artistic awakenings had come in the rudimentary Neolithic idols. It next passed through periods when a desire for decoration and for logical rigour reigned in turn; and it completed its course in the polymorphic and multi-coloured abundance of Hellenistic fantasy. But Greek art did not, in fact, die at the end of the Hellenistic period. It survived by fertilizing Roman art, and becoming assimilated into a new aesthetic.

ARCHITECTURE

Building first took place on Greek soil in the form of modest huts, in the Neolithic period. True settlements like the acropolis of Dimini were extremely complex. They were, however, a far cry from the lavish arrangements of the 2nd-millennium Cretan palaces, which show real virtuosity in architectural composition. In the plans of the Mycenaean Age simplicity prevailed. Fortresses were equipped with ramparts and such original forms as the tholos tomb were developed.

The Geometric period was not particularly brilliant in the field of architecture. In the 7th century, on the other hand, a fair range of experiments were attempted, as can be seen on the island of Samos in Ionia, for example; or in Crete where the house of god, the temple, had a number of different shapes. The Thermum site in Aetolia presents an interesting succession of temple plans, from the start of the 1st millennium to the 7th century when the peripteral colonnade enclosing the chamber of the divine statue first appeared. There then emerged a distinction that was to be of crucial importance: the separation in style of Asiatic Greek buildings from those in Greece proper. It was the two-pronged tongue of Greek architecture which embraced both the Ionic and the Doric styles. The Ionic style quite quickly showed grandiose ambitions and went in for rich ornamentation. Doric architecture preferred a sober, rigorous approach and was early cultivated in the western parts of Greece, where it was to have a splendid future. However the Doric order in no way gave rise to monotony: its usage was varied with many different formulas and it even went so far as to incorporate Ionic features. In the east, buildings took on progressively ampler proportions. But the Ionic style could be applied just as well to enormous stone halls such as the temple of Apollo at Didyma or the tombs of the Hellenized princes of Lycia and Caria as to small buildings like the Siphnian Treasury.

During the Hellenistic period the Doric and Ionic styles followed their own courses. But temple construction was not the sole task that builders aspired to. They integrated their buildings into vast complexes with *agorai* surrounded by porticoes, and applied themselves to the development of great urban projects. Sometimes it was the logical mind that prevailed, and at other times a versatility that sought to adapt to the nature of the terrain was needed. In either case, man's daily life, his domestic well-being and leisure activities, were taken into account.

Only by considering the succession of materials employed can one understand the forms of Greek temples. The transition from wood to stone was a gradual process. That explains certain details which appear to be purely decorative but whose role was originally functional. Columns and their capitals played an essential part in building aesthetics from the Minoan period up to the end of the Hellenistic period. At first, in the Cretan palaces, columns were wider at the top, but subsequently they narrowed as they went up and were decorated with fluting, sometimes with sharp arrises (Doric style), and sometimes separated by fillets (Ionic style). Capitals evolved over the centuries: the Doric profile gradually became elongated; the Ionic or Corinthian accumulated more and more motifs. But it was not just the capital that provided a surface for decoration: socles, walls and gutters all lent themselves to the same purpose.

Very soon sculpture was added to the decorative repertoire. Works of monumental sculpture had existed since the Mycenaean period. But the real birth of sculpture was in the 7th century and it was not until the 6th century that it established itself as a fundamental feature in architecture. Sculpture could appear on columns, which were either carved in partial relief or virtually replaced by caryatids. It insinuated itself into the upper parts of the Doric temple where the metope—the panel separating two triglyphs—offered favourable ground for the execution of small pictures. It unrolled a continuous band of decoration on the entablature of some Ionic buildings. Finally, it populated the triangular space in pediments by setting up figures that grew increasingly more numerous and yet looked ever more at home.

Climatic conditions in Greece are such that painted decorations on buildings have to a large extent disappeared. From the pre-Hellenic age there remain only a few large fragments of Cretan or Mycenaean frescoes. The Thera site daily reveals more evidence of a school of Cycladic painters who had no cause to envy the Minoans, as we have seen.

But nearly all evidence for the historic period has completely disappeared, although the literature is packed with names of artists and mentions of works. We can only imagine Classical pictures from Pausanias' descriptions. An idea of the decoration on Hellenistic houses can only be obtained by studying the painted adornment of Roman villas. Mosaic art has left us more, as for example at Delos, where in some of the houses the floor still glows with vibrant colours. From Neolithic huts to the monumental complexes of Pergamon or Miletus, the builders of Hellas steadily took over the art of construction, first in honour of the gods and then in the service of man. Their decorative language was to haunt our consciousness for a long time, as we are constantly reminded when we walk along our own city streets.

SCULPTURE

The first sculpted shapes in the Aegean world were rudimentary Neolithic clay or stone figurines, most often female, with very naturalistic expressions. The Cycladic idols, which were mainly abstract in form, may seem totally unlike them even though they succeeded them chronologically. A transition does, however, exist, as can be seen on a number of sites. There is, moreover, considerable variation in Cycladic figurines. They are evidence of the earliest use of marble quarries in an island world which, 2000 years later, was to put marble to the most glorious uses.

When the Cycladic artists cut and polished figures nearly a metre and a half long, they were creating true sculptures. Such dimensions were not to be found in the Minoan productions of the 2nd millennium. The Cretans seemed not to have been familiar with large-scale sculpture and were content carefully to chip out tiny objects. The same appears to have been the case with Mycenaean art in general, although there are some examples such as the Lion Gate (Mycenae) and certain other recent discoveries that are exceptions to this rule.

In the Geometric Age there are still no great works of sculpture. The bronze-workers and terracotta modellers were developing forms which, while obeying the rigid aesthetic canons of the time, sought more and more to reproduce observed features. The early Oriental contributions showed a similar tendency. From the end of the 8th century the various elements were falling into place and true groups were being composed in a very subtle style.

But it was the 7th century that was to prove decisive for the future of Greek sculpture. It was then that the Daedalic style (attributed in legend to the famous craftsman Daedalus) appeared as a reaction against the angular, spaced-out Geometric forms. Frontal figurines were produced from rigid blocks cut out of different materials (clay, wood, ivory, and also limestone and even marble), which for the first time respected the proportions of the body. Seventh-century artists finally managed to make their creations life-sized and then moved quickly on to gigantic dimensions.

Perhaps Egypt helped them to take this decisive step. It was at any rate in the middle of this Orientalizing century that large-scale marble sculpture evolved. In the last two decades there appeared the first specimens of that extremely prolific series of kouroi and korai, young naked men and draped girls who honoured the gods with their beauty.

Starting with these fundamental archetypes, it is possible to follow the evolution of the male and female types. The first kouroi were colossal and they were only later scaled down to life-size dimensions. They were carved by artists who knew how to combine sharper and sharper observation with the particular decorative stylization of their native regions. Along with naked kouroi there appeared offering-bearers, horsemen, warriors and clothed men standing, sitting or lying down. By the end of the Archaic period, the male anatomy had been mastered, but it was still frozen in a rigid style. The shock-waves of the Persian wars brought freedom to the sculptors, and from 480 B.C. bodies were presented in relaxed, naturally balanced postures.

The athletes of the Severe style were making real movements. High Classicism, however, was enamoured of the harmony it pursued with its calculations of proportions, and it reintroduced the male body into an unreal world, the world of reason. After the Apollos of Phidias, which expressed the ideals of a generation, at the end of the 5th and in the 4th century a greater animation was introduced into the bodies of men and gods, and different poses were used to convey the instability and anxiety of the times. With Lysippos came the return of the athletic ideal, now articulated in real space. This reassertion of realism was to develop throughout the Hellenistic period. Musculature told tales of ageing or suffering, or slackened into a soft sensuality.

The female type went through a parallel evolution from the Archaic period onwards. But the fact that the korai were clothed gave rise to skilful variations in their drapery, which with their hair-styles was a pretext for every kind of decorative trick. The Severe style then reacted against ornamentation. Its drapery was as simple as its faces were serious. Corresponding to the Apollos of high Classicism were Athenas with firm expressions and calm, timeless strength. However, it was not until the end of the 5th century that proper homage began to be paid to femininity, which then came to be glorified in the 4th century by Praxiteles. The female form finally emerged from its veils and was totally revealed—no longer subject to the influence of ideals relating to virility. Sensually undulating forms blossomed into a triumphant fullness in the Hellenistic period. Interest in themes outside the Classical register can also be found in statues of boys and young girls, and even very young children, and their charming poses are admirably caught.

Although statuary groups were cultivated from the Archaic period on, they were made up of independent figures. Not until the early 5th century did compositions appear in which each figure was complemented by the figure that accompanied it. Hellenistic sculptors created many increasingly complex ensembles, in which decorative effects were sometimes applied to excess.

Another mode of expression in Greek sculpture was relief. This technique had pre-Hellenic antecedents but is mainly represented in votive or funerary steles. Their design varied according to period and region. The most prestigious was the Attic stele, although it underwent an eclipse in the first half of the 5th century. Figures on these reliefs grew in number and were eventually enclosed in a framework with an architectural structure. During the Hellenistic period decorative motifs began to appear, based on natural objects and features, and progressively taking over the background.

Relief art was closely bound up with religious observances and so it is the form most often found among extant specimens. Reliefs range in quality from the sublime relief from Eleusis to a humble ex-voto carved clumsily but piously by a provincial artist.

CERAMICS

Painted pottery is a very important discipline in the history of Greek art.

From the Neolithic period on, the shapes of the pottery and its incised or painted decorations were diversified in response to influences from the Orient. Some of the motifs were extremely refined. A similar ebb and flow can be seen in the Cycladic vases of the 3rd millennium, during the Early Bronze Age, although with a certain impoverishment which must signify some change in the degree of eastern influences. From the Early Minoan Age, Cretan workshops were producing goods of quality, such as the mottled pottery which prefigured the marvellous series of Kamares-style vases. This group, named after the Mount Ida cave where excavations have revealed the best specimens, offers subtly stylized decorations that are truly feasts of colour. No idea of constraint seems to have impeded the artists' inspiration. With their 'floral' and 'marine' designs the Cretan painters—without forsaking stylization—were nevertheless evolving towards naturalistic forms. They subsequently regressed to more conventional modes when Mycenaean influences began to make themselves felt. But the deliberately abstract and rigorously organized Achaean style always met with resistance, whether in Cycladic pottery, where Thera shone brightest, or in Crete itself. And yet the Mycenaeans produced innumerable vases and devised new shapes such as the 'stirrup-cup' and 'champagne-cup'. The popularity of their wares is illustrated by finds stretching from the Near East all the way across to Sicily, and the famous 'warrior vase' is proof of the high quality they could achieve.

After the watershed at the end of the 2nd millennium, painted-vase art emerged again on Greek soil with the Geometric style. This was the major discipline of the period. There was an astonishing diversity of invention in the shapes of the receptacles, but the designs were restricted by rigid limits. They could range in size from the tiniest flask to funerary urns as big as a man. Geometric motifs were applied with an increasingly acute sense of composition which took into account the architecture of the vase. Undulating lines, chevrons, zig-zags and hound's-tooth patterns were arranged in carefully selected zones. Eventually human figures appeared among these abstract designs, mainly in funerary or battle scenes. At first they were rendered in simplified schemas, but little by little the silhouettes became life-like and their contours began to step outside the dominant aesthetic principles. The Geometric inspiration weakened and, in time, died. It had been honoured in all sectors of the Greek world, with regional variations which were in fact dialects of the same language. By this point, Athens had taken the lead.

Next came Orientalizing pottery. Ornamentation from the East unrolled its floral volutes, first of all within the former Geometric framework. The workshops all plunged eagerly into use of the new images—demons and heroes transcribing epic and mythological scenes. Naturally such Orientalization could be felt most strongly in the iconography of eastern Greece, as that region was nearer the sources, and in Crete which was situated on the sea-route from the Levant. However, it also affected production in the islands (Melos, Paros, Naxos, Euboea, etc.), the mainland workshops (Athens, Boeotia) and the western Greek art centres (Megara Hyblaea). Each factory found its own way of assimilating the exotic elements. But Corinth stood out clearly from the rest. The small perfume vases it exported to all the Mediterranean markets were supreme both in quality and in quantities produced. There it was that the black-figure technique was invented (glazed silhouettes with incised details picked out in red and white, as we have seen), which was to be of prime importance for the history of Greek pottery; and the centre exercised a strong influence on all other styles. The Corinthians knew, moreover, how to use the double register: decorations of a purely Orientalizing tradition, together with those consisting of the great figurative pictures that were beginning to appear at the end of the 7th century—with silhouettes against a pictorial background bereft of any 'fill-in' features.

The pre-eminence of the isthmus city was, nevertheless, to be challenged and then threatened by the Attic workshops in the first half of the 6th century. The Athenian painters had adopted the Corinthian black-figure style, but had soon adapted it to their own genius by using it to illustrate lively scenes whose skilful composition went beyond purely decorative effects. After a spirited contest, Athens was left master of the field. The Amasis Painter and the 'minor masters' worked on the smallest scale, creating graceful miniatures. The famous painter and potter Exekias, on the other hand, brought to his work the spirit of the epic frescoes whose solemnity prefigured the tragic accents of Athenian theatre.

Alongside these two great centres, many other factories were creating shapes and images which would in each case perpetuate their particular genius—e. g. in eastern Greece, Laconia, Boeotia and southern Italy, where a colony of Chalcis, Rhegion, produced wares in great abundance.

The 6th century was the period when the range of shapes and forms in which Greek vases might be made was more or less permanently fixed. It is not possible to review this here in detail. Briefly, the large vases —the kraters, deinoi and later the stamnoi—were used to mix beverages, which were then put into oinochoai so that they could be poured into cups—kantharoi or skyphoi—from which the banqueters drank direct. The cup evolved particularly rapidly and moved towards a general similarity of form. The amphora was very common and used in many ways, notably as a reward in competitions at the great Panathenaic games. The three-handled hydriai were used for carrying water.

Greece

The end of the Archaic period was the golden age of Greek pottery, and it was at its most brilliant in Athens. Artists were signing their work more often at this time—an indication that they were aware of their own importance. But nobody knows the name of the painter who invented the red-figure technique, which was to make available a far richer means of expression. The Andokides Painter (his name is taken from the name of the potter with whom he collaborated) reversed the colours: figures were kept in the natural colour of the clay and the ground became that of the slip. It was thus possible to fill out details not only by means of dry or mechanical incision, but also by brushwork which could achieve graded effects. The Attic masters of red-figure work very soon reached the pinnacle of their art. An artist like the painter Euphronius, towards the end of the 6th century, could compose elaborate pictures in which concern for detail (anatomy is perfectly rendered) does not detract from highly ambitious and profoundly inspiring subject-matter.

At the start of the 5th century Attic pottery maintained this high aesthetic level, despite the upheavals caused by the Persian wars. Painters like Douris achieved a perfect style in the decoration of the sides and inside tondo of cups. The scenes depicted were taken from mythology, and also from daily life, in which athletic exercises played a large part. Victory against the Persians, paradoxically, depressed the art of vase-painting. It was large-scale painting that had attracted the people of talent, and an increase in resources led to the industrialization of workshops, which meant that the best was often threatened by the less good. Certainly there were excellent masters who managed to adapt vase imagery first to the new pre-Classical styles and then to the Classical ideal as glorified by sculpture. But the ceramicists no longer held the prime position they had occupied at the end of the Archaic period. An exception, however, is the beautiful series of lekythoi. On these funerary receptacles tomb scenes on a white ground were adorned with various contrasting colours after firing.

The end of the 5th century saw the arrival of scenes including women with swirling draperies—these did not always escape preciosity. The last era in the history of Greek pottery can be more rapidly described. In the 4th century—apart from the 'Kerch style': Attic vases produced by order of the barbarian princes on the coasts of the Black Sea—the factories of Greece proper were starting to die out. But the torch was taken up by the more youthful southern Italian and Sicilian schools which, before coming of age, had always been dominated by the Attic style. Now they developed self-confidence and established their own characteristics. In Lucania, Apulia and Campania and particularly at Paestum, as well as in Sicily, vases were turned whose shapes had no links with the Greek past, which were enlivened with a great number of coloured decorations. The influence of the theatre can be seen again here. The activities of these workshops ceased at the end of the 4th century.

In the Hellenistic period, Greek pottery declined to the status of a minor art. There were many attempts to blaze new trails, but the use of superadded paint, of vivid polychrome on a white ground, and of relief, failed to redeem the mediocrity of decoration from which figures had virtually disappeared, and whose inspiration had faltered.

Despite a few sporadic successes, Hellenistic pottery succumbed to the decadence that had been inherent in the craft since early Classical times.

MINOR ARTS

'Minor arts' is a convenient expression, but it is only applicable to Greek art if the adjective 'minor' refers to size rather than quality. Many of the countless statuettes and objects and implements that came out of Greek workshops are in no way inferior—certainly as far as talent is concerned—to the reputedly 'major' works.

Every material was used, and for multiple purposes. There was bronze, of course, and its well-mastered metallurgy offered an inexhaustible range of possibilities. But there were also silver, ivory and wood; and the plasticity of clay and the hardness of stone were equally exploited. That most precious of metals, gold, paid homage to the gods with its brilliance, and adorned men, accompanying them right into the darkness of the tombs.

Bronze figurines present a condensed history of the human form as transcribed by successive generations of artists. From the bent bodies of worshipping Minoans one passes to the disjointed forms of Geometric warriors. The Daedalic style is well illustrated by small sculptures, as are the various 6th-century styles, when each workshop had its own trade marks. Up to the time of the Persian wars forms were constantly evolving while remaining faithful to Archaic models. All this changed with the Classical period, when the subjects treated by the grand masters of sculpture came to hold sway and the smiths imitated them in small bronze works. The Hellenistic period brought back to the workshops the richness and freedom of inspiration they had known in the Archaic period. To the traditional factories were added art centres which flowered in the Hellenized zones: Syria, Egypt, Asia Minor. The repertoire was enlarged: along with figurines of divinities (of which Aphrodite and Dionysos made up the bulk), were effigies of Hellenistic princes and statuettes reflecting popular themes, especially at Alexandria.

The diversity of bronze techniques is seen in the production of certain implements. The circular-handled cauldrons of the Geometric period had already combined hammered and cast elements. This duality is reflected again in Orientalizing cauldrons in which the casting process was progressively gaining ground: moulded decorations—animal protomes, busts of sirens—developed considerably as a result.

In the field of armoury, the Mycenaeans—after the Minoans—created ceremonial arms using very skilful techniques. For centuries the various pieces of a warrior's equipment offered the bronzeworkers areas for decoration, which they filled with relief-work or engraved motifs. More peaceful were toilet articles such as caryatid mirrors, and among these one can find some of the best illustrations of the transition from Archaism to Classicism. Many utensils were embellished with figured decorations: incense-holders, lids of boxes, handles on receptacles. Bronze lay at the centre of everyday life. With silver and gold it provided material for the coin workshops, whose art grew constantly more refined: some of the silver coins from Sicily are sheer masterpieces.

Another precious material was ivory, which was worked with virtuosity from Minoan times and never went out of fashion. This material was chosen to immortalize the features of the family of Alexander the Great. Particular mention should be made of wood. Although climatic conditions in Greece militate against the preservation of objects made in this material, there are many indications that its use was extremely widespread. The rare statues that still exist unfortunately cannot give an exact idea of the artistic role that wood played, in particular in the creation of large-scale sculpture. Some think it may have been a determining factor.

There is, at the same time, an abundance of terracotta figurines which have come down to us. The discipline of 'coroplastics'—modelling in terracotta—was born in Greece with art itself and was practised until the end of the Hellenistic period. Minoan and Mycenaean artists had no qualms about giving that humble material the features of their goddesses. After the bell-idols of the Geometric period, the mould appeared in the 7th century, and this technique stimulated the workshops' activities. All subjects were treated by these craftsmen, but above all, of course, they depicted the human figure; and one can follow its iconographic development from Archaism up to the Hellenistic period. As with bronze-working, the various factories had technical and aesthetic traditions which usually enable one to identify them despite the effects of outside influences, imitations and the 'remoulding' process. The 4th century was the high-point of terracotta modelling. It was the time of the famous Tanagra figurines, graceful young girls richly adorned, whose form and dress are astonishingly varied and whose originality never ceases to surprise us. But Boeotia was not the only centre of creativity. In the course of the Hellenistic period many other regions were to become renowned for the quality of their products, and particularly the Anatolian coast. Who has not heard of Myrina? From this city's necropolis came hundreds of figurines, dominated by the aerial forms of Victory and Eros. Their interest is increased by the fact that they bear the signatures of some thirty artists, whose individual inspiration and styles can thus be followed.

Alongside use of the soft material of clay, Greek artists had learned how to work little objects of hard stone, particularly in the early periods in the Cyclades and Crete. Lastly, goldwork, into the techniques for which the artists of Hellas were initiated by the lessons of the Orient, produced masterpieces in every period. Pre-Hellenic jewellery, Archaic finery, Classical and Hellenistic ornaments rival each other in finesse and technical virtuosity. Notable examples are the Daedalic pendants, the Graeco-Scythian objects discovered to the north of the Black Sea, and the hoard of objects recently exhumed from the tomb at Vergina in Macedonia which may be the grave of King Philip II.

As is the case with other civilizations, the minor arts of Greece put us in direct contact with daily life, whether the forms used are sacred or profane. Of one thing we can be sure: in the creative gestures of the humblest artisan, artistic quality and a sense of beauty were never sacrificed.

CONCISE BIBLIOGRAPHY

ARIAS, P.E., and HIRMER, M. *Le Vase grec.* Paris, 1962.

BEAZLEY, J.D. *Attic Black-figure Vase-painters.* Oxford, 1956.

——————— *Attic Red-figure Vase-painters.* Oxford, 1963.

——————— and ASHMOLE, B. *Greek Sculpture and Painting.* Cambridge, 1966.

BERVE, H., and GRUBEN, G. *Griechische Tempel und Heiligtümer.* Munich, 1961. 2nd ed., 1978. *Greek Temples, Theatres and Shrines,* trans. Richard Waterhouse. London, 1963.

BOARDMAN, J. *Athenian Black-figure Vases.* London, 1974.

——————— *Athenian Red-figure Vases.* London, 1975.

——————— *Greek Gems and Finger Rings.* London, 1971.

CHARBONNEAUX, J. *Les Bronzes grecs.* Paris, 1958. *Greek Bronzes,* trans. Katherine Watson. London, 1962.

——————— *La Sculpture grecque archaïque.* Paris, 1939.

——————— *La Sculpture grecque classique.* Paris, 1943.

COCHE DE LA FERTE, E. *Les Bijoux antiques.* Paris, 1956.

COLDSTREAM, J.N. *Greek Geometric Pottery.* London, 1968.

——————— *Geometric Greece.* London, 1977.

DEMARGNE, P. *Naissance de l'art grec.* L'Univers des Formes. Paris, 1964. *The Origins of Greek Art,* trans. Stuart Gilbert and James Emmons. London, 1964.

FRANKE, P.R., and HIRMER, M. *Die griechische Münze.* Munich, 1964.

LENGYEL, LANCELOT. *Chefs-d'œuvre des monnaies grecques.* Montrouge, 1952.

LULLIES, R., and HIRMER, M. *La Sculpture grecque.* Paris, 1971. *Greek Sculpture.* London, 1960.

MARTIN, R. *Monde grec,* in *Architecture Universelle.* Fribourg, 1966.

MARTIN, R., CHARBONNEAUX, J., and VILLARD, F. *Grèce archaïque.* L'Univers des Formes. Paris, 1968. *Archaic Greek Art,* trans. James Emmons and Robert Allen. London, 1971.

——————— *Grèce classique.* L'Univers des Formes. Paris, 1969. *Classical Greek Art,* trans. James Emmons. London, 1972.

——————— *Grèce hellénistique.* L'Univers des Formes. Paris, 1970. *Hellenistic Art,* trans. Peter Green. London, 1973.

MOLLARD-BESQUES, S. *Les Terres-cuites grecques.* Paris, 1963.

PAPAIOANNOU, K. *L'Art grec.* Paris, 1972.

RICHTER, G.M.A. *The Sculpture and Sculptors of the Greeks.* 4th rev. ed. New Haven, 1970.

ROBERTSON, M. *Greek Painting.* Geneva, 1959.

ZERVOS, C. *L'Art de la Crète néolithique et minoenne.* Cahiers d'Art. Paris, 1970.

——————— *L'Art des Cyclades du début à la fin de l'Age du Bronze.* Cahiers d'Art. Paris, 1957.

——————— *La Civilisation hellénique, XIe-VIIIe siècle.* Cahiers d'Art. Paris, 1969.

——————— *Naissance de la civilisation en Grèce.* Cahiers d'Art. Paris, 1963.

MAJOR MUSEUMS

Austria
Kunsthistorisches Museum, Vienna

Denmark
Ny-Carlsberg Glyptotek, Copenhagen
National Museum, Copenhagen

England
British Museum, London
Ashmolean Museum, Oxford

France
Musée du Louvre, Paris
Cabinet des Médailles de la Bibliothèque Nationale, Paris

Germany, East
Staatliche Museen, East Berlin

Germany, West
Glyptothek, Munich
Antikensammlungen, Munich
Martin von Wagner Museum, Würzburg
Badisches Landesmuseum, Karlsruhe

Italy
Museo Nazionale, Rome
Museo del Vaticano, Rome
Museo della Villa Giulia, Rome
Museo dei Conservatori, Rome
Museo Capitolino, Rome
Museo Nazionale, Naples
Museo Nazionale, Syracuse
Museo Nazionale, Palermo

Switzerland
Antikenmuseum, Basle

U.S.A.
Metropolitan Museum, New York
Museum of Fine Arts, Boston
J. Paul Getty Museum, Malibu, California

U.S.S.R.
Hermitage Museum, Leningrad

THE GREEK WORLD

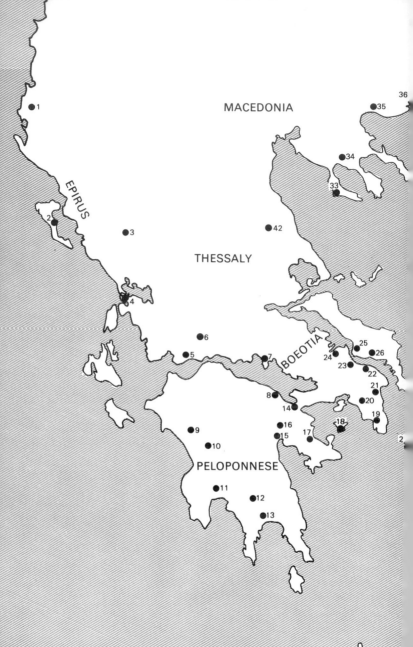

MACEDONIA

●35

36

●34

●33

EPIRUS

●1

●2

THESSALY

●3

●42

●4

●6

●5

●7

BOEOTIA

●25

●24

●26

●23

●22

●21

●8

●20

●14

●19

●18

2

●9

●16

●15

●17

●10

PELOPONNESE

●11

●12

●13

CRETE

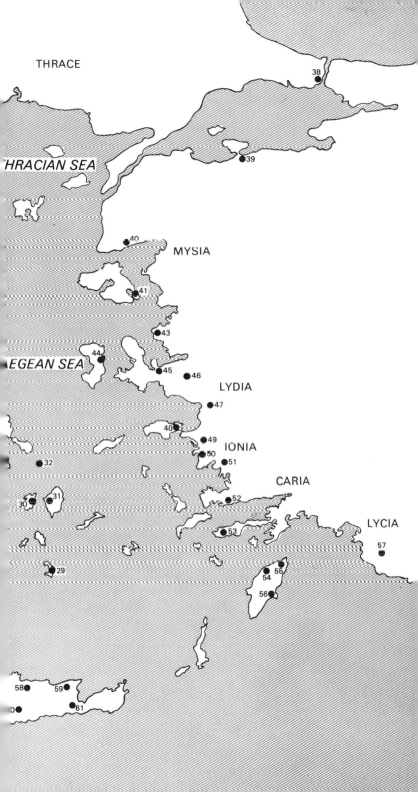

THRACE

THRACIAN SEA

MYSIA

AEGEAN SEA

LYDIA

IONIA

CARIA

LYCIA

38

39

40

41

43

44

45

46

47

48

49

50

51

52

53

57

55

54

56

32

31

30

29

58

59

61

60

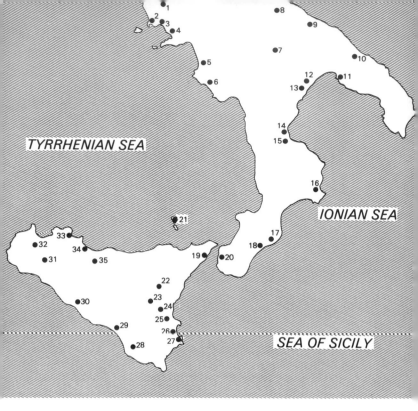

MAGNA GRAECIA
AND SICILY

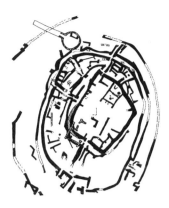

1   Plan of the acropolis at Dimini (Thessaly), Late Neolithic, c. 3700–3200 B.C.

2   Plan of the palace at Mallia (Crete), Middle Minoan, c. 2000–1650 B.C.

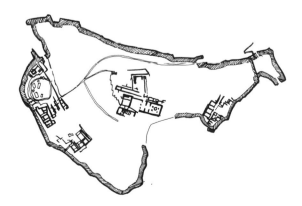

3   Plan of the acropolis at Mycenae, Mycenaean, 14th–13th c. B.C.

4
Plan of the 'Little Palace' at Knossos (Crete), Late Minoan, 15th c. B.C.

5
Restored western façade, palace at Knossos, end of Middle, beginning of Late Minoan, *c.* 1700–1400 B.C.

6
Palace of King Nestor at Pylos, Mycenaean, 13th c. B.C.

7
A road in Santorini (Thera), Middle Cycladic III–Late Cycladic I, 16th c. B.C.

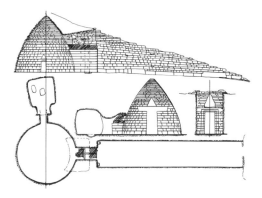

8   The 'Treasury of Atreus', Mycenae, monumental tomb: section and plan, Mycenaean, *c.* 1330 B.C.

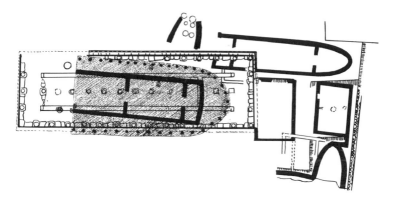

9   Thermum (Aetolia), plans of 9th-c. (black), 8th-c. (grey) and 7th-c. buildings

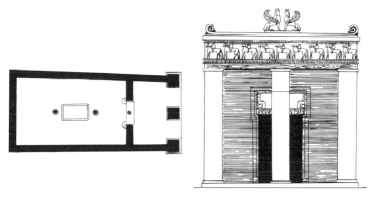

10
Prinias, temple A: plan, 7th c. B.C.

11
Prinias, temple A: restored façade

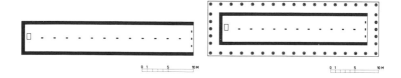

12
Samos, Hekatompedon, *c.* 800 B.C.

13
Samos, Hekatompedon, *c.* 700 B.C.

14 Restored façade of the temple of Artemis, Corfu, *c.* 600 B.C.

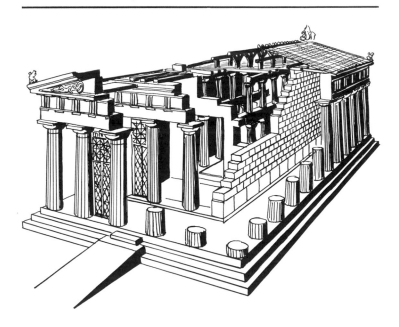

15 Oblique view of the temple of Athena Aphaia, Aegina, beginning of 5th c. B.C.

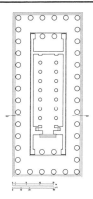

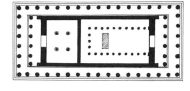

16
Plan of the temple of Hera, Poseidonia (Paestum), c. 450 B.C.

17
Plan of the Parthenon, Athens Acropolis, 447–432 B.C.

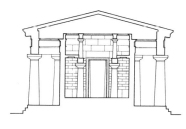

18
Section of the temple of Hera, Poseidonia (Paestum), c. 450 B.C.

19
Section of the Parthenon, Athens Acropolis, 447–432 B.C.

20
Reconstructed view of the interior of the temple of Apollo Epikourios, Bassae, 2nd half of 5th c. B.C.

21
Mixture of Doric and Ionic orders, temple of Athena, Poseidonia (Paestum), end of 6th c. B.C.

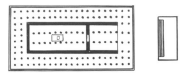

22
Plan of the temple of Rhoikos with its altar, Samos, *c.* 580–540 B.C.

23
Plan of the temple of Apollo, Didyma, Hellenistic period

24
Restoration of the façade of the Siphnian Treasury at Delphi, 530–525 B.C.

25
Lower part of the temple of Athena Nike, Athens Acropolis, *c.* 420 B.C.

26
Restoration of the Nereid Monument at Xanthos (Lycia), *c.* 400 B.C., B.M.

27
Narrow south side of the Sarcophagus of Alexander, marble, *c.* 310 B.C., Sidon, Archaeol. Mus., Istanbul

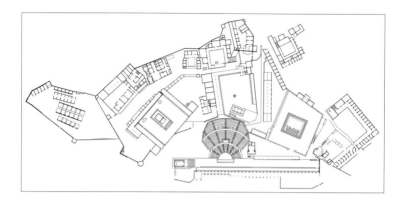

28   Plan of the acropolis of Pergamon, 3rd 2nd c. B.C.

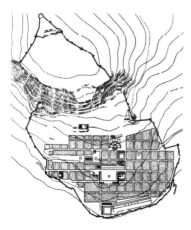

29
Plan of the city of Priene, end of 4th c.
B.C.

30
Plan of the agora at Pergamon, 3rd–
2nd c. B.C.

31
Restored façade of a tomb, painted stucco on limestone, 1st half of 3rd c. B.C., Lefcadia

32
Propylon, sanctuary of Athena, Pergamon, limestone and marble, H. 8.80 m., 2nd c. B.C., St. Mus., E. Berlin

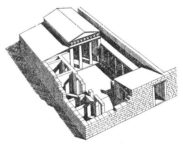

33
Restoration of the theatre at Priene, 3rd c. B.C.

34
Restored view of a house at Priene

35   Altar consecrated to Zeus and Athena, Pergamon, marble, L. 36.44 m., W. 34.20 m., c. 180 B.C., St. Mus., E. Berlin

36
Minoan columns and capitals: northern entrance of the palace at Knossos

37
Capital from the façade, Treasury of Atreus: restoration, Mycenae, green stone, 13th c. B.C., B.M.

38
Palm capital, Arcadia, limestone, abacus 49 × 50 cm., 7th c. B.C., Herakleion Mus.

39
Aeolic capital, Larissa, limestone, H. 1.45 m., end of 7th, early 6th c. B.C., Archaeol. Mus., Istanbul

40
Anta-capital, Poseidonia (Paestum), limestone, H. 73.4 cm., c. 540 B.C., Paestum Mus.

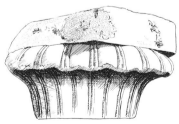

41
Palm capital, Massaliot Treasury, Delphi, marble, end of 6th c. B.C., Delphi Mus.

42
Doric capital, Delphi, tufa, abacus dimensions 80 × 80 cm., end of 7th c. B.C., Delphi Mus.

43
Doric capital, Aegina, temple of Athena Aphaia, marble, H. of column 5.272 m., beginning of 5th c. B.C.

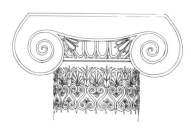

44
Ionic capital, temple of Polycrates, Heraion of Samos, end of 6th c. B.C.

45
Ionic capital, temple of Artemis, Sardis, marble, H. 81 cm., 3rd c. B.C.

46
Corinthian capital: reconstruction, Bassae, marble, H. c. 65 cm., 5th c. B.C., fragments in Nat. Mus., Athens

47
Corinthian capital: reconstruction, Ai Khanum, hypostyle hall, limestone, H. 92 cm., beginning of 2nd c. B.C.

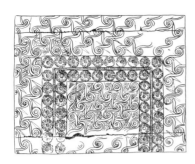

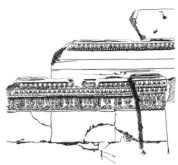

48
Ceiling in the chamber of a tholos, Orchomenos of Boeotia, green schist, originally 3.74 × 2.75 m., 14th c. B.C.

49
Wall and entablature ornamentation, Athens Acropolis, Erechtheion, marble, end of 5th c. B.C.

50
Gutter, Delphi, tholos, marble, H 54 cm., c. 370 B.C., Delphi Mus.

51
Gutter, Delphi, temple of Apollo, marble, mid-4th c. B.C., Delphi Mus.

52
Masonry course decoration, Delphi, Siphnian Treasury, marble, c. 530–525 B.C.

53
Masonry course decoration, Epidaurus, tholos, marble, 370–330 B.C., Epidaurus Mus.

54   Lion Gate, Mycenae, stone, 13th c. B.C.

55
Sculpture on a restored façade, Prinias, limestone, H. of frieze 84 cm., 620–600 B.C., Herakleion Mus.

56
Decoration under the lintel of the temple at Prinias

57
Restored entablature, temple at Thermum, wood and terracotta, metopes 88 × 99 cm., end of 7th c. B.C.

58
Entablature, Priene, temple of Athena, marble, H. 2.11 m., 2nd half of 4th c. B.C., St. Mus., E. Berlin

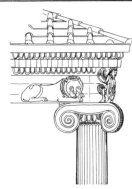

59
Relief from a column drum, Didyma, temple of Apollo, marble, H. 27 cm., *c.* 540–520 B.C., St. Mus., E. Berlin

60
Restoration of the upper parts of the temple of Apollo at Didyma: lion and gorgon

61
Reliefs from a column drum, Ephesus, marble, H. of bust on left 59 cm., legs 1 m., 550–540 B.C., B.M.

62
Restoration of the lower part of the column, with its socle, Didyma, temple of Apollo

63
Relief decorating a column drum, Ephesus, temple of Artemis, marble, H. 1.82 m., *c.* 340 B.C., B.M.

64
Pilaster capital with animal decoration, Didyma, temple of Apollo, marble, H. 90 cm., 3rd–2nd c. B.C.

66
Caryatid, Delphi, unidentified treasury, marble, H. 84 cm., *c.* 540–530 B.C., Delphi Mus.

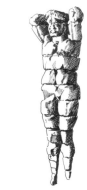

65
Caryatid, Delphi, Siphnian Treasury, marble, H. *c.* 2 m., *c.* 525 B.C., Delphi Mus.

67
Telamon, decoration, Agrigento, temple of Olympian Zeus, limestone, H. *c.* 8 m., *c.* 460 B.C., Agrigento Mus.

68
Caryatid, Athens Acropolis, Erechtheion, marble, H. 2.31 m., *c.* 415 B.C., B.M.

69
Column of dancers: tripod support, Delphi, marble, H. of figures 2.08 m., *c.* 335–325 B.C., Delphi Mus.

70
Metope (?), Mycenae, limestone, H. 40 cm., 2nd half of 7th c. B.C., Nat. Mus. Athens

71
Relief: divine triad, Gortyn, temple of Apollo, limestone, H. 1.50 m., c. 630–620 B.C. Herakleion Mus.

72
Metope: two girls in flight, Poseidonia (Paestum), sandstone, H. 78 cm., c. 550–540 B.C., Paestum Mus.

73
Metopes: two girls dancing, Poseidonia (Paestum), sandstone, H. 85 cm., 510–505 B.C., Paestum Mus.

74
Metope: Herakles and the Cerynian stag, Delphi, marble, H. 67 cm., 490–485 B.C., Delphi Mus.

75
Metope: Herakles and Kyknos, Delphi, Athenian Treasury, marble, H. 67 cm., 490–485 B.C., Delphi Mus.

76
Metope: Athena with Herakles and Atlas, Olympia, marble, H. 1.60 m., *c.* 460 B.C., Olympia Mus.

77
Metope: Herakles and the bull of Crete, Olympia, marble, H. 1.60 m., *c.* 460 B.C., Louvre and Olympia Mus.

78
Metope: Hera and Zeus, Selinus, temple of Hera, tufa and marble, H. 1.62 m., c. 460 B.C., Palermo Mus.

79
Metope: Actaeon and Artemis, tufa and marble, Selinus, temple of Hera, H. 1.62 m., *c.* 460 B.C., Palermo Mus.

80
Metope: centaur and Lapith, Athens, Parthenon: Doric frieze on south side, marble, H. 1.34 m., 448–440 B.C., B.M.

81
Metope: Lapith and centaur, marble, H. 1.34 m., 448–440 B.C., Athens, Parthenon: Doric frieze on south side

82   Frieze: Herakles banqueting, Assos, temple of Athena, trachyte, H. 49 cm.,
c. 540–530 B.C., Louvre.

83   Frieze: gathering of the gods, Delphi, Siphnian Treasury, marble, H. 65 cm.,
c. 530–525 B.C., Delphi Mus.

84
Frieze: the gods, Athens, Parthenon:
Ionic frieze on east side, marble, H.
1.06 m., 440–432 B.C., Acropolis Mus.

85
Frieze: notables surrendering a city,
Xanthos, Nereid Monument, marble,
H. 63 cm., c. 400 B.C., B.M.

86
Frieze (interior): centaur and Lapiths, Bassae, temple of Apollo Epikourios, marble, H. 70 cm., *c.* 420 B.C., B.M.

87
Frieze: man and horse, marble, H. 1.06 m., 440–432 B.C., Athens, Parthenon: west Ionic frieze

88
Frieze: battle of Plataea (479 B.C.), Athens, temple of Athena Nike, marble, H. 48 cm., 425–421 B.C., B.M.

89
Frieze: battle of Greeks and Amazons, Halicarnassus, Mausoleum, marble, H. 89 cm., *c.* 350 B.C., B.M.

90   Sarcophagus of Alexander: lion hunt, Sidon, marble, L. 3.18 m., H. of frieze 58.5 cm., *c.* 305 B.C., Archaeol. Mus., Istanbul

91
Frieze (interior): combat of Greeks
and Amazons, Bassae, marble, H.
63 cm., *c.* 420 B.C., B.M.

92
Frieze: battle scene, Xanthos, Nereid
Monument, marble, H. 1.01 m., *c.* 400
B.C., B.M.

93
Frieze: Zeus and the giant Porphyrios,
Pergamon, marble, H. 2.30 m., *c.*
180–160 B.C., St. Mus., E. Berlin

94
Frieze: Athena and giant Alkyonios,
Pergamon, marble, H. 2.30 m., *c.*
180–160 B.C., St. Mus., E. Berlin

95–96
Frieze: combat of Greeks and
Amazons, Magnesia, marble, H. of
frieze 70 cm, *c.* 125 B.C., Louvre

97   East pediment of the temple of Athena Aphaia, Aegina: reconstruction,
        L. *c.* 7.25 m., Glyptothek, Munich

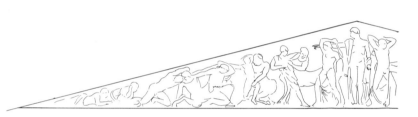

98   East pediment of the temple of Zeus, Olympia: reconstruction, L. 26.40 m.,
        Olympia Mus.

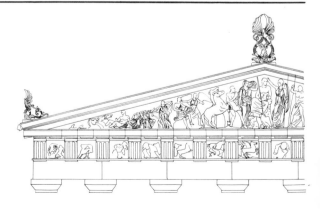

99   East pediment and Doric frieze of the Parthenon: reconstruction, L. *c.* 32 m.,
        Athens Acropolis

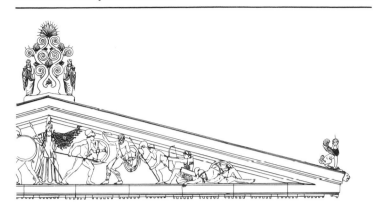

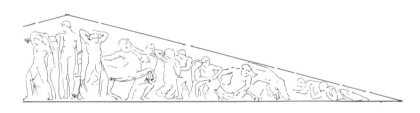

100
Fresco of the 'Parisienne', palace of Knossos, H. of fragment 25 cm., *c.* 1500–1450 B.C., Herakleion Mus.

101
Fresco of spring, house in Thera, *c.* 1500 B.C., Nat. Mus., Athens

102
Fisherman: painted vase, Phylakopi of Melos, terracotta, H. of figure 17 cm., *c.* 1650 B.C., Nat. Mus., Athens

103
Fresco of a fisherman, house in Thera, *c.* 1500 B.C., Nat. Mus., Athens

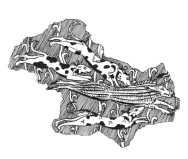

104
Fresco of a boar hunt, Tiryns, W. of conserved portion 43 cm., 13th c. B.C., Nat. Mus., Athens

105
Polychrome metope: reconstruction, two women undressing, Thermum, temple of Apollo, H. 95 cm., *c.* 625 B.C.

106   Painted cupola in a royal tomb: homage to the princely couple, fresco, H. of frieze 55 cm., *c.* 300 B.C., Kazanlak

107
Painted decoration on the wall of the tomb at Kazanlak

108
Wall painting: Perseus freeing Andromeda, after Nikias, fresco original *c.* 330 B.C., Pompeii, Nat. Mus., Naples

109
Mosaic: stag hunt, signed by Gnosis, beginning of 3rd c. B.C., Pella

110
Mosaic: Dionysos on a leopard, 2nd half of 2nd c. B.C., Delos, House of the Masks

111
Female figurine, Nea Nikomedia (Thessaly), terracotta, H. 17 cm., 5900–5200 B.C., Beroea Mus.

112
Female figurine, Chaeronea, painted terracotta, H. 12 cm., 5200–4200 B.C., Chaeronea Mus.

113
Female figurine, Pharsalus, terracotta, H. 7 cm., Middle Neolithic, 5200–4200 B.C., Volos Mus.

114
Kourotrophic figurine, Sesklo, terracotta, H. 16 cm., Late Neolithic, 4200–3200 B.C., Nat. Mus., Athens

115
Standing female figurine, marble, H. 13.5 cm., Late Neolithic, 4th millennium B.C., Weert, Smeets Coll.

116
Seated female figurine, marble, H. 19 cm., Late Neolithic, 4th millennium B.C., Mus. Royaux, Brussels

117
Head of a female figurine, Pyrasos, terracotta, H. 3.4 cm., Middle Neolithic, 5200–4200 B.C., Volos Mus.

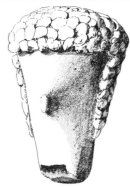

118
Head of a figurine, Corinth, terracotta, H. 6.8 cm., Late Neolithic, 4200–3200 B.C., Corinth Mus.

119
Head of a figurine, Dikili Tash, terracotta, H. 1.3 cm., Late Neolithic, 4200–3200 B.C., Kavalla Mus.

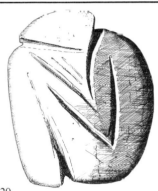

120
Seated figurine, Magula Karamurlar, stone, H. 4 cm., Early Neolithic, 5900–5200 B.C., Volos Mus.

121
Seal, Nessonis, D. 3.3 cm., Middle Neolithic, 5200–4200 B.C., Larissa Mus.

122
Figurine: pack-animal, Sitagroi, terracotta, W. 17 cm., Late Neolithic, 4200–3200 B.C., Philippi Mus.

123
Schematic female idol, Despotiko, marble, H. 12 cm., Early Cycladic I, 3200–2700 B.C., Nat. Mus., Athens

124
Female idol, Naxos, marble, H. 20.8 cm., Early Cycladic I, 3200–2700 B.C., Ashmolean Mus.

125
Head of female idol, Amorgos, marble, H. 35.5 cm., Early Cycladic II, 2700–2300 B.C., Louvre

126
Lyre-player, Keros, marble, H. 22.5 cm., Early Cycladic II, 2700–2300 B.C., Nat. Mus., Athens

127
Female idol, Amorgos, marble, H. 1.485 m., Early Cycladic II, 2700–2300 B.C., Nat. Mus., Athens

128
Man's head, Knossos, terracotta, H.
5 cm., Middle Minoan I–II, 2000–1700
B.C., Herakleion Mus.

129
Man's head, Knossos, ivory, H.
4.5 cm., Late Minoan 1, c. 1550 B.C.,
Herakleion Mus.

130
Funerary mask said to be of Agamemnon, Mycenae, gold, H. 31.5 cm., 16th
c. B.C., Nat. Mus., Athens

131
Female head, Acropolis, Mycenae,
painted stucco, H. 16.8 cm., Mycenaean, c. 1300 B.C., Nat. Mus., Athens

132
Female head, Amyclae, terracotta, H.
8.5 cm., Late Geometric, end of 8th c.
B.C., Nat. Mus., Athens

133
Warrior's head, Amyclae, terracotta,
H. 11.5 cm., Late Geometric, end of
8th c. B.C., Nat. Mus., Athens

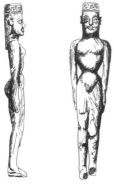

134
Female figurine, Dipylon Gate, north-west of Athens, ivory, H. 24 cm., *c.* 730 B.C., Nat. Mus., Athens

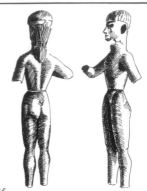

135
Man, probably Apollo Dreros, bronze, H. 80 cm., Late Geometric, *c.* 700 B.C., Herakleion Mus.

136
Warrior, Karditsa, bronze, H. 28 cm., Late Geometric, end of 8th c. B.C., Nat. Mus., Athens

137
Statuette of Apollo, Thebes, bronze, H. 20 cm., beginning of 7th c. B.C., Mus. of Fine Arts, Boston

138
Charioteer, Olympia, bronze, H. 13.6 cm., Late Geometric, *c.* 725 B.C., Olympia Mus.

139
Hero and centaur: Herakles and Nessos (?), bronze, H. 11 cm., end of 8th c. B.C., Metropolitan Mus.

140
Naxian female statue, Delos, Sanctuary of Artemis, marble, H. 1.75 m., c. 650 B.C., Nat. Mus., Athens

141
Seated woman, Gortyn, limestone, H. 80 cm., 1st half of 7th c. B.C., Herakleion Mus.

142
Bust of seated woman, Astritsi, limestone, H. 1.04 m., c. 650 B.C., Herakleion Mus.

143
'Lady from Auxerre', limestone, H. 75 cm., c. 640–630 B.C., Louvre

144
Bust of seated woman, Eleutherna, limestone, H. 57 cm., c. 600 B.C., Herakleion Mus.

145
Woman's head (?), Axos, limestone, H. 16.2 cm., 590–570 B.C., Herakleion Mus.

146
Head of Attic kouros, Dipylon Gate north-west of Athens, marble, H. 44 cm., *c.* 600 B.C., Nat. Mus., Athens

147
Head of Boeotian kouros, Ptoan (Boeotia), limestone, H. 33 cm., *c.* 580 B.C., Nat. Mus., Athens

148
Attic kouros, Sounion, marble, H. 3.05 m., *c.* 600 B.C., Nat. Mus., Athens

149
Kouros: back view, Sounion, marble, H. 1.65 m., 600–590 B.C., Nat. Mus. Athens

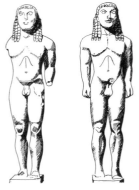

150
Argive twin kouroi: Kleobis and Biton (?), Delphi, marble, H. 2.16 m., 590–580 B.C., Delphi Mus.

151
Kouros, marble, H. 1.80 m. (body), 575–550 B.C., Vathy Mus., Samos, Archaeol. Mus., Istanbul (head)

152
Corinthian (?) kouros, Tenea, marble,
H. 1.53 m., *c.* 560–550 B.C., Glypto-
thek, Munich

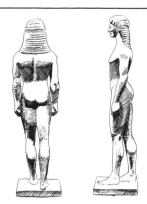

153
Back view and profile of Tenea kouros

154
Boeotian kouros, Ptoan (Boeotia),
marble, H. 1.60 m., *c.* 530 B.C., Nat.
Mus., Athens

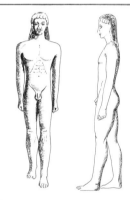

155
Cycladic kouros, Melos, marble, H.
2.14 m., *c.* 550 B.C., Nat. Mus., Athens

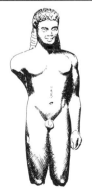

156
Parian kouros, Paros, marble, H.
1.035 m., 540–530 B.C., Louvre

157
Attic kouros: funerary statue of Croe-
sus, Anavysos (Attica), marble, H.
1.94 m., 530 B.C., Nat. Mus., Athens

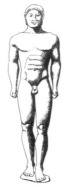

158
Attic kouros, Attica, marble, H. 2.11 m., *c.* 540–530 B.C., Glyptothek, Munich

159
Attic kouros: funerary statue of Aristodikos, Attica, marble, H. 1.95 m., *c,* 500 B.C., Nat. Mus., Athens

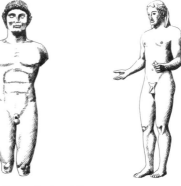

160
Kouros, known as the 'Strangford Apollo', Anaphi, marble, H. 1.01 m., *c.* 500–490 B.C., B.M.

161
Kouros, Piraeus, bronze, H. 1.92 m., *c.* 530–520 B.C., Nat. Mus., Athens

162
Ear of a kouros from Sounion, *c.* 600 B.C.

163
Ear of the Aristodikos kouros, *c.* 500 B.C.

164
Statue by Rhombos, 'Moschophoros',
Athens Acropolis, marble, H. 96 cm.,
c. 570 B.C., Acropolis Mus.

165
'Rampin Horseman', Athens, marble,
H. of head 29 cm., c. 550–540, Louvre
(head) and Acropolis Mus.

166
Seated man, Didyma, marble, H.
1.55 m., c. 560 B.C., B.M.

167
Draped man by Dionysermos,
marble, H. 69 cm., c. 630 B.C., Louvre

168
Reclining man (from a group), Samos,
marble, L. 1.60 m., by Geneleos, c. 560
B.C., Vathy Mus., Samos

169
Torso of warrior, Sparta, marble, H.
85 cm., c. 490–480 B.C., Sparta Mus.

170
Youth's head, the 'Blond Boy', Athens
Acropolis, marble, H. 25 cm., *c.* 490–
480 B.C., Acropolis Mus.

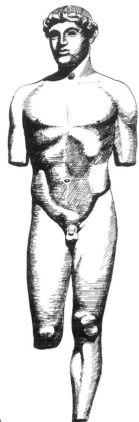

171
Youth, Agrigento, marble, H. 1.10 m.,
c. 480 B.C., Civic Mus., Agrigento

172
Ephebe by Kritios, Athens Acropolis,
marble, H. 82 cm., *c.* 480 B.C., Acropolis Mus.

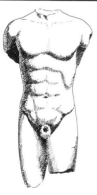

173
Male torso, Miletus, marble, H.
1.32 m., *c.* 480 B.C., Louvre

174
Male torso, Leontini, marble, H.
1.03 m., *c.* 490 B.C., Archaeol. Mus.,
Syracuse

175
Zeus with lightning, or Poseidon, His-
tiaea (in the sea), bronze, H. 2.09 m., *c.*
460 B.C., Nat. Mus., Athens

176
Man's head, 'Chatsworth Apollo',
Cyprus, bronze, H. 31.7 cm., *c.* 460
B.C., Cyprus, B.M.

177
Discus thrower (Discobolos), marble,
Roman copy after Myron, Rome, H.
1.55 m., *c.* 450 B.C., Nat. Mus., Rome

178
The river-god Alpheus, from pediment, Olympia, temple of Zeus,
marble, *c.* 460 B.C., Olympia Mus.

179
Charioteer: detail from a group,
Delphi, bronze, H. 1.80 m., *c.* 475 B.C.,
Delphi Mus.

180
'Kassel' Apollo, Rome, marble, H. 2 m., Roman copy after Phidias, *c.* 450–440 B.C., Kassel Mus.

181
Dionysos: figure from the corner of a pediment, Parthenon, marble, H. 1.30 m., *c.* 440–432 B.C., B.M.

182
'Tiber' Apollo, Rome, marble, H. 2.04 m., Roman copy after Phidias (or Kalamis), *c.* 450 B.C., Nat. Mus., Rome

183
'Omphalos' Apollo, Athens, marble, H. 1.76 m., copy after Kalamis, *c.* 460–450 B.C., Nat. Mus., Athens

184
The Doryphoros, Pompeii, marble, H. 2.12 m., Roman copy after Polykleitos, *c.* 440 B.C., Nat. Mus., Naples

185
The Diadoumenos, Delos, marble, H. 1.95 m., Roman copy after Polykleitos, *c.* 430 B.C., Nat. Mus., Athens

186
Discus thrower, Rome, marble, H. 1.67 m., Roman copy after Naukydes, end of 5th c. B.C., Louvre

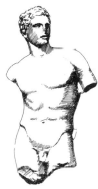

187
Ares, marble, H. 2.11 m., Roman copy after Alkamenes, end of 5th c. B.C., Louvre

188
The Pothos, Rome, marble, H. 1.80 m., Roman copy after Skopas, c. 350 B.C., Capitoline Mus., Rome

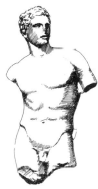

189
Meleager, Santa Marinella, marble, H. 1.23 m., after Skopas, c. 340–330 B.C., Fogg Mus., Cambridge, Mass.

190
Satyr pouring, marble, H. 1.50 m., Roman copy after Praxiteles, c. 360 B.C., Louvre

191
Apollo Sauroktonos, marble, H. 1.49 m., Roman copy after Praxiteles, c. 350–330 B.C., Louvre

192
Portrait of an African, temple of Apollo, Cyrene, bronze, H. 30.5 cm., end of 4th c. B.C., B.M.

193
Portrait of a wrestler, Olympia, bronze, H. 28 cm., attributed to Silanion, *c.* 325 B.C., Nat. Mus., Athens

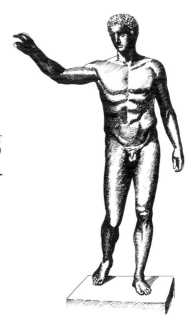

194
Ephebe of Marathon, Gulf of Marathon, bronze, H. 1.30 m., *c.* 340 B.C., Nat. Mus., Athens

195
Athlete of Ephesus, bronze, H. 1.92 m., *c.* 350 B.C., Ephesus Mus., Vienna

196
Youth of Antikythera, Antikythera, bronze, H. 1.94 m., *c.* 350 B.C., Nat. Mus., Athens

197
Victorious athlete, bronze, life-size, work of Lysippos or his circle, end of 4th c. B.C., J. Paul Getty Mus., Malibu

198
Alexander with lance, Lower Egypt, bronze, H. c. 17 cm., Hellenistic copy after Lysippos, c. 330 B.C., Louvre

199
Herakles in repose, Perugia, bronze, H. 43.5 cm., Hellenistic copy after Lysippos, c. 330–320 B.C., Louvre

200
Hermes fastening his sandal, marble, H. 1.54 m., Roman copy after Lysippos, end of 4th c. B.C., Louvre

201
Wounded Gaul, marble, H. 83 cm., Roman copy after a group from Pergamon, 2nd c. B.C., Louvre

202
Warrior in combat: 'Borghese gladiator', Anzio, marble, H. 1.99 m., c. 100 B.C., Louvre

203
Portrait of Demosthenes, marble, H. 2.07 m., Roman copy after Polyeuktos, c. 280 B.C., Vatican Mus.

204
Portrait of a philosopher, Delphi, marble, H. 2.07 m., c. 250 B.C., Delphi Mus.

205
Statue, said to be of Hippokrates, Cos, marble, c. 150–100 B.C., Cos Mus.

206
Poseidon of Melos, sanctuary of Poseidon, Melos, marble, H. 2.17 m., c. 130 B.C., Nat. Mus., Athens

207
Sleeping satyr, Rome, marble, H. 2.15 m., c. 200 B.C. (Bernini restoration), Glyptothek, Munich

208
Boxer, Rome, bronze, H. 1.28 m., beginning of 1st c. B.C., Nat. Mus., Rome

209   Alexander's family: Olympias, Alexander, Philip and two unidentified
portraits, Vergina, ivory, H. 3 cm., 3rd quarter of 4th c. B.C., Salonica Mus.

210
Portrait of Alexander ('Azara herm'),
Tivoli, marble, H. 68 cm., after Lysip-
pos, c. 330 B.C., Louvre

211
Portrait of Alexander, Pergamon,
marble, H. 42 cm., c. 160 B.C., Arch-
acol. Mus., Istanbul

212
Youth, from the sea at Agde: Hellenistic sovereign (?), bronze, H. 1.32 m.,
2nd c. B.C. (?), Louvre (vault)

213
Head of Helios, Rhodes, marble, H.
55 cm., c. 150 B.C., Archaeol. Mus.,
Rhodes

214
Menander, Tarquinia, marble, H.
46.2 cm., Roman copy, beginning of
3rd c. B.C., Dumbarton Oaks Coll.

215
Portrait of Flamininus (?), Delphi,
marble, H. 27 cm., beginning of 2nd c.
B.C., Delphi Mus.

216
Portrait of Hesiod (?), Herculaneum,
bronze, Roman copy, end of 2nd c.
B.C., Nat. Mus., Naples

217
Portrait of Cleopatra VII (?), limestone, H. 27 cm., c. 40 B.C., B.M.

218
Portrait of a Greek, Delos, bronze,
H. 32.5 cm., c. 100 B.C., Nat. Mus.,
Athens

219
Sleeping woman, marble, Roman
copy, c. 180 B.C., Nat. Mus., Rome

220
Attic kore, Keratea, marble, H.
1.93 m., *c.* 570-560 B.C., St. Mus., E.
Berlin

221
Kore with pomegranate, Athens
Acropolis, marble, H. 99.5 cm., *c.* 560
B.C., Acropolis Mus.

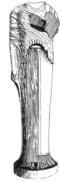

222
Samian kore dedicated by Cheramyes
('Hera of Samos'), Samos, marble, H.
1.92 m., *c.* 560 B.C., Louvre

223
Kore, Ornithe, back view, Samos,
marble, H. 1.68 m., work of Geneleos,
c. 560–550 B.C., St. Mus., E. Berlin

224
Attic Nike: akroterion, temple of
Apollo, Delphi, marble, H. 1.13 m., *c.*
520–510 B.C., Delphi Mus.

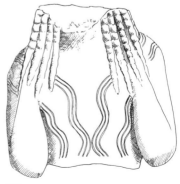

225
Bust of kore, Chios, marble, H. 55 cm.,
c. 570 B.C., Chios Mus.

226
'Peplos kore', Athens Acropolis, marble, H. 1.17 m., *c.* 530 B.C., Acropolis Mus.

227
Kore, Athens Acropolis, marble, H. 55.5 cm., *c.* 520 B.C., Acropolis Mus.

229
Head of kore, marble, Athens Acropolis, H. of statue 1.82 m., *c.* 530–520 B.C., Acropolis Mus.

228
Head of 'Peplos kore' (see No. 226)

230
Torso of kore, Delos, marble, H. 1.34 m., *c.* 500 B.C., Nat. Mus., Athens

231
Head of kore, Athens Acropolis, marble, H. 14.5 m., *c.* 510 B.C., Acropolis Mus.

232
Nike dedicated by Kallimachos, Athens Acropolis, marble, restored H. 1.40 m., *c.* 490 B.C., Acropolis Mus.

233
Woman in a peplos, Xanthos, marble, H. 1.25 m., *c.* 470 B.C., B.M.

234
'Angelito' Athena, Athens Acropolis, marble, H. 89.5 cm., *c.* 480 B.C., Acropolis Mus.

235
Aphrodite ('Esquiline Venus'), marble, H. 1.55 m., Roman copy, *c.* 450 B.C., Mus. dei Conservatori, Rome

236
Athena Lemnia (detail), marble, Roman copy after Phidias, Civic Mus., Bologna

237
Athena Parthenos (by Barbakeion?), Athens, marble, H. 94 cm., after Phidias, *c.* 447 B.C., Nat. Mus., Athens

238
Wounded Amazon, marble, H.
1.83 m., Roman copy after Polykleitos,
440–430 B.C., St. Mus., E. Berlin

239
Wounded Amazon, marble, H.
2.02 m., Roman copy after Kresilas,
440–430 B.C., Capitoline Mus., Rome

240
Wounded Amazon, marble, H.
2.25 m., after Phradmon, 440–430 B.C.,
Villa Doria Pamphili, Rome

241
Wounded Amazon, marble, Roman
copy after Phidias, 440–430 B.C., Villa
Hadriana, Tivoli

242
Nike: victory trophy, Olympia,
marble, H. 2.16 m., work of Paionios
of Mende, 420 B.C., Olympia Mus.

243
Nereid or nymph, 'Nereid Monu-
ment' from Xanthos (Lycia), marble,
H. 1.66 m., c. 400 B.C., B.M.

244
Aphrodite 'Genetrix', marble, H. 1.64 m., Roman copy after Kallimachos, end of 5th c. B.C., Louvre

245
Maenad in ecstasy, marble, H. 45 cm., Roman copy after Skopas, c. 350 B.C., St Skulpturensammlung, Dresden

246
Aphrodite of Knidos, marble, H. 2 m., Roman copy after Praxiteles, c. 340 B.C., Vatican Mus.

247
Artemis Brauronia ('Diana of Gabies'), marble, H. 1.65 m., after Praxiteles, c. 345 B.C., Louvre

248
Head of Aphrodite of Knidos ('Kaufmann head'), marble, H. 35 cm., after Praxiteles, c. 340 B.C., Louvre

249
'Aphrodite of Arles', marble, H. 1.94 m., Roman copy after Praxiteles, 350–330 B.C., Louvre

250
Themis, Rhamnous, marble, H. 2.22 m., work of Chairestratos, *c.* 300 B.C., Nat. Mus., Athens

251
Aphrodite ('Callipygian Venus'), marble, H. 1.52 m., Roman copy, 2nd c. B.C., Nat. Mus., Naples

252
Aphrodite ('Venus de Milo'), Melos, marble, H. 2.02 m., end of 2nd c. B.C., Louvre

253
Aphrodite kneeling, Villa Hadriana, marble, H. 1.06 m., copy after Doidalsas, *c.* 250 B.C., Nat. Mus., Rome

254
'Heyl Aphrodite', Pergamon, terracotta, H. 30 cm., *c.* 150 B.C., St. Mus., E. Berlin

255
Artemis, Milan, marble, H. 1.10 m., Roman copy, 2nd c. B.C., Archaeol. Mus., Milan

256
Muse: Polyhymnia (?), Rome, marble,
H. 1.59 m., Roman copy, end of 2nd c.
B.C., Capitoline Mus., Rome

257
Nike ('Victory of Samothrace'),
marble, H. 2.45 m., 180–160 B.C.,
Louvre

258
Ariadne sleeping, marble, L. 1.50 m.,
Roman copy, 200–150 B.C., Louvre

259
Old woman at market, marble, 2nd c.
B.C., Metropolitan Mus.

260   Hermaphrodite sleeping, marble, L. 1.48 m., Roman copy, 200–150 B.C.,
Louvre

261
Young girl running: Atalanta (?), marble, H. 1.24 m., 3rd–2nd c. B.C., Louvre

262
Little girl with dove, in the Ilissos, marble, H. 74 cm., *c.* 300 B.C., Nat. Mus., Athens

263
Young boy: 'ephebe of Tralles', Tralles, marble, H. 1.45 m., 100–50 (?) B.C., Archaeol. Mus., Istanbul

264
Winged genius: Agon (?), from the sea at Mahdia, bronze, H. 1.40 m., 200–150 B.C., Bardo Mus., Tunis

265
Little serving-boy, Taranto, sandstone, H. 64 cm., St. Mus., E. Berlin

266
Eros sleeping, Rhodes (?), bronze, L. 78.1 cm., *c.* 200 B.C., Metropolitan Mus.

267
Zeus abducting Ganymede: akroterion, Olympia, terracotta, H. 1.10 m.,
c. 480 B.C., Olympia Mus.

268
The 'Tyrannicides', marble, H.
1.95 m., Roman copy after Kritios and
Nesiotes, 477 B.C., Nat. Mus., Naples

269
Athena and Marsyas, marble, Roman
copy after Myron, c. 460 B.C., Frank-
furt and Vatican Mus.

270
Prokne and Itys, Athens, marble, H.
1.92 m., attributed to Alkamenes, end
of 5th c. B.C., Acropolis Mus.

271
Eirene (Peace) and Ploutos (Wealth),
Rome, marble, H. 1.99 m., Roman
copy, 370 B.C., Glyptothek, Munich

272
Nereid on horseback, Epidaurus,
temple of Asclepios, marble, H.
78 cm., 370 B.C., Nat. Mus., Athens

273
Artemis the huntress ('Diana of Versailles'), marble, H. 2 m., Roman copy after Leochares, c. 340 B.C., Louvre

274
Leda and the swan, marble, H. 1.32 m., Roman copy after Timotheos, c. 370 B.C., Capitoline Mus., Rome

275
Hermes and the child Dionysos, Olympia, marble, H. 2.15 m., Praxiteles (?), c. 340 B.C., Olympia Mus.

276
Child with goose, marble, H. 92 cm., Roman copy after Boethos, 3rd c. B.C., Louvre

277
Apollo and Marsyas, Mantineia, marble, H. 98 cm., workshop of Praxiteles, c. 320 B.C., Nat. Mus., Athens

278
Three muses, Mantineia, marble, H. 98 cm., workshop of Praxiteles, c. 320 B.C., Nat. Mus., Athens

279
Punishment of Marsyas, marble, Roman, after a Pergamon group, *c.* 210–200 B.C., Uffizi and Louvre

280
Jockey, from the sea at Artemision, bronze, H. of jockey 84 cm., *c.* 150–100 B.C., Nat. Mus., Athens

281
Death of Laocoön and his children, marble, H. 2.42 m., end of 2nd c. (?) B.C., Vatican Mus.

282
Aphrodite, Eros and Pan, Delos, marble, H. 1.29 m., *c.* 100 B.C., Nat. Mus., Athens

283
Eros and Psyche ('Capitoline kiss'), marble, H. 1.25 m., Roman copy, 200–150 B.C., Capitoline Mus., Rome

284
Tyche of Antioch, marble, H. 89.5 cm., Roman copy after Eutychides, *c.* 300 B.C., Vatican Mus.

285
Funerary relief: hunting scene (?),
Mycenae, limestone, H. 1.34 m., 16th
c. B.C., Nat. Mus., Athens

286
Sphinx: top of a funerary stele,
Athens, marble, H. 63 cm., c. 560 B.C.,
Kerameikos Mus., Athens

287
Stele of the 'Discophoros', Dipylon
Gate, Athens, marble, H. 34 cm., c.
560 B.C., Nat. Mus., Athens

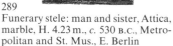

288
Funerary stele of a boxer, Athens,
marble, H. 23 cm., c. 540 B.C.,
Kerameikos Mus., Athens

289
Funerary stele: man and sister, Attica,
marble, H. 4.23 m., c. 530 B.C., Metropolitan and St. Mus., E. Berlin

290
Funerary stele of an athlete, Thebes, marble, H. 1.40 m., c. 550 B.C., Boston Mus.

291
Votive relief: offerings to a heroized couple, Chrysapha, marble, H. 87 cm., c. 540 B.C., St. Mus., E. Berlin

293
Funerary stele: hoplite running, Athens, marble, H. 1.02 m., c. 510 B.C., Nat. Mus., Athens

292
Funerary stele, Belanidera, marble, H. 2.02 m., work of Aristokles, c. 520–510 B.C., Nat. Mus., Athens

294
Votive (?) relief: goddess mounting a chariot, Athens Acropolis, marble, H. 1.205 m., c. 500 B.C., Acropolis Mus.

395

295
Funerary stele: man playing with his dog, Sardis (?), marble, H. 2.50 m., *c.* 480 B.C., Nat. Mus., Naples

296
Votive relief: ephebe greeting the divinity, marble, H. 48 cm., *c.* 460 B.C., Nat. Mus., Athens

297
Funerary stele: little girl with doves, Paros, marble, H. 80 cm., *c.* 450 B.C., Metropolitan Mus.

298
Funerary stele (fragment): two women, Pharsalos, marble, H. 60 cm., *c.* 470 B.C., Louvre

299
Funerary stele of a doctor, marble, H. 1.40 m., *c.* 480 B.C., Antikenmus., Basle

300
Funerary stele: ephebe, little slave, animals, Salamis, marble, H. 1.04 m., *c.* 430 B.C., Nat. Mus., Athens

301
Votive relief: 'pensive Athena',
Athens Acropolis, marble, H. 54 cm.,
c. 460 B.C., Acropolis Mus.

302
Relief decorating a passage: Hermes
and one of the graces, Thasos, marble,
H. 92 cm., c. 470 B.C., Louvre.

303
Votive (?) relief ('Disc of Milo'): Aphrodite, Melos, marble, t. D. 44.8 cm.,
c. 460 B.C., Nat. Mus., Athens

304
Relief: Athens and Samos, Athens
Acropolis, marble, W. 56 cm., 403–402
B.C., Acropolis Mus.

305
Cult relief: Demeter, Triptolemos,
kore, Eleusis, marble, H. 2.20 m., c.
450 B.C., Nat. Mus., Athens

306
Funerary stele of Dexileos, Athens, marble, H. 1.40 m., 394–393 B.C., Kerameicos Mus., Athens

307
Funerary stele of Hegeso, Kerameikos cemetery, marble, H. 1.58 m., end of 5th c. B.C., Nat. Mus., Athens

308
Funerary stele: Kriton and Timarista, Rhodes, marble, H. 2.09 m., c. 400 B.C., Rhodes Mus.

309
Funerary stele: man and woman, Rhamnous, marble, H. 1.81 m., c. 320 B.C., Nat. Mus., Athens

310 'Lycian' sarcophagus, Sidon, marble, L. 2.535 m., end of 5th c. B.C., Archaeol. Mus., Istanbul

311
Votive relief: Dionysos and actors, Piraeus, marble, H. 55 cm., *c.* 410 B.C., Nat. Mus., Athens

312
Relief: Victory undoing her sandal, temple of Athena Nike, marble, H. 1.06 m., *c.* 410 B.C., Acropolis Mus.

313
Votive relief: abduction of Basile by Echelos, New Phaleron, marble, H. 70 cm., *c.* 400 B.C., Nat. Mus., Athens

314
Maenad dancing, marble, H. 1.435 m., neo-Attic copy after Kallimachos, end of 5th c. B.C., Conservatori, Rome

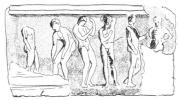

315
Votive relief: nymphs, Hermes and Pan in a grotto, marble, H. 70 cm., *c.* 320 B.C., Nat. Mus., Athens

316
Base with relief of athletes, Athens Acropolis, marble, H. 48 cm., end of 4th c. B.C., Acropolis Mus.

317
Relief from a monument: horse and black groom, Athens, marble, H. 2 m., *c.* 300 B.C., Nat. Mus., Athens

318
Funerary stele of the Thasian Nike, Tenos, marble, H. 1.64 m., 2nd c. B.C., Nat. Mus., Athens

319
Pictorial relief: huntsman satyr, marble, H. 1.88 m., 2nd–1st c. B.C., Louvre

320
Relief: apotheosis of Homer, Bovillae, marble, H. 1.18 m., work of Archelaos of Priene, *c.* 125 B.C., B.M.

321
Archaistic votive relief: Apollo and Nike, marble, H. 47 cm., 1st c. B.C., Louvre

322
Votive relief: Dionysos at a poet's house, marble, H. 79 cm., 1st c. B.C., Louvre

323
Vase with painted incisions, Liano-kladhi, terracotta, H. 14.4 cm., 5900–5200 B.C., Nat. Mus., Athens

324
Restoration of vase decoration, Thessaly, terracotta, Early Neolithic, 5900–5200 B.C., Larissa Mus.

325
Bowl, Otzaki Magula, terracotta, H. 9 cm., Middle Neolithic, 5200–4200 B.C., Volos Mus.

326
Flat-handled cup, Tsani Magula, terracotta, H. 10.5 cm., Middle Neolithic, 5200–4200 B.C., Volos Mus.

327
Spherical vase, Dimini, terracotta, H. 25.5 cm., Late Neolithic, 4200–3200 B.C., Nat. Mus., Athens

328
Bowl, terracotta, H. 10.5 cm., Late Neolithic, 4200–3200 B.C., Volos Mus.

329
Pan-shaped receptacle, Syros, terracotta, W. 28 cm., Early Cycladic II,
2700–2300 B.C., Nat. Mus., Athens

330
Kernos, terracotta, H. 34.3 cm., Early
Cycladic III, c. 2000 B.C., B.M.

331
Modelled vase, hedgehog-shaped,
Syros, terracotta, H. 10.8 cm., 2700–
2300 B.C., Nat. Mus., Athens

332
Rhyton: bull and acrobat, Messara,
terracotta, H. 19.5 cm., c. 2000–1700
B.C., Herakleion Mus.

333
Beak-spouted jug ('fired' pottery),
Vasiliki, terracotta, H. 33.5 cm., c.
2300–2200 B.C., Herakleion Mus.

334
Beak-spouted jug, Melos, terracotta,
H. 23.3 cm., Early Cycladic III, c.
2300–2100 B.C., B.M.

335
Jug (Kamares-style), Phaistos, terracotta, H. 26 cm., Middle Minoan II,
c. 1800 B.C., Herakleion Mus.

336
Footed krater (Kamares-style), Phais-
tos, terracotta, H. 45.5 cm., *c.* 1800 B.C.,
Herakleion Mus.

337
Beak-spouted jug: ears of corn, Thera,
terracotta, H. 21.3 cm., *c.* 1600–1500
B.C., Nat. Mus., Athens

338
Double-handled pithos (Palace style),
Knossos, terracotta, Late Minoan III,
c. 1400–1200 B.C., Herakleion Mus.

339
Krater, Orchomenos of Boeotia, terra-
cotta, Middle Helladic, *c.* 2000–1700
B.C., Nat. Mus., Athens

340
Pithos, Koraku, terracotta, H.
41.5 cm., Middle Helladic, *c.* 2000–
1700 B.C., Corinth Mus.

341
Gourd, Palaikastro, terracotta, H.
28 cm., Late Minoan I, *c.* 1500 B.C.,
Herakleion Mus.

342
Stirrup-vase, Attica, terracotta, H.
24.3 cm., Mycenaean, *c.* 1250 B.C.,
Nat. Mus., Copenhagen

343
Oenochoe, Egypt, terracotta, H.
25 cm., Late Minoan I, *c.* 1500 B.C.,
Archaeol. Mus., Marseilles

344
Beak-spouted jug, Katsamba, terracotta, H. 49.5 cm., Late Minoan II,
15th c. B.C., Herakleion Mus.

345
Krater: departure of warriors,
Mycenae, terracotta, H. 40 cm., *c.* 1200
B.C., Nat. Mus., Athens

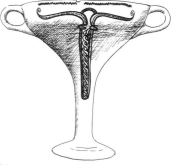

346
'Champagne' cup, Zygouries, terracotta, H. 40 cm., Mycenaean, 14th–
13th c. B.C., Corinth Mus.

347
Attic amphora, Nea Ionia, terracotta,
H. 57.2 cm., Proto-Geometric, begin-
ning of 10th c. B.C., Nat. Mus., Athens

348
Attic amphora, Attica, terracotta, H.
73 cm., Early Geometric, 9th c. B.C.,
Nat. Mus., Athens

349
Attic pyxis, Kerameikos cemetery,
terracotta, H. 21 cm., beginning of 8th
c. B.C., Kerameikos Mus., Athens

350
Attic krater, terracotta, H. 56 cm.,
Middle Geometric, end of 9th c. B.C.,
Louvre

351
Attic oenochoe, terracotta, H. 22 cm.,
Late Geometric, 750–725 B.C., Louvre

352
Boeotian oenochoe, Thebes, terracotta, H. 51 cm., Late Geometric, end
of 8th c. B.C., Louvre

353
Corinthian skyphos, terracotta, H.
11 cm., Proto-Corinthian Geometric,
c. 740 B.C., Louvre

354
Rhodian kantharos, Rhodes, terracotta, H. 18.7 cm., Late Geometric,
750–725 B.C., Louvre

355
Corinthian lebes: sailing-boat, terracotta, H. 22.6 cm., Late Geometric,
end of 8th c. B.C., Royal Ontario Mus.

356
Cretan oenochoe, terracotta, H.
19.7 cm., Late Geometric, end of 8th c.
B.C., Louvre

357
Argive cup, Tiryns, terracotta, H.
13 cm., Late Geometric, end of 8th c.
B.C., Nauplia Mus.

358
Melian krater: chariot, Melos, terra-
cotta, H. 26.5 cm., end of 8th c. B.C.,
Fabregat Mus., Béziers

359
Detail of a Boeotian kantharos: dance scene, terracotta, H. of vase 15 cm., *c.* 725 B.C., Dresden

360
Detail of an Attic amphora: mourners, terracotta, H. of vase 77.7 cm., 750–725 B.C., Metropolitan Mus.

361
Attic amphora: lying-in-state, near Athens, terracotta, H. 1.55 m., *c.* 750 B.C., Nat. Mus., Athens

362
Attic krater, Dipylon Gate, Athens, terracotta, H. 1.23 m., Late Geometric, *c.* 740 B.C., Nat. Mus., Athens

363
Rhodian plate: battle of Menelaos and Hector, Rhodes, terracotta, D. 38.5 cm., *c.* 600 B.C., B.M.

364
Melian plate: Bellerophon and the Chimaera, Thasos, terracotta, *c.* 660 B.C., Archaeol. Mus., Thasos

365
Rhodian oenochoe, terracotta, H. 39.5 cm., *c.* 650 B.C., Louvre

366
Megarian pithos, Megara Hyblaea, terracotta, *c.* 630 B.C., Nat. Mus., Syracuse

367
Rhodian oenochoe (detail of No. 365): wild goat

368
Cretan jug (detail), Arcadia, terracotta, t. H. 31.8 cm., *c.* 630 B.C., Herakleion Mus.

369
Proto-Attic loutrophoros: sphinx, dancers and musician, chariots, terracotta, H. 80 cm., *c.* 700 B.C., Louvre

370
Naxian amphora: animals face to face, Thera, terracotta, H. 82 cm., *c.* 650 B.C., Nat. Mus., Athens

371
Amphora (detail): Ulysses' men blind Polyphemus, Eleusis, terracotta, t. H. 1.42 m., *c.* 650 B.C., Eleusis Mus.

372
Proto-Argive krater (detail): blinding of Polyphemus, Argos, terracotta, H. 24 cm., *c.* 660 B.C., Argos Mus.

373
Proto-Attic oenochoe, Athens, terracotta, H. 9.5 cm., *c.* 660 B.C., Nat. Mus. Athens

374
Euboean krater: women and sphinx, Eretria, terracotta, H. 72 cm., *c.* 620 B.C., Nat. Mus., Athens

375
Kotyle: crouching dog, terracotta, H.
19 cm., *c.* 660 B.C., B.M.

376
Oenochoe, Cumae, terracotta, H.
33.4 cm., *c.* 700 B.C., Nat. Mus., Naples

377
Aryballos: abduction of Helen,
Thebes, terracotta, H. 7 cm., *c.* 675
B.C., Louvre

378
Aryballos with woman's head: hoplite
battle, terracotta, H. 6.8 cm., *c.* 640
B.C., Louvre

379
Olpe, Etruria, terracotta, H. 28.8 cm.,
c. 630 B.C., Louvre

380
Oenochoe: rows of animals, Etruria,
terracotta, H. 27.8 cm., *c.* 620 B.C.,
Louvre

381
Corinthian aryballos: griffin-bird, Nola, terracotta, H. 17.5 cm., *c.* 600 B.C., St. Mus., E. Berlin

382
Krater: banquet in honour of Herakles, Cerveteri, terracotta, H. 46 cm., *c.* 600 B.C., Louvre

383
Corinthian alabastron: winged demon, Tanagra, terracotta, H. 23.5 cm., *c.* 600 B.C., Louvre

384
Corinthian cup (tondo): female head, Etruria, terracotta, D. 22.7 cm., *c.* 570 B.C., Louvre

385
Attic deinos and stand: hoplite duel, Cerveteri, terracotta, H. 93 cm., *c.* 590 B.C., Louvre

411

386
Attic amphora: Achilles kills Penthesilea, terracotta, H. 41.5 cm., *c.* 540 B.C., B.M.

387
Attic amphora: Achilles and Ajax playing dice, Vulci, terracotta, H. 61 cm., *c.* 540 B.C., Vatican Mus.

388
Attic amphora (detail): Dionysos and maenads, Vulci, terracotta, H. 33 cm., *c.* 530 B.C., Cabinet des Médailles

389
Chalcidian krater: Andromache and Hector, terracotta, H. 45.7 cm., *c.* 550–530 B.C., Würzburg Mus.

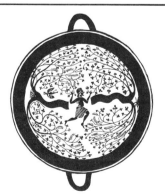

390
Ionian cup (tondo): birdcatcher, terracotta, D. 23.5 cm., *c.* 550 B.C., Louvre

391
Laconian cup (tondo): Achilles ambushing Troilus, terracotta, D. 18.5 cm., *c.* 580 B.C., Louvre

392
Attic cup (the 'Siana'): banquet, Taranto, terracotta, H. of vase 13 cm., *c.* 560 B.C., Nat. Mus., Taranto

393
Boar-headed Boeotian kantharos, terracotta, H. with handle 17 cm., *c.* 560 B.C., Louvre

394
Attic lipped cup: chariot race, Tarquinia, terracotta, H. 17 cm., *c.* 540 B.C., Nat. Mus., Tarquinia

395
Attic cup: Theseus and the Minotaur, terracotta, H. 26.5 cm., *c.* 540 B.C., Antikensammlungen, Munich

396
Attic cup with eyes, terracotta, D. 11.5 cm., *c.* 535 B.C., Antikensammlungen, Munich

397
Attic red-figure cup: maenads, terracotta, H. 11.5 cm., *c.* 490 B.C., Käppeli Coll., Lucerne

400
Psykter: satyrs at play, terracotta, H. 28 cm., *c.* 490 B.C., B.M.

398–399
Two-tongued amphora, Vulci, terracotta, H. of ground 18.1 cm., *c.* 520 B.C., Antikensammlungen, Munich

401
Bell-krater (detail): Ganymede, Etruria, terracotta, H. 33 cm., *c.* 490 B.C., Louvre

402
Panathenaic-type amphora: Herakles, Vulci, terracotta, *c.* 490 B.C., Von Wagner Mus., Würzburg

403
Lekythos: Apollo and Muses, terracotta, H. 17.5 cm., *c.* 490 B.C., Louvre

404 Calyx-krater: preparations for an expedition, or infernal scene (?), Orvieto, terracotta, H. 53 cm., *c.* 460 B.C., Louvre

405 Cup (detail): death of Priam, Vulci, terracotta, D. 32.5 cm., *c.* 490 B.C., Louvre

406
Lekythos: young huntsman, Gela, terracotta, H. 38.7 cm., *c.* 460 B.C., Mus. of Fine Arts, Boston

407
Cup (tondo): Zeus and Ganymede, Spina, terracotta, *c.* 460 B.C., Archaeol. Mus., Ferrara

408
Cup (tondo): Achilles and Penthesilea, Vulci, terracotta, D. 43 cm., *c.* 460 B.C., Antikensammlungen, Munich

409
Cup (tondo): punishment of Tityus, Vulci, terracotta, D. 39.5 cm., *c.* 450 B.C., Antikensammlungen, Munich

410
Bone-shaped vase: Aeolus and the breezes, terracotta, W. 17.2 cm., *c.* 460 B.C., B.M.

411
Amphora: Achilles, Vulci, terracotta, H. 60 cm., *c.* 440 B.C., Vulci, Vatican Mus.

416

412
Stamnos: Kaineus and Centaurs, Vulci, terracotta, H. 36 cm., *c.* 440 B.C., Mus. Royaux, Brussels

413
Lekythos (white-ground): deceased on his tomb, Eretria, terracotta, H. 48 cm., *c.* 430 B.C., Nat. Mus., Athens

414
Oenochoe: game of 'ephedrismos', Nola, terracotta, H. 17.5 cm., *c.* 420 B.C., St. Mus., E. Berlin

415
Epinetron (thigh-guard): wedding preparations, Eretria, terracotta, W. 26 cm., *c.* 420 B.C., Nat. Mus., Athens

416
Hydria: rape of Leukippos' daughters, Herakles in garden, terracotta, H. 52.2 cm., *c.* 410 B.C., B.M.

417
Nuptial lebes: wedding gifts, Kerch, terracotta, H. 46 cm., *c.* 335 B.C., Hermitage

418
Calyx-krater from Paestum, theatrical scene, Lipari, terracotta, H. 41 cm., *c.* 370 B.C., Lipari Mus.

419
Apulian cylindrical amphora: funerary building, terracotta, H. 1.26 m., *c.* 350–300 B.C., Louvre

420
Lucanian nestoris: departure of warriors, terracotta, H. 44.5 cm., *c.* 400 B.C., Louvre

421
Lucanian pelike: Orestes, Electra and Hermes, terracotta, H. 43 cm., *c.* 350 B.C., Louvre

422
Apulian volute-krater: ephebe and woman honouring a statue, terracotta, H. 40 cm., *c.* 350 B.C., Louvre

423
Campanian amphora: warrior's departure, terracotta, H. 54 cm., *c.* 350–325 B.C., B.M.

424
Lagynos: garlands, terracotta, H.
20.1 cm., *c.* 230–180 B.C., B.M.

425
Gnathia-style oenochoe: theatrical
mask, Nola, terracotta, H. 31 cm., *c.*
350 B.C., Louvre

426
Amphora with reliefs: Dionysos and
panther, Melos, terracotta, H.
45.5 cm., *c.* 300 B.C., Louvre

427
Bowl with reliefs (lower portion):
floral decoration, terracotta, 3rd–2nd
c. B.C., Louvre

428
'Hadra' hydria, terracotta, *c.* 290–230
B.C., Nat. Mus., Athens

429
'Centuripe-style' krater: mistress and
servants, Centuripe, terracotta, H.
56 cm., 3rd c. B.C., Catania Univ.

419

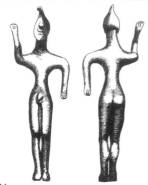

430
Cretan worshipper, Tylissos, bronze,
H. 16.5 cm., Late Minoan I, *c.* 1500
B.C., Herakleion Mus.

431
Argive warrior with a javelin (front
and back), Olympia, bronze, H.
16.5 cm., 750–700 B.C., Olympia Mus.

432
Carved Cretan plaque: two hunts-
men, Crete, bronze, H. 18.3 cm., *c.* 630
B.C., Louvre

433
Cretan carrying ram (kriophoros),
Crete, bronze, H. 18 cm., *c.* 620 B.C., St.
Mus., E. Berlin

434
Small Samian kouros (profile and
back), Heraion of Samos, bronze, H.
19 cm., *c.* 580 B.C., Vathy Mus., Samos

435
Small Laconian (?) kouros ('Apollo
with collar'), Delphi, bronze, H.
40 cm., *c.* 530–520 B.C., Delphi Mus.

436
Argive statuette: Herakles fighting,
Mantinea, bronze, H. 13 cm., *c.* 460
B.C., Louvre

437
Peloponnesian statuette: Zeus the
Thunderer, Dodona, bronze, H.
18.9 cm., *c.* 450 B.C., Louvre

438
Polykleitan statuette: ephebe making
a libation, bronze, H. 21.8 cm., *c.* 430
(?) B.C., Louvre

439
Statuette in the style of Naukydes:
Phrixos, bronze, H. 16.5 cm., *c.* 400
B.C., J. Paul Getty Mus., Malibu

440
Ionian statuette: discus thrower,
bronze, H. 18.6 cm., *c.* 450 B.C., Louvre

441
Argive statuette: wrestler, bronze, H.
20 cm., beginning of 4th c. B.C., Louvre

442
Praxitelean statuette: Aphrodite adorning herself, bronze, H. 26 cm., 3rd c. B.C., B.M.

443
Praxitelean statuette: Aphrodite in modesty, Saida (Syria), bronze, H. 23.2 cm., 3rd c. B.C., Louvre

444
Aphrodite unfastening her sandal, Syria, bronze, H. 30.8 cm., end of 3rd c. B.C., Louvre

445
Corinthian statuette: bather, Beroea, bronze, H. 25 cm., 350–300 B.C., Antikensammlungen, Munich

446
Statuette, copy of the 'Tyche of Antioch', Tortosa, bronze, H. 16 cm., Hellenistic period, Louvre

447
Veiled dancer ('Baker Dancer'), bronze, 3rd c. B.C., Metropolitan Mus.

448
Alexandrian statuette: strolling merchant, Alexandria, bronze, H. 9 cm., 2nd c. B.C., Louvre

449
Gracco-Syrian statuette: Adonis, Saida (Syria), bronze, H. statuette 24.3 cm., 2nd c. B.C., Louvre

450
Alexandrian statuette: priest of Isis, Hermonthis, bronze, H. 13.3 cm., 2nd c. B.C., Louvre

451
Alexandrian statuette: hunchback, bronze, H. 6.6 cm., c. 250 B.C., Kunst und Gewerbe Mus., Hamburg

452
Alexandrian statuette: singer, Châlon-sur-Saône, bronze, H. 20 cm., end of 2nd c. B.C., Bibliothèque Nat.

453
Alexandrian group: wrestlers, bronze, H. 17.9 cm., 3rd c. B.C., Louvre

454
Cretan statuette: chamois, Hagia Triada, bronze, L. 5.5 cm., Late Minoan I, *c.* 1500 B.C., Herakleion Mus.

455
Attic statuette: stag, Kerameikos, terracotta, H. 26.6 cm., *c.* 950 B.C., Kerameikos Mus., Athens

456
Corinthian statuette: horse, Olympia, bronze, H. 16 cm., Late Geometric, *c.* 740 B.C., St. Mus., E. Berlin

457
Laconian statuette: horse, Olympia, bronze, H. 5.5 cm., Late Geometric, end of 8th c. B.C., Olympia Mus.

458
Peloponnesian statuette: horse, bronze, H. 12 cm., end of 8th c. B.C., Allard Pierson Mus., Amsterdam

459
Attic horse decorating a vase, Athens, terracotta, H. 12.4 cm., 750–725 B.C., Kerameikos Mus., Athens

460
Cauldron with circular handles, on a tripod, Olympia, bronze, H. 64 cm., *c.* 800 B.C., Olympia Mus.

461
Stand decoration: Apollo and Herakles, Olympia, bronze, H. 46.7 cm., end of 8th c. B.C., Olympia Mus.

462–463
Attic statuettes: Theseus and Minotaur (?), Olympia, bronze, *c.* 700 B.C., Nat. Mus., Athens, and Louvre

464
Circular handle, Olympia, bronze, H. 15.4 cm., Middle Geometric, beginning of 8th c. B.C., Olympia Mus.

465
Statuette decorating a cauldron, Olympia, bronze, H. 14.4 cm., 750–725 B.C., Olympia Mus.

425

466
Reconstructed cauldron decoration: griffins, lions and sirens, bronze, D. 65 cm., early 7th c. B.C., Olympia

467
Cauldron and tripod: griffins, Ste Colombe, bronze, H. of vat 32 cm., 6th c. B.C., Châtillon-sur-Seine Mus.

468
Griffin protome, cauldron decoration, Olympia (?), bronze, H. 25 cm., 675–650 B.C., private coll., Athens

469
Griffin protome, cauldron decoration, Olympia, bronze, H. 22 cm., beginning of 7th c. B.C., Olympia Mus.

470
Cauldron handle attachment: 'siren', oriental object, bronze, H. of bust 6 cm., end of 8th c. B.C., Olympia Mus.

471
Cauldron handle attachment: 'siren', Olympia, bronze, H. of bust 6 cm., beginning 7th c. B.C., Olympia Mus.

472   Dagger: lion hunt, Mycenae, bronze, gold and niello, L. 23.8 cm., 16th c.
B.C., Nat. Mus., Athens

473
Helmet and cuirass, Argos, bronze, H.
of helmet 46 cm., cuirass 47.4 cm., Late
Geometric, 750–700 B.C., Argos Mus.

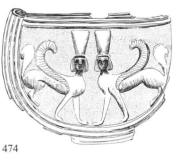

474
Cretan armour: two sphinxes face to
face, Afrati, bronze, H. 17.4 cm., c. 620
B.C., Metropolitan Mus.

475
Illustrated shield armlet, Olympia,
bronze, 6th c. B.C., Olympia Mus.

476
Laconian caryatid mirror, Hermione, bronze, H. of figure 19 cm., *c.* 540 B.C., Antikensammlungen, Munich

477
Laconian caryatid mirror, bronze, H. 35.5 cm., *c.* 530 B.C., Metropolitan Mus.

478
Peloponnesian caryatid mirror, Hermione, bronze, H. 41.2 cm., *c.* 460 B.C., Louvre

479
Caryatid mirror from western Greece, Camarina, bronze, H. 15.8 cm., *c.* 460 B.C., Nat. Mus. Copenhagen

480
Caryatid incense-burner, Delphi, bronze, H. of figure 16 cm., *c.* 460 B.C., Delphi Mus.

481
Lid of boxed mirror: Herakles and Auge, bronze, D. 6.5 cm., Louvre

482
Volute-krater handle: gorgon, Italy, bronze, H. 24 cm., 6th c. B.C., Louvre

483
Oenochoe handle: female head, Greece, bronze, H. 17.5 cm., 600–550 B.C., Louvre

484
Mirror attachment: Elektra with urn of Agamemnon, Locri, bronze, W. 11.2 cm., c. 400 B.C., Reggio Mus.

485
Mirror attachment: Silenus and youth, Medina, bronze, W. 10 cm., c. 380 B.C., Nat. Mus., Reggio

486
Hydria handle: figure of Eros, Myrina, bronze, H. 26.5 cm., end of 4th c. B.C., Louvre

487
Hydria handle: figure of siren, bronze, H. 19 cm., end of 5th c. B.C., Louvre

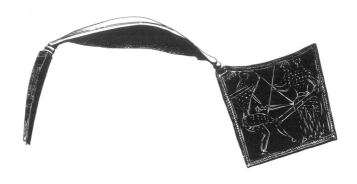

488   Boeotian fibula with plaque: Herakles against the Molionides, Mount Ida grotto (Crete), bronze, H. of plaque 6 cm., Late Geometric, *c.* 700 B.C., Nat. Mus., Athens

489
Scales (?): Nike, Athens, bronze, H. 34 cm., 5th c. B.C., Louvre

490
Strainer, bronze, W. of remains 20.8 cm., end of 4th c. B.C., Metropolitan Mus., Bastis Coll.

491
Kantharos, Derveni, bronze, H. 9.4 cm., end of 4th c. B.C., Salonica Mus.

492
Lantern, Derveni, bronze, H. 41.8 cm., end of 4th c. B.C., Salonica Mus.

493
Coin of Syracuse: head of the nymph Arethusa, silver, D. 2.3 cm., *c.* 485–478 B.C., Cabinet des Médailles, Paris

494
Coin from Syracuse: head of the nymph Arethusa, silver, D. 3.4 cm., *c.* 480 B.C., Cabinet des Médailles, Paris

495
Coin from Cos: figure of a discus thrower, silver, *c.* 475 B.C. (type), Nat. Mus., Athens

496
Coin from Cos: crab, emblem of the city, silver, reverse of No. 495

497
Coin from Syracuse: head of the nymph Arethusa, silver, D. 2.9 cm., *c.* 400 B.C., Cabinet des Médailles, Paris

498
Coin from Syracuse: head of the goddess Persephone, silver, D. 3.6 cm., *c.* 400 B.C., Cabinet des Médailles

499   Cretan acrobat, Knossos, ivory, L. 29.5 cm., Late Minoan I, *c.* 1500 B.C.,
       Herakleion Mus.

500
Divine triad, Mycenae, ivory, H.
7.3 cm., Mycenaean, *c.* 1450 B.C., Nat.
Mus., Athens

501
Cretan sacred knot, Knossos, ivory,
Middle Minoan, *c.* 1800 B.C., Hera-
kleion Mus.

502
Element from a lyre: kneeling youth,
Samos, ivory, H. 14.5 cm., end of 7th c.
B.C., Nat. Mus., Athens

503
Laconian male head, Sparta, ivory, H.
4.6 cm., end of 8th c. B.C., Nat. Mus.,
Athens

504
Samian divine couple: Zeus and Hera
(?), wood, H. 19.1 cm., c. 630–600 B.C.,
Samos

505
Female statuette, Palma Monte-
chiaro, wood, H. 16 cm., beginning of
6th c. B.C., Nat. Mus., Syracuse

506
Female statuette, probably Hera,
Samos, wood, H. 28.7 cm., c. 630 B.C.,
Tigani Mus., Samos

507
Panel from a sarcophagus: Hera (?),
Kerch, gilded wood, H. 21 cm., begin-
ning of 4th c. B.C., Hermitage

508
Short side of the sarcophagus
decorated with No. 507, W. 1.09 m.

433

509
Mycenaean female idol, Tiryns, terracotta, H. 13.7 cm., Mycenaean, *c.*
1400–1200 B.C., Louvre

510
Female statuette from the Cyclades,
Melos, terracotta, H. 18 cm., *c.* 1200
B.C., Archaeol. Mus., Melos

511
Male statuette, Olympia, terracotta,
H. 13 cm., Geometric, Olympia Mus.

512
Cretan idol: goddess with poppies,
Gazi, terracotta, H. 77.5 cm., 12th c.
B.C., Herakleion Mus.

513
Boeotian bell-idol with movable legs,
Thebes, terracotta, H. 33 cm., Late
Geometric, end of 8th c. B.C., Louvre

514
Boeotian bell-idol with movable legs,
Boeotia, terracotta, H. 39.5 cm., Late
Geometric, end of 8th c. B.C., Louvre

515
Cycladic wailing woman, Thera, terracotta. H. 32 cm., *c.* 650 B.C., Thera Mus.

516
Boeotian female idol, Tanagra, terracotta, H. 15.3 cm., 600–550 B.C., Louvre

517
Modelled vase from the 'Aphrodite group', Rhodes, terracotta, *c.* 530 B.C., Louvre

518
Corinthian female figurine, Magna Graecia, terracotta, H. 14.2 cm., beginning of 5th c. B.C., Louvre

519
Female figurine from Boeotia, carrying a cist, terracotta, end of 5th c. B.C., Canellopoulos Coll., Athens

520
Attic figurine of seated draped woman, terracotta, H. 30 cm., beginning of 5th c. B.C., Louvre

521
Melian plaque with a relief: death of Actaeon, with Artemis, terracotta, H. 20 cm., *c.* 460 B.C., Nat. Mus., Naples

522
Votive plaque from Locri: woman arranging clothes, terracotta, H. 26 cm., *c.* 460 B.C., Nat. Mus., Taranto

523
Pan, Anthedon, terracotta, H. 21 cm., *c.* 350 B.C., St. Mus., E. Berlin

524
Youth with lantern, Tanagra, terracotta, H. 27.5 cm., *c.* 250 B.C., Louvre

525
Magna Graecia figurine: maenad dancing, Locri, terracotta, H. 19 cm., *c.* 400 B.C., Nat. Mus., Reggio

526
Young woman and Eros, Taranto, terracotta, H. 31.2 cm., *c.* 350 B.C., Nat. Mus., Taranto

527
Tanagran statuette: draped woman,
Boeotia, terracotta, H. 32 cm., *c.* 330–
320 B.C., Louvre

528
Another view of No. 527

529
Myrinian statuette: Nike in flight,
Myrina, terracotta, H. 37.5 cm., begin-
ning of 2nd c. B.C., Louvre

530
Myrinian statuette: Eros in flight,
Myrina, terracotta, H. 36.5 cm., 2nd c.
B.C., Louvre

531
Statuette of actor: parodying a tragic
heroine, Boeotia, terracotta, H.
21.5 cm., end of 4th c. B.C., Louvre

532
Myrinian group: couple seated on a
bed, Myrina, terracotta, H. 28 cm.,
150–100 B.C., Louvre

533
Cycladic lugged vase, marble, H. 26.2 cm., Early Cycladic I, *c.* 3200–2700 B.C., private coll., Basle

534
Cycladic lugged goblet, marble, H. 10.5 cm., Early Cycladic I, *c.* 3200–2700 B.C., private coll., Basle

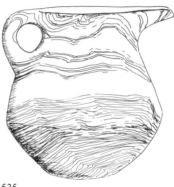

535
Cretan jug, Mochlos, alabaster, H. 12 cm., Early Minoan II, *c.* 2400 B.C., Herakleion Mus.

536
Cretan flask, Mochlos, steatite, H. 7 cm., Early Minoan II, *c.* 2400 B.C., Herakleion Mus.

537
Cretan rhyton: mountain shrine, Zakro, steatite and gilt, Late Minoan I, *c.* 1500 B.C., Herakleion Mus.

538
Cretan rhyton: homage to a chief, Hagia Triada, steatite, H. 11.5 cm., *c.* 1500 B.C., Herakleion Mus.

539
Cretan ceremonial axe: panther, Mallia, steatite, L. 15 cm., *c.* 2000–1700 B.C., Herakleion Mus.

540
Mycenaean duck-headed bowl, Mycenae, rock crystal, L. 13.2 cm., 16th c. B.C., Nat. Mus., Athens

541
Cretan goddess with serpents, Knossos, faience, H. 29.5 cm., Late Minoan I, *c.* 1500 B.C., Herakleion Mus.

542
Cretan papyrus-bunch lamp, Knossos, red porphyry, H. *c.* 45 cm., *c.* 1600 B.C., Herakleion Mus.

543
Cretan seal impression: male head, Knossos, steatite, D. 1.5 cm., *c.* 1600 B.C., Herakleion Mus.

544
Cretan seal impression: warrior in a chariot, Vaphio, sard, D. 2.5 cm., *c.* 1500 B.C., Nat. Mus., Athens

545
Pre-Hellenic goblet, Euboea (?), gold, H. 9.5 cm., Chalcolithic, 3rd millennium, Benaki Mus., Athens

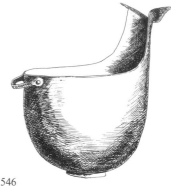

546
Cycladic sauce-boat, Heraeum of Arcadia (?), gold, H. 17 cm., Early Cycladic III, c. 2200 B.C., Louvre

547
Mycenaean rhyton: head of lioness, Mycenae, gold, H. 14 cm., 16th c. B.C., Nat. Mus., Athens

548
Cretan rhyton: bull's head, Knossos, gold and steatite, H. 35.6 cm., c. 1500 B.C., Herakleion Mus.

549
Casket: larnax of Philip II (?), Vergina, gold and glass paste, 20.7 × 41 × 34 cm., 350–325 B.C., Salonica Mus.

550
Lid of a box: nereid and sea monster, Taranto, gold and silver, D. 10 cm., end of 2nd c. B.C., Nat. Mus., Taranto

551
Relief: altar, Mycenae, gold, H. 7.5 cm., 16th c. B.C., Nat. Mus., Athens

552
Cretan jewellery: bee pendant, Mallia, gold, max. L. 5 cm., Middle Minoan, c. 1700 B.C., Herakleion Mus.

553
Cretan jewellery: pendant of the master of animals, Mallia (?), gold, H. 6 cm., 17th c. B.C., B.M.

554
Cretan jewellery: pendant, gold, Middle Minoan III, 17th c. B.C., B.M.

555
Cretan double-axe, bronze covered with gold, L. 45 cm., Late Minoan II, c. 1500 B.C., Herakleion Mus.

556
Disc from a Cretan sword: acrobat, Mallia, gold, D. 7 cm., Middle Minoan, c. 1700 B.C., Herakleion Mus.

441

557   Attic funerary bandeau: animal battles, Attic, gold, L. 38.5 cm., Late Geometric, *c.* 750 B.C., Louvre

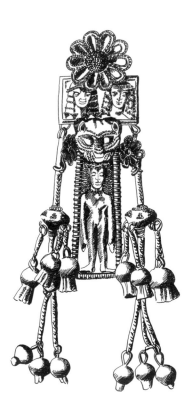

559
Rhodian pendant: centaur huntsman, Kamiros, gold, H. of plaque 4.2 cm., *c.* 630 B.C., B.M.

558
Rhodian pendant, Kamiros, electrum, H. 8 cm., *c.* 630–620 B.C., Louvre

560
Rhodian plaque, dress ornament: griffin, Delphi, gold, W. 10 cm., *c.* 570–560 B.C., Delphi Mus.

561
Graeco-Scythian pectoral: pastoral scenes, Tolstaïa Mogila, gold, D. 30.6 cm., 4th c. B.C., Kiev Mus.

562
Graeco-Scythian comb: battle scene, gold, H. 12.6 cm., beginning of 4th c. B.C., Hermitage

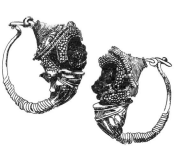

563
Graeco-Macedonian medallion: bust of Artemis, gold, D. 11.5 cm., 3rd c. B.C., Nat. Mus., Athens, Stathatos Coll.

564
Ear-rings: negroid heads, gold and amber, H. 1.93 cm., Hellenistic period, Louvre

Etruria and the Etruscans

by François Baratte and Catherine Metzger
Curators, Department of Greek and Roman Antiquities,
Louvre

Drawings by Marie Bévillard and Marie-Lise Bordreuil

ETRURIA AND THE ETRUSCANS

The Etruscan civilization dates from *c.* 750 B.C., and flourished in the territory between the Adriatic Sea, the Arno and the Tiber. The origin of the Etruscans has been passionately debated—whether they came from elsewhere or were autochthonous; but whatever the answer to this question, modern research has made it clear that they gradually developed a distinct character, continuous with the Iron Age cultures that came before them, in particular with the Villanovan civilization.

THE VILLANOVAN CIVILIZATION

Although it was present in the whole of the peninsula, the Villanovan culture was especially vigorous in the central region, which was later to constitute the Etruscan territory proper. It was marked by the beginnings of urban organization, with farmers gradually replacing shepherds, at least in some regions. For its funerary customs it adopted cremation in characteristic biconical urns which were deposited in pit-tombs, covered with stones and accompanied by abundant chattels: a sign of some sort of belief in an after-life for the deceased.

In art, it is classed as a Geometric civilization, in contact with the Mediterranean basin cultures and with those of Danubian Europe; and its productions show a mainly industrial bias, being almost exclusively devoted to objects of domestic life or ceremony, such as fairly crude, hand-made pottery with incised or sometimes summary plastic decorations, or objects founded or hammered in bronze. Stylistically, this art was marked by attempts to represent life-like figures, human and animal, but the tendency was towards abstraction. The Villanovan civilization had, indeed, an acute sense of decorative function without any concern at all for narration.

It was a time of growing maturity, its productions being lively in observation and execution but still at the level of craftwork, and incapable of the theoretical treatment of formal problems.

ARCHAIC ETRUSCAN ART

In the second half of the 8th century a new, and decisive, factor came into play: the beginning of Greek colonization in Sicily and southern Italy. This corresponded to the birth of a distinct Etruscan civilization; at this time the cities of southern Etruria were flourishing as the result of a substantial increase in maritime trade and the exploitation of rich coastal mines.

In about 750 B.C. an extraordinary qualitative leap was made in Etruscan art. It was associated not with a cultural upheaval but with a considerable increase in wealth, as is shown by the chattels in the great inhumation tombs at Caere, one of the power centres of the period, and at Praeneste, a city in Latium under very strong Etruscan influence. The latter was rich in precious objects, many of them imported from the Orient, and shows in striking fashion the effect on Etruria of the Orientalizing movement which was at that time inspiring the whole of the Mediterranean basin. Its artisans assimilated Orientalizing themes with remarkable facility and showed the greatest skill in developing refined techniques of gold-work (filigree, granulation) and ivory carving.

Orientalizing Etruscan art was not confined to luxury goods but is seen also in the development of a special technique, called *bucchero*, to provide cheaper pottery as a substitute for more precious vessels. Bucchero ceramics were made of a fairly fine black paste, relatively thick, and took on metalware shapes, often with abundant relief decoration. The production of this ware was accompanied by a large-scale import trade in Greek vases, first Corinthian, then Attic from the middle of the 6th century, and the settlement of Greek potters in Etruria. On the level of craftsmanship, then, it is not hard to explain the development of an imitative Etruscan pottery, although really strong individual personalities are sometimes revealed.

Etruscan art throughout the Archaic period appears to have followed much the same path as Greek art, and, when in the 6th century Orientalizing influences began to fade, Etruscan artists echoed motifs from the main Greek figurative tradition, although they never really managed to assimilate the basic stylistic content.

This phenomenon can be seen particularly in sculpture. Artisans of centres such as Caere and Vulci, at first using local volcanic stone, created some original works of sculpture. With their repertoire of animals (deer), fantastic monsters (sphinxes, centaurs) and even human beings, these works bore witness to a growing Ionian influence, but also to the typically Etruscan inability to conceive genuinely organic forms. Sculpture was essentially funerary in character and gives an idea of the part played by religion in the development of Etruscan art. Concern with death and the conceptions of the after-life as a mirror-image of life on earth play a vital role.

Such concerns are also reflected in the wall paintings, which showed a remarkable development; they were doubtless used to decorate both secular and religious buildings, but their principal use was on the walls of monumental tombs. Paintings have been found in many cities—Chiusi, Vulci, Caere and above all Tarquinia. Mineral or vegetable colours were used, restricted in range, to begin with at least, and sometimes applied direct to the tufa wall, or else to a plastered surface. The preliminary sketch, incised or in charcoal, was an important stage in the operation.

Wall paintings are often considered to be one of the favourite Etruscan art forms. They exhibit, nevertheless, considerable Greek influence, in the canon of the human form, for example—so much so that the hand of an Ionian artist may be seen in some of them. Recent discoveries in Paestum in southern Italy show that these works were not as isolated as had once been supposed. Nevertheless, the general orientation of the iconography seems specific. Mythological or fantastical themes were rare, because they were remote from the Etruscan spiritual tradition which was seeking to create an atmosphere of real life for its dead. The main concern was to make the tomb into a house of eternity: so that decoration proliferated and gradually spread over everything; banquets, dances and games were favourite subjects, often linked with religious preoccupations. Nature almost always played a part in the scene and was deliberately shown as abundant.

The thing that first strikes one about Etruscan decoration is the variety of tone, from solemn restraint to relaxed exuberance, together with a play of colour and a mastery in designs that were still tied to the 6th century by Archaic conventions. Liveliness of observation and execution characterizes Etruscan art, and allied to great technical skill, it explains its success in bronze-work and terracotta architectonic decoration, two fields connected with modelling.

Etruscan bronze-workers were much renowned in antiquity for their numerous productions ranging from utensils for use in daily life, candelabra, basins, tripods—very much in favour—to mounted reliefs and decorative or religious statuettes.

Architecture was mainly ephemeral, because the buildings were for the most part constructed of wood; and this explains why, except for the tombs, so few Etruscan monuments have come down to us. Great importance was accorded to decoration, even to the detriment of the structure to which it was applied; and there was a multiplicity of terracotta elements, friezes, acroteria, antefixes, already present in Greek architecture but proliferating here and developing a rich repertoire of monstrous Gorgons and subtly observed heads.

Specifically Etruscan, however, were the great modelled statues, destined to embellish not pediments, as was the case in Greece, but roof rampants or ridge-tiles. Those found in the Portonaccio temple at Veii dating from the end of the 6th or beginning of the 5th century B.C. furnish what are certainly the most prestigious though not the only examples. These works, which are technically quite remarkable, provide more evidence of Greek influence, in this case Ionian, in the style of faces and taste for curves. But the features are all exaggerated, even the smiles on the faces—another example of Etruscan disdain for the organic nature of the composition as a whole that was the hallmark of Greek art. Nevertheless, there was clearly a very strong personality expressing itself at Veii: perhaps, as has been suggested, the very same Vulca, of Veientine origin, that Pliny describes to us as directing the terracotta decoration of the temple to Jupiter Capitolinus in Rome.

The same traits—Ionian influence adapted to an Etruscan repertoire and presented in an inorganic fashion, allied to exceptional technical skills—are found again in the two great contemporary terracotta sarcophagi in Caere. An astonishing intensity of observation and feel for rendering gestures has been brought to these creations so that a superb vitality and spirituality emanate from the couples, qualities that inform the very best and most beautiful of Etruscan works.

THE CLASSICAL PERIOD
(6TH–5TH CENTURY)

The end of the 6th century and the first years of the 5th marked the apogee of Etruscan civilization. This was the moment of greatest political power and widest geographical expansion—into the Po plain in the north and down to Campania in the south. Culturally it was producing its finest works, in such direct contact with the Greeks that one can perceive the first echoes of the Severe style that in Greece preceded the transition to Classicism proper.

But the flame was delicate and ephemeral. By the first quarter of the 5th century there was already a harsh and rapid decline. According to annalistic tradition, the last Etruscan king was expelled from Rome in 509, and off Cumae in 474 the Etruscan fleet suffered annihilation at the hands of the forces of Syracuse. The influence of the Etruscans was on the wane: they were to lose control of Campania and from the 4th century on had to face Roman expansion—the fall of Veii in 396 was symbolic of the shift in power.

A period of withdrawal set in, marked in the economic sphere by a decline in commercial activity. Etruscan art was, for the time being at least, cut off from new stimuli from outside, mainly from the Greek world. This isolation was the more serious in that their constant refusal to come to grips with theoretical aesthetic problems had deprived the Etruscans of any capacity for autonomous creative development. It is worthwhile emphasizing here the extent to which the concern of Classical art for balance and universality was alien to them, preoccupied as they were with detail rather than with the whole.

The political, economic and cultural retreat was accompanied by a serious moral and religious crisis. Doubt, even anguish over man's fate after death, appeared, with the result that realism in art gave way to a world of almost nightmarish fantasy. These tendencies can be seen particularly in wall paintings, which were affected besides by an obvious slackening of pace. Bloody and violent legends began to appear, separation scenes, infernal monsters.

THE HELLENISTIC AND ROMAN PERIOD

Hellenistic art with its leanings towards the picturesque and grandiloquent, would probably have seemed more comprehensible to the Etruscans than Classical art, more in line with their sympathies. That would explain the revival of Greek influence on the art of Etruria from the end of the 4th century. Technical mastery still existed but it was from then on a mechanical, spiritless exercise. The Etruscans continued to rely on familiar themes, interpreted sometimes with brilliance, often with superficiality.

The Etruscan taste for the rapid pen-portrait, the sketch, and amusing or disquieting iconography can, however, be found whenever the subject lent itself to such treatment, such as in certain sculptures (Civita Alba pediments, pillage of the Delphic shrine by the Galatae) and in ceramics. The latter were once more under the strong influence of Greek ware, either directly or through the trade with southern Italy. They were predominantly craft in character but capable at times of charming expressiveness.

Most characteristic of this period is undoubtedly the series of bronzes with engraved decoration, the mirrors and cists. Here the Etruscan artisan's high technical ability can frequently be seen, his love of drawing and his spontaneity, with a repertoire at times typically local and at times directly inspired by Greece. Praeneste, the city in Latium most influenced by the Etruscans, dominated the industry. But the finest example in its richness of decoration and quality of execution, the Ficoroni cist, found in a tomb at Praeneste, is typical of Etruscan art as a whole as it evolved from the end of the 4th century. Based on a cartoon which had been borrowed from Greek painting (an episode from the story of the Argonauts), it displays an incomparable firmness of line and quality of design. The accompanying inscription, however, apprises us of the fact that it is the work of an artist, probably Campanian, who is working in Rome for a noble family from Praeneste: it is already becoming more and more difficult to distinguish Etruscan art from that of the other peoples of Italy.

Etruscan art had now become the art of Etruria, in the geographical sense, which did not prevent it from the occasional attainment of distinction or from producing works of craftsmanship and quality. Examples of this can be seen in the field of funerary sculpture, where innumerable sarcophagi and cinerary urns were turned out, decorated with reliefs whose themes were often borrowed from the Hellenistic repertoire.

The most striking feature of this last period is undoubtedly the increased attention paid to the individual. In the 4th century there had developed a concern, not perhaps for true portraits that reproduced a person's actual features, but at least for individualized physiognomies (Tarquinia, Tomb of the Shields). Effigies were still of an extremely generic nature, marked by the Hellenistic preference for a psychological image that took into account, above all else, the social or physical category to which the subject belonged.

From the 2nd century on, a general tendency towards self-assertion was developing in the Italic world. It resulted in a spate of honorific statues and its effects were felt even in Rome itself. Following this trend, facial representations moved increasingly towards portraiture without in any way rejecting the peculiarly Etruscan taste for exaggeration—even caricature—nor really abandoning the inorganic nature of Etruscan art, which remained one of its fundamental characteristics. The aristocracy in each of the cities of Etruria had provided the impetus. The Roman conquerors allowed this nobility to survive only so long as it was useful to them. With the massacres under Sulla and then Octavian, the Etruscan nation disappeared: and with it its art. More brilliant than that of its neighbours, it was more fragile too, depending on a relatively shallow layer of society. When this class was destroyed, Etruscan art merged into that of Rome, and the legacy it bequeathed in the end amounted to very little.

CONCISE BIBLIOGRAPHY

BEAZLEY, J.D. *Etruscan Vase-painting.* Oxford, 1947.
BIANCHI BANDINELLI, R., and GIULIANO, A. *Les Etrusques et l'Italie avant Rome.* L'Univers des Formes. Paris, 1973.
BLOCH, R. *Les Etrusques.* Geneva, 1970.
BOETHIIUS, A., and WARD-PERKINS, J.B. *Etruscan and Roman Architecture.* Harmondsworth, 1970.
GRANT, M. *The Etruscans.* London and New York, 1980.
MANSUELLI, G.A. *Les Etrusques et les commencements de Rome* Paris, 1963.
MANSUELLI, G.A. *Les Etrusques et les commencements de Rome.* Paris, 1963.
PALLOTTINO, M. *Etruscan Painting.* Geneva, 1952. *La Peinture étrusque.* Geneva, 1962.
———————— and TUCKER, H. & J. *Art of the Etruscans.* London, 1955.
SPRENGER, M., and BARTOLONI, G. *Die Etrusker, Kunst und Geschichte.* Munich, 1977.

MAJOR MUSEUMS

France	Musée du Louvre, Paris
Italy	Museo Nazionale di Villa Giulia, Rome
	Museo Archeologico, Florence
	Museo Gregoriano Etrusco, Vatican City
	Museo Civico, Bologna
	Museo Etrusco, Chiusi
	Museo Civico, Orvieto
	Museo Archeologico Nazionale, Perugia
	Museo Archeologico, Sienna
	Museo Nazionale, Tarquinia
	Museo Etrusco Guarnacci, Volterra
West Germany	Staatliche Antikensammlungen, Munich
	Badisches Landesmuseum, Karlsruhe

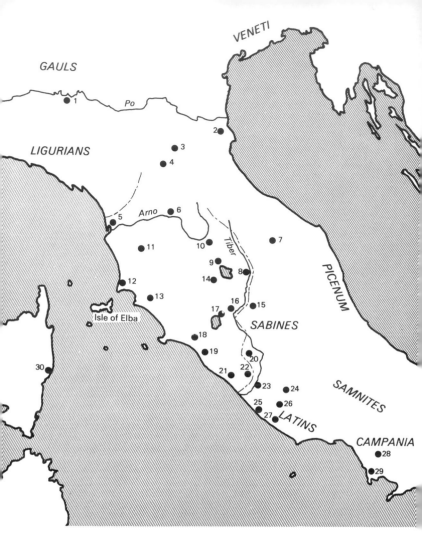

ETRURIA

1
Vase in the shape of a gourd, bronze,
H. 28 cm., 8th c. B.C., Louvre

2
Biconical vase, bronze, H. 34 cm., last
quarter of 8th c. B.C., Louvre

3
Cinerary urn, Tarquinia, terracotta
and bronze, H. of vase 71 cm., 8th c.
B.C., Archaeol. Mus., Florence

4
Cauldron with griffin heads, from
Narce, terracotta, H. 10.5 cm., 7th c.
B.C., Villa Giulia, Rome

5
Askos, terracotta, H. 17 cm., 8th c. B.C.,
Bologna (Benacci necropolis), Civic
Mus., Bologna

6
Incense-burner, bronze, Tarquinia,
8th c. B.C., Tarquinia Mus.

7
Hut-shaped cinerary urn, from Marino, terracotta, H. 26 cm., 9th–8th c. B.C., Nat. Prehistoric Mus., Rome

8
Tomb, 2nd half of 6th c. B.C., Populonia, San Cerbone necropolis

9   Tomb of the capitals, *c.* 570 B.C., Necropolis, Caere

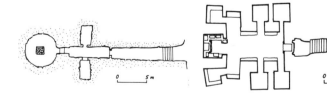

10
Montagnola tomb, *c.* 600 B.C., Quinto Fiorentino

11
Tomb of the Volumnii, mid-2nd c. B.C., near Perugia

12
Temple model, from Vulci, terracotta, H. 22 cm., 1st half of 1st c. B.C., Villa Giulia, Rome

13
House-shaped cinerary urn, Chiusi (?), volcanic stone, H. 43 cm., 2nd c. B.C., Archaeol. Mus., Florence

14   Reconstruction of an Archaic Etruscan temple

15
Gorgon-headed antefix, from Veii, terracotta, H. 48 cm., end of 6th c. B.C., Villa Giulia, Rome

16
Antefix with the head of a black man, from Caere, terracotta, H. 26 cm., beginning of 5th c. B.C., Louvre

17
Male statuette, from Caere, painted
terracotta, H. 47 cm., 2nd half of 7th c.
B.C., Mus. dei Conservatori, Rome

18
Funerary stele of Aulus Titus, from
Volterra, volcanic stone, H. 1.70 m., c.
550 B.C., Volterra Mus.

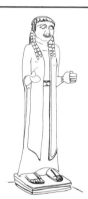

19
Centaur, from Vulci, volcanic stone,
H. 77 cm., 590–580 B.C., Villa Giulia,
Rome

20
Offering-bearer, from Vulci, plaster,
H. 85 cm., 570–550 B.C., B. M.

21
Lion, from Vulci (?), volcanic stone,
7th c. B.C., Vatican Mus.

22
Winged lion, from Vulci (?), volcanic
stone, H. 71 cm., mid-6th c. B.C., Ménil
Foundation, Houston

23
Married couple: detail from a sarcophagus, from Caere, terracotta, c. 510–500 B.C., Louvre

24
Apollo, from Veii, painted terracotta, H. 1.80 m., end of 6th c. B.C., Villa Giulia, Rome

25
Head of Hermes (Mercury), from Veii, painted terracotta, H. 37 cm., end of 6th c. B.C., Villa Giulia, Rome

26
Head of a god, from Volterra, local marble, H. 31 cm., 520–480 B.C., private coll., Volterra

27
Male head, from Casale di Conca, terracotta, H. 25 cm., c. 490 B.C., Villa Giulia, Rome

28
Canopic vase, from Dolciano, terracotta, H. 27 cm., 500–480 B.C., Chiusi Mus.

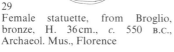

29
Female statuette, from Broglio, bronze, H. 36 cm., *c.* 550 B.C., Archaeol. Mus., Florence

30
Female statuette, bronze, 520–500 B.C., Cabinet des Médailles, Paris

31
Statuette of a male votary, from Monteguragazza, bronze, H. 24 cm., *c.* 480 B.C., Civic Mus., Bologna

32
Statuette of a female votary, from Monteguragazza, bronze, H. 24 cm., *c.* 480 B.C., Civic. Mus., Bologna

33
Athena (Minerva) Promachos, from Perugia, bronze, 5th c. B.C., Louvre

34
Javelin thrower, from Caere, bronze, H. 45 cm., 490–470 B.C., Louvre

35
Votive head, from Veii, terracotta, H. 17 cm., 430–420 B.C., Villa Giulia, Rome

36
Youth's head, from Cagli, bronze, H. 14 cm., 1st half of 4th c. B.C., Villa Giulia, Rome

37
Cinerary statue: mother, Chianciano, limestone, H. 1 m., 2nd half of 5th c. B.C., Archaeol. Mus., Florence

38
Aphrodite (?) (Venus), from Lake Nemi, bronze, H. 50 cm., 4th c. B.C., Louvre

39   Sarcophagus cover: the deceased reclining, from Tarquinia (Tomb of the Partunu), marble, W. 2.43 m., end of 4th c. B.C., Tarquinia Mus.

40
Frieze: pillaging of Delphic shrine, Civita Alba, terracotta, 180–150 B.C., Civic Mus., Bologna

41
Pediment: Dionysus discovers Ariadne, from Civita Alba, terracotta, 180–150 B.C., Civic Mus., Bologna

42
Bust of Apollo, from Falerii, terracotta, H. 80 cm., end of 4th c. B.C., Villa Giulia, Rome

43
Head with Phrygian cap, from Caere, terracotta, H. 32 cm., 1st half of 1st c. B.C., Villa Giulia, Rome

44
Portrait: Brutus (?), bronze, H. 69 cm.,
1st quarter of 3rd c. (?) B.C., Mus. dei
Conservatori, Rome

45
Male head, from San Giovanni
Lipioni, bronze, H. 27 cm., 3rd–2nd c.
B.C., Cabinet des Médailles, Paris

46
Portrait of a youth, from central
Etruria, bronze, H. 23 cm., 2nd half of
3rd c. B.C., Archaeol. Mus., Florence

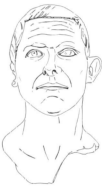

47
Votive head, from Caere, terracotta,
H. 32 cm., 1st half of 1st c. B.C., Villa
Giulia, Rome

48   Chimaera, bronze, L. 1.28 m., 4th c. B.C., Archaeol. Mus., Florence

49
Canopus, terracotta, H. 50 cm., 2nd half of 6th c. B.C., Louvre

50
Lid of cinerary urn, from Perugia, bronze, W. 69.3 cm., end of 4th–beginning of 3rd c. B.C., Hermitage

51
Sarcophagus cover: couple, from Vulci, limestone, L. 2.43 m., end of 4th c. B.C., Mus. of Fine Arts, Boston

52
Sarcophagus: couple, Città della Pieve, alabaster, W. 1.23 m., end of 5th c. B.C., Archaeol. Mus., Florence

53
Cinerary urn: voyage of the deceased, from Volterra, alabaster, 3rd–2nd c. B.C., Guarnacci Mus., Volterra

54
Cinerary urn, from Chiusi, alabaster,
H. 49 cm., mid-2nd c. B.C., Sienna
Mus.

55
Cinerary urn, from Volterra, terra-
cotta, 2nd c. B.C., Guarnacci Mus.,
Volterra

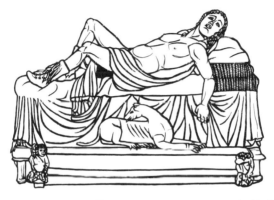

56   Urn cover: Adonis, from Tuscany, terracotta, H. 63 cm., 2nd half of 2nd c.
B.C., Vatican Mus.

57   Lid of cinerary urn: deceased couple, terracotta, H. 41 cm., 1st half of 1st
c. B.C., Volterra Mus.

463

58
Painted plaque: Iphigenia carried to
sacrifice (?), Caere, H. 1.25 m., 3rd
quarter of 6th c. B.C., Louvre

59
Horseman, wall painting, 550–540
B.C., Tarquinia, Tomb of the Bulls

60
Pair of dancers, wall painting, c. 530
B.C., Tarquinia, Tomb of the
Lionesses

61
Dancing girl, wall painting, c. 510–
490 B.C., Tarquinia, Tomb of the
Acrobats

62   Pair of dancers, wall painting, c. 480–470 B.C., Tarquinia, Tomb of the Triclinium

63
Man with cup and flute-player, wall painting, *c.* 510 B.C., Tarquinia, Tomb of the Baron

64
Man and his slave, wall painting, 2nd half of 4th c. B.C., Vulci, François Tomb

65   Wrestling scene, wall painting, beginning of 5th c. B.C., Chiusi, Tomb of the Monkey

66
Portrait of the founder of the tomb, wall painting, 350–325 B.C., Tarquinia, Tomb of the Shields

67
Female bust, wall painting, 375–350 B.C., Tarquinia, Tomba dell'Orco

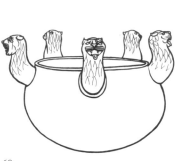

68
Cauldron with lion protomes, from Caere, bronze, D. 47 cm., mid-7th c. B.C., Vatican Mus.

69
Fragment of a tripod, from Fonte Ranocchio, bronze, 3rd quarter of 6th c. B.C., Antikensammlungen, Munich

70   Fragment of chariot decoration, from Castel San Marano, bronze, 540–530 B.C., Antikensammlungen, Munich

71
Perfume vase: woman's head, bronze, H. 10 cm., 2nd half of 3rd c. B.C., Louvre

72
Oenochoe in the shape of a youth's head, from Gabii, bronze, H. 32 cm., 4th c. B.C., Louvre

73
Candelabrum, bronze, H. 92 cm., mid-5th c. B.C., Vatican. Mus.

74
Draped figure, crown of candelabrum (No. 73)

75
Fragment of candelabrum: dancer, from Vulci, bronze, c. 500 B.C., Karlsruhe Mus.

76
Candelabrum base: dancing girl, bronze, 1st quarter of 5th c. B.C., B.M.

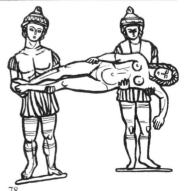

77
Foot of the Ficoroni cist, from Palestrina (Praeneste), bronze, 3rd quarter of 4th c. B.C., Villa Giulia, Rome

78
Handle of the Barberini cist, from Palestrina (Praeneste), bronze, end of 4th c. B.C., Villa Giulia, Rome

467

80
Detail of engraving on Ficoroni cist
(see No. 79)

79
Ficoroni cist, Palestrina (Praeneste),
bronze, H. 77 cm., 3rd quarter of 4th c.
B.C., Villa Giulia, Rome

81
Mirror: divination scene, from Vulci,
bronze, D. 18 cm., 1st half of 4th c.
B.C., Vatican Mus.

82
Engraved mirror, from Bomarzo,
silver, D. 10.5 cm., c. 350 B.C., Archaeol. Mus., Florence

83
Engraved mirror, from Palestrina
(Praeneste), bronze, W. 33.6 cm.,
mid-3rd c. B.C., Villa Giulia, Rome

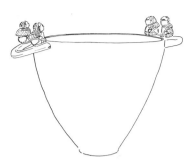

84
Skyphos, from Palestrina (Praeneste), gold, H. 7.9 cm., 640–620 B.C., Bernardini tomb, Villa Giulia, Rome

85
Fibula disc, from Caere, gold, W. 31.5 cm., 670–650 B.C., Regolini-Galassi tomb, Vatican Mus.

87
Necklace, silver, L. 30 cm., 7th c. B.C., Louvre

86
Pendant in the shape of a head of Achelous, gold, H. 4 cm., 6th c. B.C., Louvre

88
Bracelet, gold, L. 18 cm., 7th c. B.C., Louvre

89
Fibula, from Marsiliana d'Albegna, gold, W. 15.5 cm., 2nd quarter of 7th c. B.C., Archaeol. Mus., Florence

90
Fibula, from Vetulonia, gold, W. 15.6 cm., 3rd quarter of 7th c. B.C., Archaeol. Mus., Florence

91
Lion fibula, gold, W. 9.7 cm., 5th c. B.C., Louvre

92
Fibula, gold, W. 8 cm., 4th c. B.C., Louvre

93
Fibula, gold, W. 7 cm., 4th c. B.C., Louvre

94
Ear-ring, gold, H. 9 cm., 4th–3rd c. B.C., Louvre

95
Caryatid chalice, bucchero, H. 19 cm.,
700–670 B.C., Louvre

96
Vase with sculpted decoration, Caere,
bucchero, H. 26 cm., 3rd quarter of 7th
c. B.C., Vatican Mus.

97
Globular amphora, bucchero, H.
10 cm., beginning of 7th c. B.C., Louvre

98
Globular amphora with incised
decoration, bucchero, H. 14 cm., 2nd
half of 7th c. B.C., Louvre

99
Skyphos, bucchero, H. 11 cm., 2nd
half of 7th c. B.C., Louvre

100
Kantharos, bucchero, H. 10 cm., 2nd
half of 7th c. B.C., Louvre

101
Vase with incised decoration, from Caere, bucchero, end of 7th c. B.C., Vatican Mus.

102
Vase with sculpted and incised decoration, Orvieto, bucchero, end of 7th c. B.C., Archaeol. Mus., Florence

103
Oenochoe with polychrome decoration, Veii, painted terracotta, 1st half of 6th c. B.C., Metropolitan Mus.

104
Oenochoe with relief, from Chiusi, bucchero, H. 36 cm., 2nd half of 6th c. B.C., Archaeol. Mus., Florence

105
Duck-shaped askos, terracotta, L. 18 cm., end of 4th c.–3rd c. B.C., Louvre

106
Vase in the shape of a leg, bucchero, H. 20 cm., 2nd half of 6th c. B.C., Louvre

Rome

by François Baratte and Catherine Metzger
Curators, Department of Greek and Roman Antiquities,
Louvre

Drawings by Marie Bévillard and Marie-Lise Bordreuil

ROME

Roman art has been defined by neo-Classical critics as a chapter —the last—in Greek art, deteriorating as it moved away from Classical canons. Such a view, which denies Rome any artistic originality, has for many years affected our judgement of Roman art. It now appears superficial and is unacceptable. Greek artists and models were certainly the main contributors in the development of the Roman creative tradition, and its ties with Hellenic culture were always fundamental to its evolution. But Rome had developed a new ideology —together with a different political, social and economic structure—which was bound to engender new forms.

THE ORIGINS

Recent research has much increased our knowledge of the civilizations of Latium and Rome during the proto-historic and Archaic periods. Their evolution was broadly parallel to that of civilizations in Etruria, with a few interesting differences, particularly in Rome itself: cremation, for example, was practised earlier there, from the 10th or 9th century onwards, in typical hut urns, many of which were discovered in the earliest of the Roman necropolises on the site of the future Forum. But what is most surprising is the modest character of the culture that came to light there, especially in the Orientalizing period when the rich material in the tombs of Caere or Praeneste, or even in their immediate neighbourhood, had no equivalent in the city.

Thanks mainly to the Etruscans, Rome was a city from the 6th century B.C., but it may be misleading to talk about 'Roman' art before the end of the 3rd century. This is chiefly because of the political and moral climate at the time. With its strength fully stretched in creating the city and then expanding it, the ruling class looked upon art with suspicion and considered it to be an extravagant dissipator of energy: it was to be reserved for the gods. Nevertheless, one can discern an artistic culture in Archaic Rome, developing from three main elements which became apparent simultaneously or in sequence.

The Etruscan element came first and was all the more vigorous because it was accompanied in the 6th century by political control. According to tradition, the relief decoration on the temple to Jupiter Capitolinus was effected in 509 by the Etruscan Vulca. The second element was Italic, and was supplied by peoples indigenous to eastern and north-eastern Latium. These peoples introduced a taste for firm structure and a vitality that at times approached expressionism. Finally there was the Greek element, present from Archaic times because of contact with Campania and continued by the resettlement of Greek artisans in Rome itself, where they were responsible for the decoration of the temple of Ceres at the beginning of the 5th century. This Greek influence was continually and decisively reinforced from the 3rd century on by great families such as the Scipios, who were enamoured of Greek culture, and, most dramatically, by Rome's military expansion—first into southern Italy and then towards the east. In this respect, the capture of Tarentum in 272, Syracuse in 212 and Corinth in 146 proved symbolic: through these gateways Rome received an unimaginable abundance of riches, artisans and works of art, which were to revolutionize the Romans' ways of thought and of life.

ART AT THE END OF THE REPUBLIC

The last centuries before the Christian era were formative periods. During the 3rd and 2nd centuries Rome had been flooded with the works brought from the Greek world; but this was more a reflection of the conqueror's need to prove himself by display of the arts than a sign of true aesthetic sensibility.

The time came, however, during the 2nd century, when the ruling class decided it was no longer enough to reuse imported works and themes. Art was the medium by which the privileged individual could celebrate his relation to the gods or the state, or by which the state itself could be celebrated as guarantor of its citizens' well-being. As such it needed to develop a repertoire better adapted to the ideology of those who were responsible for the city, than imported works could provide.

It was inevitably an eclectic art, because of the disparate elements which constituted it. These various influences were not only welcomed: they could actually be juxtaposed, undigested, within the same work—a conception fundamentally foreign to Greek art. Moreover, artists of Greek origin played an important part in its development. They had settled in Rome in large numbers, as we have seen, and from the 2nd century on applied themselves to the production of the kind of iconography that their patrons demanded (relief 'of Domitius Ahenobarbus'). Often their work was based on cartoons used in earlier times in Greece itself.

This art was concentrated in three domains: architecture, portrait sculpture and painting.

Architecture, significantly, took up the formulas elaborated in Hellenistic art, but carried the sense of overall organization almost to an extreme: buildings that made up a complex were conceived as part of a whole (Fortuna sanctuary at Praeneste, beginning of 1st century B.C.). The use of rubble instead of chipped stones allowed particularly daring technical solutions.

Portraiture was the perfect example of an art placed at the service of the upper classes of society, whether in Rome or in the Italian provincial cities: we need only note the ancestor portraits which were the reserve of patrician families who used them on special occasions for ostentatious public display. Towards the end of the 2nd century and in the 1st century, above all in the ancient Italic cities, there was a definite tendency to develop the image of an aristocracy rooted in the land, unpolished and hard-working, austere, characterized physically by time-worn features. Clearly, what emerged here was not only the wish for a personal, individualized portrait, but also the affirmation of participation in a group, with the self expressed as part of that group. Such quasi-naturalistic elements are sometimes thought to be quintessentially Roman. It would be wrong, however, to exaggerate their importance: in Rome, at least, they were tempered by the influence of Hellenistic psychological portraiture which frequently prescribed touching, idealized character types. Lastly, some of the less favoured classes, such as the freedmen, emulated their betters, using portrait art to assert both their existence and their individuality.

Painting did not escape such a partially ideological role, although the few scraps that survive give a rather imprecise idea of the importance of historical, triumphal painting. However, this period was significant for its development of decorative mural painting, which belongs to the realm of a private, more disinterested art. As with architecture, Greek influence was strong in this field, especially in iconography; but, again, a unity was imposed on wall decoration in a way which appears to have been markedly Roman. At first, it was very architectonic, emphasizing the main divisions of the wall structure ('1st Style' in the traditional classification); then in the 1st century it became integrated into a new system ('2nd Style'), and an illusionistic style was born which sought to suggest a succession of receding backgrounds opening into infinity: this was an original creation on the part of artists working both in Rome and in central Italy.

THE CENTURY OF AUGUSTUS

The 1st century before Christ, a period of intense creative activity, was also a time of serious political unrest. Civil wars broke out, which did not end until 27 B.C. when Caesar's nephew, Octavian, accepted the title Augustus from the Senate and established a new regime, the Principate. That led to the gradual and empirical organization—under the guise of a return to Republican traditions (Augustus presented himself as 'the first among equals')—of a system strongly influenced by Hellenistic monarchical concepts. Augustus was to implement policies of social, economic and religious regeneration to which he himself was temperamentally drawn and for which Italy craved after the unstable period through which it had passed.

Art, in all its aspects, was one element in these policies. Art illustrated the basic characteristics of the regime the more clearly because throughout Augustus' long reign it showed a special brilliance. With respect to style, at least, the influence of Greek Classicism is evident. But it was a somewhat artificial reversion to a mannered Classicism, which, though at times capable of creative invention, was mostly cold and rhetorical. The ideological and intellectual content was radically different from that of Classical Greek art: in official monuments it conveyed a discreet but effective celebration of the emperor as the guarantor of order in the world, of the efficient running of the state and the felicity of its citizens. The deliberately allegorical style of this art with its elitist and partisan elements frequently gave it the character of court art, even if many of its features could also be found in the private domain. This official art form, and its Hellenizing elements of formal perfection and extreme coldness, continued to be dominant, with some variations, under Augustus' immediate successors and was to persist beyond the end of the 1st century. The continuity and longevity of the tradition suggest that its emergence was not solely due to the efforts of one man, Augustus, but that it in fact contained something inherent in Roman art. Greek culture was always to be the educator of the Roman ruling classes.

However, certain artistic stirrings in the second half of the 1st century blossomed during the 2nd century into an assertion of some originality.

ROMAN ART UNDER THE FLAVIANS AND THE FIRST ANTONINES (69–160)

In 69 the crisis that resulted in Nero's death also brought to power Vespasian, the first representative of the Flavian dynasty. His provincial, bourgeois origins no doubt explain in some measure the subsequent move away from Classicizing art. In sculpture, notably, a concern with space gradually asserted itself and reliefs gained a new profundity (Arch of Titus in the Forum). From then on, subjects moved not as if on a stage, but in real space, the viewer's space.

The new spirit became predominant under the Antonine dynasty. After Domitian's catastrophic reign and his assassination in 96, Nerva and then Trajan reestablished political stability and economic prosperity in the Empire. The policies of Trajan favoured the provincial middle classes, and it is significant that the affirmation of an original Roman art went hand in hand with the development of forms associated with precisely those groups in the Roman population that had their roots in Italic culture. They tended to turn their backs on the naturalistic laws expressed in Greek art in favour of conventions that organized space and objects according to a relative importance determined in advance.

Official art proliferated and owed much to the creative genius of one exceptional character, Apollodorus of Damascus, a man of Syrian origin who was an adviser to the emperor, an architect and the overseer of works on the great complex that constituted the Forum of Trajan, the most finished of the imperial *fora.* It was Apollodorus who exploited the full potential of bricks in architecture and built the monumental markets on the periphery of the Quirinal hill. He also undoubtedly developed the historical relief, with rare mastery, and brought it to a perfect balance of form and feeling. Trajan's Column, which was dedicated in 113 in celebration of victorious campaigns against the Dacians, shows such perfection. Creating a new form, this illustrated column developed a new, perfectly compatible artistic language, which showed a remarkable capacity for invention and composition. Obvious narrative and historical concerns—e.g. the glorification of the emperor—were accompanied by emotional and moral reflections on such themes as the conduct of the prince near his soldiers and citizens; the nature of war, the horrors of which were never dissimulated; and relations between men— a genuine respect for the adversary is clearly seen on the relief. It was a political work, certainly, but balanced by a humanity which elevates those first years of the 2nd century into a Golden Age of Roman art.

WINDS OF CHANGE: ROMAN ART IN THE SECOND HALF OF THE 2ND CENTURY

Such harmony and balance began to be threatened from the middle of the 2nd century. As with any art that has reached maturity, that of the Romans was affected by academicism, by a mechanical and rhetorical repetition of formulas that were drained of significance. But more importantly, new forces were at work which would change Roman art profoundly from *c.* 160, during the rule of the emperor Marcus Aurelius, the Stoic philosopher, who was disillusioned by the passions and nature of men. Paradoxically it was this prince, anxious to carry out his duty, however repugnant it might be, who had to face the first major invasions. His successor Commodus, assassinated in 192, was to see a totally new art style established, one that was deeply marked by the crises of the time, and that had broken with the Hellenic tradition, both from a formal and from a moral standpoint.

The rupture first appeared in a truly baroque style which was evident in sculpture just as much as in architecture: it showed a love of display, a taste for anything excessive, unstable, transitory, and a lust for violence and death. The techniques themselves changed: the increasingly frequent use of the trepan which dug deep into the marble could be seen everywhere in sculpture, in portraits and on sarcophagi, and it stressed contrasts of light and shadow. Forms became exuberant, expressing an excessive mysticism which culminated in the person of the emperor, the new Hercules. Funerary sculpture in particular was animated by a strong tendency to individualization, whilst in many cases the former naturalism was abandoned: art from then on preferred to suggest by repetition and symbolism and was assaulted by a savage irrationality. In the face of mounting danger, power was depicted more brutally, without subtlety or regard for adversaries. But the artists who vanquished the enemy in their works were actually making desperate attempts to shake off their own doubts.

THE CRISIS OF THE 3RD CENTURY

An upheaval of this kind signals a true crisis. It was contained for a while by Septimius Severus—who upon the death of Commodus seized power after a bitter struggle—but it profoundly affected the whole of the 3rd century. Although the situation was aggravated by external factors such as pressure from the barbarians, the crisis owed its virulence above all to the fact that it was structural in nature: in politics the fiction of the Principate, the balancing of power between the emperor and the Senate, was now devoid of substance; and in the arts, the old forms no longer satisfied the aspirations of an empire that had spread over the whole of the Mediterranean basin. During this period of turmoil, which was to end with Diocletian's radical reforms, society was in total confusion.

The Severan dynasty imposed an uncompromising assertion of imperial power which can be felt in its art: it was the last flowering, up until the end of the century, of the historical relief. The perfection of architectural forms was accompanied by great novelties in decoration: in a composition of superimposed reliefs—borrowed perhaps from certain forms of painting—one can observe a rejection of traditional narrative art in favour of a symbolism which used schema and repetition for its effects (Arch of Septimius Severus in the Forum). This sometimes deliberately summary sculpture testified to the growing importance of provincial and popular currents that were quite alien to Hellenic culture.

A rapid succession of soldier-emperors after 235 made it difficult to carry out any policy of creating major works, especially in the field of monumental sculpture. Portraits and funerary sculpture (relief sarcophagi), therefore, took on a greater significance and are the only means by which we can gain any appreciation of stylistic tendencies and spiritual changes. With their parted lips and distant gaze, the faces often transmit a sense of disillusionment if not despair; witness the portraits of children with the look of old men, as if they carried the entire burden of a disordered world. The emperors, who often came from provincial military centres, encouraged an official sculpture which used an increasingly abstract style to emphasize the physical strength that emanated from them—from that time on the only guarantee of imperial power.

But it is also worth noting that the very emperors (Maximian of Thrace and Philip the Arab) who rejected traditional forms for themselves, adopted them for portraits of their heirs. Clearly, Classical culture was still a sign that one belonged to the elite of the Roman world; it alone could confer legitimacy on a new dynasty by placing it in a tradition. That Hellenizing current, which was also very much in evidence on sarcophagus reliefs, was particularly strong under Gallienus in the 3rd century—to the extent that this has often been referred to as a period of 'renaissance', with the implication that 'Hellenization' was a deliberate policy of the sovereign. It was unquestionably a time of considerable stylistic refinement, with expressions of high moral significance and rich spiritual elevation (sarcophagus of Plotinus). But Gallienus was no doubt only keeping in motion one of the currents that ran permanently through Roman art. The Hellenizing look was, in fact, no more than a varnish: beneath the perfect form a new, geometric structure was showing through and emphasizing the growing abstraction of corporal volume. An art style was evolving which by the end of the 3rd and the beginning of the 4th century was to consist of great masses, of volumes perfunctorily contained and therefore no longer descriptive but symbolic.

That was the culmination of the artistic crisis: and it coincided with the reforms of Diocletian.

CONSTANTINIAN ART

The Tetrarchic regime instituted by Diocletian marked the start of a new phase in the evolution of the Roman world, which continued until the fall of the Western Empire in 476. The regime itself did not function for long, for it had too many internal tensions. At the beginning of the 4th century, Constantine finally succeeded in acquiring total power. He established a sort of absolute monarchy and presented himself as the new founder of the Empire, as the creation in 324 of a second capital, Constantinople, testifies. The regime was also marked by the development of a new social order. It was characterized by the integration of controversial groups such as Christians, and the admission to positions of administrative responsibility of certain elements from the lower classes, partially replacing the traditional ruling class which had been decimated by the crisis.

In art these changes were reflected in a dual tendency. During the early period the tastes of the newcomers to power overwhelmed the official art styles (Arch of Constantine in Rome), and sculpture gained characteristics that had already been seen, for analogous reasons, on some of the Severan period monuments: rigid, schematic forms, an assertion of frontality, a strict hierarchy of proportion in relation to the subject's importance, and the predominant, semi-abstract character of the imperial image.

Then occurred what, to all appearances, was a rapid revival of the Classical style, due partly to the influence of the great families of the old aristocracy still attached to their culture, and partly to that of the new elite who appropriated the Hellenizing vocabulary as a symbol of their social elevation. The result is known as the 'Constantinian renaissance', which basically followed the pattern mapped out during the 3rd century, but chose to return to the refined Classicizing formulas.

A consideration of the iconographic contributions of Christianity would be out of place here and will be presented in another volume. It should, however, be noted that the new religion had not yet produced a substantial difference in style: the same artisans carried out Christian, pagan and secular commissions. But it was to gain more power in art as patrons and workers turned to Christianity in growing numbers. Even the emperor gave generous donations to the Church and launched an ambitious programme for building basilicas.

ROMAN ART TO THE END OF THE WESTERN EMPIRE (476)

Right up to the end of the 4th century the fiction of a united empire had been maintained, even though the western half—centred on Rome—and the eastern half were developing more and more independently of one another. But on the death of Theodosius in 395 the division of the Western and the Eastern Empire was legally completed. The Orient took up the Classical heritage to an increasing extent, while the western world came under barbarian influence.

The old culture continued in iconography, and work was often of a very refined nature, as can be seen in the minor arts—the silver-work and ivories from workshops active in the great Imperial metropolises, such as Rome and Constantinople, and also in Milan, Arles, Trier, Antioch and Thessalonica. The work was made to appeal to a relatively narrow circle of dignitaries and the art often took on a notably elitist character.

This pagan Classical culture was used by some to make rather desperate assertions of the old faith in the face of a triumphant Christianity, but, devoid of substance, it eventually became for pagans and Christians alike merely an inexhaustible source of purely decorative motifs.

In 476 Odoacer deposed the last Western emperor: the barbarian kingdoms were set up and the modern nations were born. Barbarian art would now develop in most countries. Roman art would survive in Constantinople and the East where it took the Byzantine path.

CONCISE BIBLIOGRAPHY

ANDREAE, B. *L'Art de l'ancienne Rome.* Paris, 1973.
BIANCHI BANDINELLI, R. *Rome, Le Centre du pouvoir.* Paris, 1969. *Rome the Centre of Power: Roman Art to A.D.* 200. London, 1970.
——————————— *Rome. La Fin de l'art antique.* Paris, 1970. *The Late Empire: Roman Art, A.D.* 200–400. London, 1971.
BOETHIUS, A., and WARD-PERKINS, J. B. *Etruscan and Roman Architecture.* Harmondsworth, 1970.
BRILLIANT, R. *Roman Art from the Republic to Constantine.* London, 1974.
FROVA, A. *L'arte di Roma e del mondo romano.* Storia Universale dell'Arte, II, 2. Turin, 1961.
von HEINTZE, H. *Römische Kunst.* Stuttgart, 1969.
KÄHLER, H. *Rome et son empire.* Paris, 1963.
KITZINGER, ERNST. *Byzantine Art in the Making: Main Lines of Stylistic Development in Mediterranean Art, 3rd–7th Century.* London, 1977.
KJELLBERG, E., and SAFLUND, G. *Greek and Roman Art.* London, 1968.
KRAUS, T. *Das römische Weltreich.* Propyläen Kunstgeschichte, 11. Berlin, 1967.
LA BAUME, P. *Römische Kunstgewerbe zwischen Christi Geburt und 400.* Braunschweig, 1964.
PICARD, G.C. *L'Art romain.* Paris, 1962.
——————————— *L'Art romain.* Bibliothèque des Arts. Paris, 1962.
TOYNBEE, J.M.C. *The Art of the Romans.* London, 1965.

THE ROMAN EMPIRE

PANNONIA

DACIA

THRACE

MACEDONIA

AMPANIA

GREECE

CAPPADOCIA

CARIA

RHODES

CYPRUS

SYRIA

CRETE

JUDAEA

CYRENAICA

EGYPT

MAJOR MUSEUMS

Austria
Kunsthistorisches Museum, Vienna

Denmark
Ny Carlsberg Glyptotek, Copenhagen

France
Musée du Louvre, Paris
Musée de la Civilisation Gallo-Romaine, Lyons

Germany, East
Staatliche Museen zu Berlin, East Berlin

Germany, West
Glyptothek, Munich
Römisch-Germanisches Museum, Cologne

Great Britain
British Museum, London

Italy
Museo Capitolino, Rome
Museo dei Conservatori, Rome
Museo della Villa Borghese, Rome
Museo delle Terme, Rome
Museo del Vaticano, Vatican City
Museo Nazionale, Rome
Museo Nazionale, Naples

U.S.A.
Metropolitan Museum, New York
Museum of Fine Arts, Boston

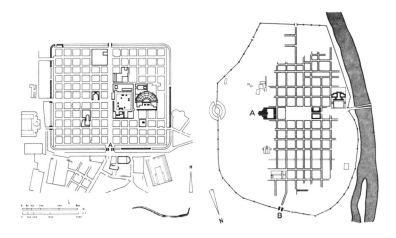

1
Timgad, plan

2
Trier, plan

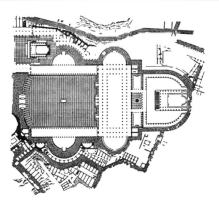

3   Rome, Forum of Trajan, plan

4
Arch of Augustus, on a bronze coin,
19–18 B.C., Ephesus

5
Arch of Claudius, on a bronze coin,
A.D. 41–45, Rome

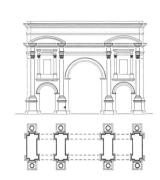

7
Arch, end of 2nd c. A.D., Timgad

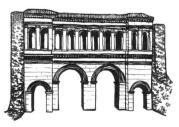

6
Arch of Trajan, A.D. 114–120, Bene-
vento

8
Porte Saint-André, 1st c. A.D., Autun

9
Temple of Jupiter Capitolinus, on a
bronze coin, *c.* 75 B.C., Rome

10
Temple of Jupiter Tonans, on a
bronze coin, *c.* 19 B.C., Rome

11   Temple of Portunus, 2nd half of 2nd c. B.C., Rome

12
Temple of Jupiter Capitolinus, on a
bronze coin, *c.* 37 B.C., Rome

13
Temple of Rome and of Augustus at
Pergamon, on a bronze coin, 19 B.C.,
Ephesus

14
Temple of Mars Ultor in Rome, on a
bronze coin, 19–15 B.C., Rome

15
Temple of Vesta in Rome, on a bronze
coin, A.D. 22, Rome

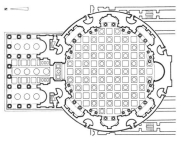

17
Baths of Caracalla, plan, beginning of
3rd c. A.D., Rome

16
Fortuna sanctuary, beginning of 1st c.
B.C., Palestrina (Praeneste), Italy

18
The Pantheon, A.D. 118–125, Rome

19   Imaginary port town, on a silver plate, *c.* A.D. 350, Kaiseraugst (Switzerland)

20   Villa, on a mosaic, 4th c. A.D., Tabarka (Tunisia)

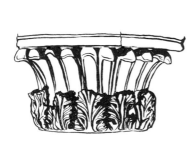

21
Capital, marble, 2nd c. A.D., Pergamon, temple of Trajan (Asia Minor)

22
Capital, marble, 1st quarter of 2nd c.
A.D., Baths of Agrippa, Rome

23
Ionic capital, marble, 1st quarter of
2nd c. A.D., Rome, Vatican Mus.

24
Composite capital, marble, 2nd c.
A.D., Basilica A, Aphrodisias (Asia
Minor)

25
Corinthian capital, marble, end of 1st
c. B.C., temple of Mars Ultor, Rome

26
Capital, temple of Concord, Rome,
marble, beginning of 1st c. A.D., Anti-
quarium of the Forum, Rome

27
Composite capital, marble, 2nd c.
A.D., Rome, Palace of the Senate,
Rome

28
Pilaster capital, marble, 2nd c. A.D.,
Exedra of Herodes Atticus, Olympia

29
Column, capital and entablature, marble, beginning of 2nd c. A.D., Baths of Agrippa, Rome

30
Cornice moulding, marble, beginning of 1st c. A.D., temple of Concord, Rome

31   Frieze, Forum of Trajan, Rome, marble, beginning of 2nd c. A.D., Vatican Mus.

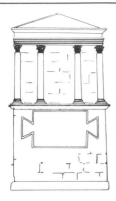

32
Mausoleum, 2nd–3rd c. A.D., Haidra
(Tunisia)

33
Mausoleum of the Ennii, 2nd c. A.D.,
Sempeter (Austria)

34
Mausoleum of the Julii, end of 1st c.
B.C., St-Rémy-de-Provence

35
Mausoleum of L. Publicius, mid-1st c.
A.D., Cologne

36
Funerary monument, mid-1st c. A.D.,
Aquileia

37
Mausoleum of A. Murcius Obulaccus,
end of 1st c. B.C., Sarsina (Italy)

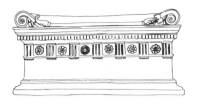

38
Sarcophagus of L. Cornelius Scipio
Barbatus, near Rome, volcanic stone,
L. 2.77 m., 3rd c. B.C., Vatican Mus.

39
Sarcophagus with ox-heads and garlands, from Augusta (Asia Minor),
marble, 2nd c. A.D., Adana Mus.

40   Sarcophagus: deceased couple, Achilles and Lycomedes, from Athenian
workshop, Rome, marble, L. 2.93 m., mid-3rd c. A.D., Capitoline Mus., Rome

41   Sarcophagus: labours of Hercules, Asia Minor workshop, marble, L.
2.58 m., 2nd half of 2nd c. A.D., Villa Borghese, Rome

42   Sarcophagus: deceased pair, the Dioscuri, marble, L. 2.18 m., 2nd half of
3rd c. A.D., Campo Santo, Pisa

43   Sarcophagus with garlands, from Rome, marble, L. 2.36 m., c. A.D. 130,
Louvre

44   Sarcophagus: deceased with geniuses, from Dougga (Tunisia), stone, 3rd c.
A.D., Dougga

45   Sarcophagus: griffins, from Rome, marble, L. 1.55 m., *c.* A.D. 140, Walters
Art Gall., Baltimore

46   Sarcophagus: massacre of the Niobids, from Rome, marble, L. 2.11 m., end
of 2nd c. A.D., Vatican Mus.

47   Sarcophagus: Dionysus (Bacchus) and Ariadne, from Rome, marble, L.
2.21 m., end of 2nd c. A.D., Ny Carlsberg Glyptotek, Copenhagen

48   Sarcophagus: marine procession, marble, L. 2.38 m., *c.* A.D. 160, Louvre

49   Sarcophagus: marine procession, from Tipasa, marble, beginning of 3rd c.
A.D., Tipasa Mus.

50
Strigil sarcophagus, marble, 2nd half
of 3rd c. A.D.

51
Funerary relief: the deceased reclining, marble, L. 1.77 m., beginning of
1st c. A.D., Terme Mus., Rome

52
Funerary altar of Amemptus, from
Rome, marble, H. 1 m., mid-1st c. A.D.,
Louvre

53
Funerary altar of Amemptus, from
Rome, marble, H. 1 m., mid-1st c. A.D.,
Louvre

55
Funerary altar of Fabia Stratonice,
marble, H. 1.35 m., early 2nd c. A.D.,
Landesmus., Karlsruhe

54
Funerary altar of Julia Victorina,
from Rome, marble, H. 1.15 m.,
beginning of 1st c. A.D., Louvre

56
Funerary stele, Au (Austria), limestone, 1st half of 1st c. A.D., Niederös-
terreichisches Landesmus., Vienna

57
Cinerary urn of Asinius Hylas, from Italy, marble, W. 42 cm., end of 1st c. A.D., Louvre

58
Funerary cippus of Saenia Calliste, from Rome, marble, H. 57 cm., Louvre

59
Funerary portrait, from Egypt, wax painting, H. 34 cm., 3rd c. A.D., Louvre

60
Funerary relief: deceased couple, from Klagenfurt (Austria), limestone, 2nd c. A.D., Klagenfurt Landesmus.

61   Sarcophagus cover: deceased, from Rome, marble, L. 1.77 m., beginning of 1st c. A.D., Terme Mus., Rome

EX·TESTAM
P·GESSI·P·L
PRIMI

ARBI
GESSIA
FAVSTI

GESSIA·P·L·FAVSTA·P·CESSIVS·P·F·ROM·P·CESSIVS·P·L·PRIMVS

62   Funerary relief: family of freedmen, marble, L. 2.04 m., 2nd half of 1st c.
B.C., Mus. of Fine Arts, Boston

63
Funerary relief: deceased couple,
from Rome, marble, H. 1.80 m., c. 50
B.C., Mus. dei Conservatori, Rome

64
Funerary relief: young girl as Venus,
from Rome, marble, H. 36 cm., beginning of 2nd c. A.D., B.M.

65   Funerary relief: deceased couple, from Rome (?), marble, B.M.

66
Altar: two maenads dancing, from Rome, marble, H. 94 cm., mid-1st c. A.D., Terme Mus., Rome

67
Altar: swans and garlands, from Arles, marble, H. 85 cm., 1st c. A.D., Lapidary Mus., Arles

68
Altar: Augustus as augur, from Rome, marble, 2nd c. A.D., Uffizi, Florence

69
Votive stele to Saturn: woman sacrificing, central Tunisia, limestone, H. 67 cm., 2nd half of 2nd c. A.D., B.M.

70
Votive stele to Saturn, from Ain Tunga (Tunisia), limestone, H. 87 cm., 3rd c. A.D., Louvre

71
Votive stele to Saturn, from Algeria, limestone, H. 60 cm., 1st c. B.C.–1st c. A.D., Guelma Mus.

72
The muse Erato, on a silver coin,
minted Rome, 69 B.C.

73
The muse Terpsichore, on a silver
coin, minted Rome, 69 B.C.

74   The muse Euterpe, on a silver coin, minted Rome, 69 B.C.

75
The muse Thalia, on a silver coin,
minted Rome, 69 B.C.

76
The muse Melpomene, on a silver
coin, minted Rome, 69 B.C.

77
Athena (Minerva) Promachos, on a
silver coin, minted Rome, A.D. 92

78
Athena, from Avenches, bronze, H.
22.3 cm., 2nd c. A.D., Schweizerisches
Landesmus., Zurich

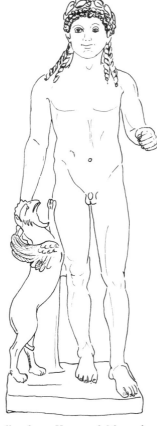

79
Diana, huntress, from Lyons, bronze,
H. 19.5 cm., 1st c. A.D., Gallo-Roman
Mus., Lyons

80
Apollo, from House of Menander,
Pompeii, marble, H. 1.05 m., begin-
ning of 1st c. B.C., Nat. Mus., Naples

81
Mars, from Coligny, bronze, H.
1.74 m., 2nd half of 1st c. A.D., Gallo-
Roman Mus., Lyons

82
Armed genius, from Augst (Switzer-
land), bronze, H. 16.6 cm., 1st c. A.D.,
Augst Mus.

83
Mercury seated, from Augst (Switzerland), bronze, H. 29 cm., 2nd half of
1st c. B.C., Augst Mus.

84
Mercury, from Odenbach, bronze, H.
21 cm., end of 1st c. A.D., Speyer Mus.

85
Mercury, good-luck amulet, from
Orange, bronze, H. 33 cm., Cabinet
des Médailles, Paris

86
Hercules and the Nemean lion, from
Avenches, bronze, H. 22.3 cm., 2nd c.
A.D., Landesmus., Zurich

87
Hercules, Rome, marble, H. 3.17 m., *c.*
A.D. 200, after a Greek 4th-c. B.C. pro-
totype, Nat. Mus., Naples

88
The emperor Commodus as Hercules,
from Rome, marble, H. 1.18 m., end of
2nd c. A.D., Conservatori, Rome

89
Sucellus, from St-Paul-Trois-
Châteaux, bronze, H. 16 cm., 2nd–3rd
c. A.D., Calvet Mus., Avignon

90
Roman lady as Omphale, marble, H.
1.82 m., beginning of 3rd c. A.D., Vatican Mus.

91
Two Romans as Mars and Venus,
marble, H. 1.80 m., beginning of 2nd c.
A.D., Louvre

92
Bacchus and Pan, from Augst, bronze, H. 18.7 cm., late 2nd c. A.D., Louvre

93
Pan and two satyrs, from Somodor (Hungary), bronze, H. 28.3 cm., 2nd c. A.D., Hungarian Nat. Mus., Budapest

94
Child Bacchus, from Vertault, bronze, H. 39 cm., 2nd–3rd c. A.D., Mus., Châtillon-sur-Seine

95
Bacchus, from Avenches, bronze, H. 66.5 cm., mid-2nd c. A.D., Avenches Mus.

96
Bacchus, head surmounted by vine-branches, from Augst, bronze, H. 23.5 cm., 1st c. A.D., Augst Mus.

97
Bacchus, decorated mount, Strasbourg, silvered bronze, H. 16 cm., Archaeol. Mus., Strasbourg

505

98
Venus arranging her hair, Gunskir-
chen (Austria), bronze, H. 14.5 cm.,
1st–2nd c. A.D., private coll.

99
Pudic Venus, Vaison, bronze, H.
25 cm., 1st–2nd c. A.D., Gallo-Roman
Mus., Lyons

100
Partly clothed goddess, Belgium
(Germany), bronze, H. 14 cm., 1st–
2nd c. A.D., Trier Mus.

101
Venus fastening her sandal, from
Kövagoszölös, bronze, H. 22.3 cm.,
2nd-3rd c. A.D., Hungarian Nat. Mus.

102
Venus with diadem, from Yakhmur
(Syria), bronze, H. 30.2 cm., Louvre

103
Venus, from Amrit (Syria), bronze, H.
22 cm., Louvre

104
Victory, from Augst, bronze, H. 63 cm., *c.* A.D. 200, Augst Mus.

105
Victory, Arch of Septimius Severus, Leptis Magna, marble, A.D. 203–204, Tripoli Mus.

106
Victory, Mauer an der Url, bronze, H. 25 cm., 3rd c. A.D., Kunsthistorisches Mus., Vienna

107
Victory-Fortuna, from Amrit (Syria), bronze, H. 20 cm., Louvre

108
Rome personified, from Rome (Esquiline), silver, H. 5.4 cm., 4th c. A.D., B.M.

109
Alexandria personified, from Rome (Esquiline), silver, H. 5.4 cm., 4th c. A.D., B.M.

110
The god Lar, from Augst, bronze, H.
32 cm., 1st c. A.D., Augst Mus.

111
Guardian spirit, from Detzem,
bronze, H. 11 cm., Rheinisches Landesmus., Trier

112
Guardian spirit, from Enns (Austria),
bronze, H. 19 cm., Enns Mus.

113
Seated Jupiter, holding a thunderbolt,
bronze, H. 17 cm., Louvre

114
Bacchus, from Vichy, gilded bronze,
H. 31 cm., Hôtel de Ville, Vichy

115
Fertility goddess, from Bavai, bronze,
H. 20 cm., 2nd c. A.D., Mariemont
Mus.

116
Jupiter Dolichenus, from Mauer an
der Url, bronze, H. 31 cm., 3rd c. A.D.,
Kunsthistorisches Mus., Vienna

117
Juno Regina, from Mauer an der Url,
bronze, H. 33 cm., 3rd c. A.D., Kunsthistorisches Mus., Vienna

118
Attis leaning against a tree-trunk,
from near Adrianopolis, bronze, H.
33 cm., Louvre

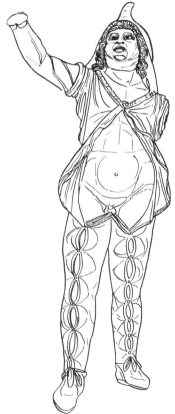

119
Winter, detail from a sarcophagus,
from Rome, marble, c. A.D. 330, Dumbarton Oaks, Washington

120
Attis, from Trier, bronze, H. 35 cm.,
Rheinisches Landesmus., Trier

121   Mithras slaying the bull, from Sidon, marble, H. 72 cm., 4th c. A.D., Louvre

122
Mithraic genius, from Sidon, marble,
H. 87 cm., 4th c. A.D., Louvre

123
Mithraic genius, from Sidon, marble,
H. 88 cm., 4th c. A.D., Louvre

124
Mithraic genius, from Sidon, marble,
H. 86 cm., 4th c. A.D., Louvre

125
Mithraic genius, from Sidon, marble,
H. 88 cm., 4th c. A.D., Louvre

126
Mithras carrying the dead bull, from
Sidon, marble, H. 80 cm., 4th c. A.D.,
Louvre

127
Chronos, time personified, from
Sidon, marble, H. 1.08 m., 4th c. A.D.,
Louvre

128
Relief: Mithras slaying the bull, limestone, 2nd c. A.D., Heddernheim

129
Three-bodied Hecate and dancers,
from Sidon, marble, H. 75 cm., 4th c.
A.D., Louvre

130   Mithras slaying the bull, from Rome, marble, 3rd c. A.D., Museo di Roma

131
Spring, mosaic pavement, stone tesserae, La Chebba, 1st half of 2nd c. A.D., Le Bardo Mus.

132
Winter, mosaic pavement, stone tesserae, La Chebba, 1st half of 2nd c. A.D., Le Bardo Mus.

133
Spring, mosaic pavement, stone tesserae, Ain Babouch, 2nd–3rd c. A.D., Archaeol. Mus., Algiers

134
Winter, mosaic pavement, stone tesserae, Daphne (Turkey), A.D. 325–330, Louvre

135
Winter, mosaic pavement, stone tesserae, Ain Babouch, 2nd–3rd c. A.D., Archaeol. Mus., Algiers

136
Summer, mosaic pavement, stone tesserae, Ain Babouch, 2nd–3rd c. A.D., Archaeol. Mus., Algiers

137
Summer, mosaic pavement, stone tes-
serae, La Chebba, 1st half of 2nd c.
A.D., Le Bardo Mus.

138
Autumn, mosaic pavement, stone tes-
serae, La Chebba, 1st half of 2nd c.
A.D., Le Bardo Mus.

139
Summer, mosaic pavement, stone tes-
serae, Haidra (Tunisia), 4th c. A.D.,
United Nations Building, New York

140
Autumn, mosaic pavement, stone tes-
serae, Ain Babouch, 2nd–3rd c. A.D.,
Archaeol. Mus., Algiers

141
Autumn, mosaic pavement, stone tes-
serae, Haidra (Tunisia), 4th c. A.D.,
United Nations Building, New York

142
Autumn, mosaic pavement, stone tesserae, Carthage, 4th c. A.D., Carthage

143
Venus at her toilet, mosaic pavement,
stone tesserae, beginning of 3rd c. A.D.,
Khenchela (Algeria)

144
Artemis (Diana) bathing, mosaic
pavement, Philippopolis, middle of
3rd c. A.D., Suweideh Mus. (Syria)

145   Venus at her toilet, mosaic pavement, Philippopolis, mid-3rd c. A.D.,
Suweideh Mus. (Syria)

146
Female portrait, from Palombara Sabina, marble, H. 32 cm., end of 1st c. B.C., Terme Mus., Rome

147
Young girl, from Athens, marble, H. 38 cm., beginning of 1st c. A.D., Agora Mus., Athens.

148
Drusilla (?), sister of Caligula, marble, H. 44 cm., beginning of 1st c. A.D., Glyptothek, Munich

149
Agrippina the Younger, marble, H. 39 cm., mid-1st c. A.D., Württembergisches Landesmus., Stuttgart

150
Female portrait, from Rome, marble, H. 24 cm., end of 1st c. A.D., Vatican Mus.

151
Faustina, wife of Antoninus Pius, on a bronze coin, minted Rome, mid-2nd c. A.D.

152
Sabina, wife of Hadrian, on a bronze coin, minted Rome, A.D. 134–136,

153
Sabina, on a bronze coin, minted Rome, A.D. 132–134

154
Orbiana, wife of Severus Alexander, on a bronze coin, minted Rome, A.D. 225

155
Herennia Etruscilla, wife of Decius Trajan, on a bronze coin, minted Rome, A.D. 249–251

156
Female portrait, marble, H. 68 cm., A.D. 240–250, Glyptothek, Munich

157
Female portrait, from Constantinople, marble, H. 53 cm., beginning of 6th c. A.D., Metropolitan Mus.

158
Funerary relief: woman and daughter, Rome, marble, H. 1.88 m., *c.* 50 B.C., Mus. dei Conservatori, Rome

159
Young woman, from Herculaneum, marble, H. 1.71 m., *c.* A.D. 42, Nat. Mus., Naples

160
Faustina, wife of Antoninus Pius, from Rome, marble, H. 1.97 m., *c.* A.D. 140, Mus. dei Conservatori, Rome

161
Female statue, from Cyrene, marble, H. 2.10 m., mid-2nd c. A.D., Louvre

162
Vestal, from Roman Forum, marble, H. of remains 1.21 m., 1st quarter of 2nd c. A.D., Terme Mus., Rome

163
Marriage scene, detail from a sarcophagus from Rome, marble, *c.* A.D. 275, Terme Mus., Rome

164
L. Mammius Maximus, from theatre at Herculaneum, bronze, H. 2.12 m., *c.* A.D. 50, Nat. Mus., Naples

165
Titus, from Rome, marble, H. 1.96 m., *c.* A.D. 80, Vatican Mus.

166
Augustus as priest, from Rome, marble, H. 2.17 m., end of 1st c. B.C., Terme Mus., Rome

167
Priest, from Lyons, bronze, H. 16.7 cm., 1st half of 1st c. A.D., Gallo-Roman Mus., Lyons

168
Consul waving the *mappa,* from Rome, marble, 4th c. A.D., Mus. dei Conservatori, Rome

169
Person in a toga, from near Rome, marble, H. 2 m., *c.* A.D. 265, Doria Pamphili Coll., Rome

170
Emperor Julian, from Italy, marble,
H. 1.75 m., *c.* A.D. 360, Louvre

171
Senators, detail from a sarcophagus,
from Acilia, marble, H. 1.50 m., *c.* A.D.
240, Terme Mus., Rome

172
Augustus in a cuirass, from Prima
Porta, marble, H. 2.04 m., *c.* 20 B.C.,
Vatican Mus.

173
Constantine, from Rome, marble, H.
2.75 m., *c.* A.D. 320, Capitol, Rome

174
Two tetrarchs, from Constantinople,
porphyry, H. 1.30 m., beginning of 4th
c. A.D., St. Mark's Basilica, Venice

175
Probus in consular attire, on a silver
coin, A.D. 277

176
Young boy on horseback, from Borgo
Acilio, marble and alabaster, 2nd half
of 3rd c. A.D., Terme Mus., Rome

177
Equestrian statue: Marcus Aurelius,
from Rome, gilded bronze, H. 4.24 m.,
A.D. 166–180, Capitol, Rome

178
Portrait of a man, from Ostia, marble,
D. 80 cm., 1st c. A.D., Ostia Mus.

179
Portrait of a man, from Ostia, marble,
D. 80 cm., 1st c. A.D., Ostia Mus.

180
Octavian, future Emperor Augustus, on a silver coin, 29–28 B.C.

181
Augustus, on a gold coin, Oriental mint, 19–15 B.C.

182
Augustus, from Pollentia, marble, end of 1st c. B.C., private coll., Majorca

183
Augustus, marble, H. 34 cm., end of 1st c. B.C., Capitoline Mus., Rome

184
Augustus, marble, H. 44 cm., end of 1st c. B.C., Capitoline Mus., Rome

185
Augustus, marble, H. 43 cm., beginning of 1st c. A.D., Glyptothek, Munich

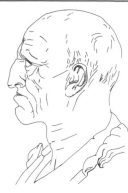

187
Male portrait, from Ofricoli, marble,
H. 35 cm., 1st half of 1st c. B.C., Tor-
lonia Coll., Rome

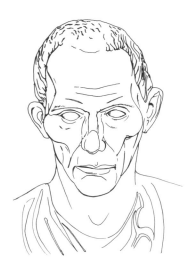

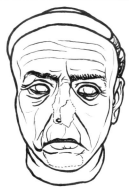

186
Male portrait, from a funerary relief,
marble, 2nd half of 1st c. B.C., Ny
Carlsberg Glyptotek, Copenhagen

188
Portrait of a priest, from Athens,
marble, H. 29 cm., c. 50 B.C., Agora
Mus., Athens

189   Funerary portraits of a couple, marble, H. 68 cm., last quarter of 1st c. B.C.,
                              Vatican Mus.

190
L. Cornelius Sulla, on a silver coin, 55
B.C., Rome

191
Vercingetorix, on a silver coin, c. 48
B.C., Rome

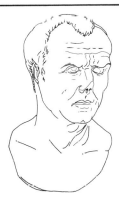

192
Pompey, marble, H. 27 cm., mid-1st c.
B.C., Ny Carlsberg Glyptotek, Copen-
hagen

193
'Marius', marble, H. 46 cm., mid-1st c.
B.C., Glyptothek, Munich

194
Nero, on a bronze coin, minted Rome,
A.D. 64–68

195
Nero, marble, H. 44 cm., A.D. 54–68,
Glyptothek, Munich

196
Vespasian, from Rome, marble, H. 29 cm., A.D. 69–79, Ny Carlsberg Glyptotek, Copenhagen

197
Vespasian, on a bronze coin, A.D. 71, Rome

198
Titus, marble, H. 48 cm., A.D. 80, Glyptothek, Munich

199
Marcellus, from Rome, marble, end of 1st c. A.D., Louvre

200
Young soldier, from near Rome, marble, H. 52 cm., c. A.D. 100, Mus. dei Conservatori, Rome

201
Trajan, from Ostia, marble, H. 39 cm., c. A.D. 120, Ostia Mus.

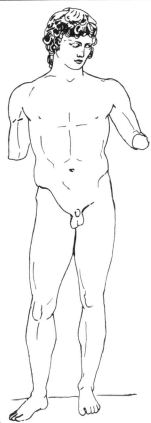

203
Antinous, marble, *c.* A.D. 140, Nat. Mus., Rome

202
Antinous, Hadrian's favourite, from Delphi, marble, H. 1.80 m., *c.* A.D. 135, Delphi Mus.

204
Idealized Augustus, from Otricoli, marble, H. 2.04 m., *c.* 20 B.C., Vatican Mus.

205
Antinous as Silvanus, from Lanuvium, marble, H. 1.42 m., *c.* A.D. 140, Rome

206
Marcus Aurelius, on a bronze coin,
minted Rome, A.D. 158

207
Hercules, from Bordeaux, bronze, end
of 2nd c. A.D., Aquitaine Mus., Bordeaux

208
Lucius Verus, from Acqua Traversa,
marble, H. 89 cm., c. A.D. 170, Louvre

209
Herodes Atticus, from Probalinthos
(Greece), marble, H. 62 cm., mid-2nd
c. A.D., Louvre

210
Gallienus, from Roman Forum,
marble, H. 38 cm., A.D. 260–268,
Terme Mus., Rome

211
Priest, from Egypt, marble, H. 29 cm.,
c. A.D. 250, St. Mus., E. Berlin

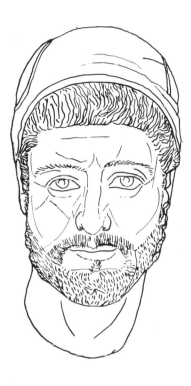

212
Theodosius II, marble, H. 25 cm., *c.*
A.D. 440, Louvre

213
Portrait of a driver, marble, H. 38 cm.,
mid-3rd c. A.D., Louvre

214
Portrait of a man, from Aphrodisias
(Turkey), marble, H. 29 cm., early 5th
c. A.D., Mus. Royaux, Brussels

215
Portrait of a man, from Egypt, wax
painting on wood, H. 33 cm., beginning of 2nd c. A.D., Louvre

216
Maximian Hercules with the Nemean lion-skin head-dress, on a bronze coin, minted Rome, end of 3rd c. A.D.

217
Diocletian, on a gold coin, minted Nicomedia, c. A.D. 294

218
Licinius, on a silvered bronze coin, minted Alexandria, beginning of 4th c. A.D.

219
Constantius Chlorus, marble, c. A.D. 315, Arch of Constantine, Rome

220
Decius, from Rome, marble, H. 78 cm., A.D. 250, Capitoline Mus., Rome

221
C. Caelius Dogmatius, from Rome, marble, H. 21 cm., c. A.D. 330, Vatican Mus.

222
Constantine, on a gold coin, minted
Siscia, A.D. 326

223
Constantine and the Sun, on a gold
coin, minted Pavia, A.D. 313

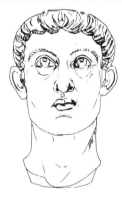

225
Constantine, from Rome, marble, H.
95 cm., c. A.D. 325, Metropolitan Mus.

226
Constantine, from Naissus, bronze, H.
24 cm., A.D. 325–330, Nat. Mus., Belgrade

224
Constantine, on a gold coin, minted
Rome, A.D. 335

227   Constantius II in his triumphal chariot, on a gold coin, minted Antioch,
c. A.D. 360

228
Arcadius, from Constantinople,
marble, H. 32 cm., *c.* A.D. 390,
Archaeol. Mus., Istanbul

229
Portrait of a man, marble, H. 30 cm., *c.*
A.D. 400, Glyptothek, Munich

230   Honorius and Maria, sard, D. 16 cm., A.D. 398, Rothschild Coll., Paris

231
Decius with rayed crown, on a bronze
coin, minted Rome, A.D. 250

232
Constantine with laurel crown, on a
silvered bronze coin, minted Rome,
A.D. 306

233
Constantine with jewelled diadem, on
a gold coin, minted Thessalonica, A.D.
327

234
Constantine (?) with jewelled diadem,
on a silver coin, minted Siscia, A.D. 336

235
Helen with jewelled diadem, on a gold
coin, minted Pavia, A.D. 325

236
Julian the Apostate with pearl
diadem, on a gold coin, minted Antioch, A.D. 362

531

237
Galloping horseman, from Orange, bronze, H. 20 cm., 2nd c. A.D., Mus. of Nat. Ant., St-Germain-en-Laye

238
Rein-rings: warrior and amazon, from Marchena (Spain), bronze, W. 18 cm., 2nd c. A.D., Louvre

240
Helmeted figure, Milan, bronze, H. 60 cm., 2nd–3rd c. A.D., Superintendence of Lombardian Ant., Milan

239
Funerary stele of a soldier, from Bingerbrück, limestone, c. A.D. 50, Kreuznach Mus.

241
Prisoner, from Brescia, gilded bronze, H. 68 cm., 2nd–3rd c. A.D., Civic Mus., Brescia

242
Helmet mask, Resca (Rumania), bronze, H. 23 cm., late 2nd c. A.D., Kunsthistorisches Mus., Vienna

243
Helmet mask, Chatalka (Bulgaria), iron and gilded bronze, H. 23 cm., early 1st c. A.D., Stara Zagora Mus.

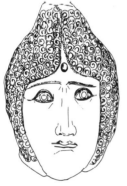

244
Helmet mask, Straubing, bronze, H. 23 cm., 1st third of 1st c. A.D., Straubing Mus.

245
Helmet mask, Plovdiv (Bulgaria), iron and silver, H. 22 cm., 1st quarter of 1st c. A.D., Plovdiv Mus.

246   Anastasius in helmet and cuirass, on a gold coin, minted Constantinople, beginning of 6th c. A.D.

247
Greave: Hercules, from Straubing, gilded bronze, H. 35 cm., 1st third of 3rd c. A.D., Straubing Mus.

248
Greave: Mars, from Regensburg-Kumpfmühl, gilded bronze, H. 35 cm., 2nd c. A.D., Regensburg Mus.

249
Phalera: Athena, Tabriz (Iran), bronze, D. 24 cm., A.D. 200–230, Prähistorische Staatssammlung, Munich

250
Greave: Mars, from Straubing, bronze, H. 36 cm., 1st third of 3rd c. A.D., Straubing Mus.

251   Horse's head-guard, from Straubing, bronze, H. 39 cm., 1st third of 3rd c. A.D., Straubing Mus.

252
Victory with trophy, from Carthage, relief, marble, c. A.D. 165, Carthage Mus.

253
Victory, from Villa della Farnesina, Rome, stucco, end of 1st c. B.C., Terme Mus., Rome

254
Emperor haranguing his troops, on a bronze coin, minted Rome, A.D. 40

255
Entrance of Magnentius into Aquileia, on a gold coin, minted Aquileia, A.D. 350

256   Triumphal procession of Titus, marble, H. 2.04 m., A.D. 80–85, Arch of Titus, Rome

257   Altar-base of Domitius Ahenobarbus: marriage of Poseidon (Neptune) and Amphitrite, from Rome, marble, H. 1.50 m., beginning of 1st c. B.C., Glyptothek, Munich

258   Altar-base of Domitius Ahenobarbus: taking the census, marble, H. 1.50 m., beginning of 1st c. B.C., Louvre

259   Septimius Severus and his two sons in a chariot, Arch of Severus, Leptis Magna, marble, H. 1.72 m., A.D. 203, Tripoli Mus.

260   Base of the column of Antoninus: cavalcade, from Rome, marble, H.
2.72 m., A.D. 160, Vatican Mus.

261   Trajan charging the barbarians, marble, H. 3 m., beginning of 2nd c. A.D.,
Arch of Constantine, Rome

262
Barbarians surrender to Marcus
Aurelius, Rome, marble, H. 3.12 m.,
A.D. 176, Conservatori, Rome

263
Legionaries, marble, H. 2.06 m., A.D.
80–90, Apostolic Chancellery, Rome,
Vatican Mus.

264
Emperor charging, from Kuzadak,
sardonyx, H. 19 cm., 2nd quarter of
4th c. A.D., Nat. Mus., Belgrade

265
Judaea conquered, on a bronze coin,
minted Rome, A.D. 80

266   Apotheosis of Sabina, in the presence of Hadrian, from Rome, marble, H.
2.68 m., A.D. 136, Mus. dei Conservatori, Rome

267   Apotheosis of Antoninus and Faustina, from Rome, marble, H. 2.72 m.,
A.D. 160, base of Antoninus column, Vatican Mus.

268   Theodosius at the hippodrome, marble, W. 3.10 m., *c.* A.D. 390, Constantinople, base of the column of Theodosius

269
Rome and Tiberius: cameo, onyx, A.D. 15–37, Kunsthistorisches Mus., Vienna

270
Hadrian sacrificing to Hercules, marble, D. 2.40 m., A.D. 130–138, Arch of Constantine, Rome

271
Septimius Severus and Julia Domna offering sacrifices, marble, H. 1.70 m., A.D. 204, near Forum Boarium, Rome

272
Funerary stele: centurion sacrificing, Rome, marble, H. 1.25 m., beginning of 3rd c. A.D., Vatican Mus.

273   Fertile Earth, marble, W. 2.40 m., 13–9 B.C., Altar of Peace of Augustus, Rome

274   Relief: rural scene, marble, H. 30 cm., 1st c. A.D., Glyptothek, Munich

275
Young women with candelabrum, ornamental plaque, from Italy, terracotta, end of 1st c. B.C., Louvre

276
Corybantes dancing the Pyrrhica, ornamental plaque, terracotta, H. 50 cm., end of 1st c. B.C., B.M.

277   Myrtilus and Oenomaus, ornamental plaque, terracotta, end of 1st c. B.C., Metropolitan Mus.

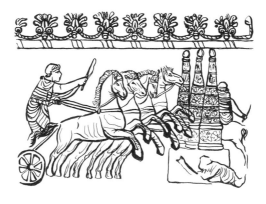

278   Chariot in the hippodrome, ornamental plaque, terracotta, 1st c. A.D., B.M.

279   Open-air banquet: detail from a plate, from Cesena, nielloed silver, 4th
          c. A.D., Biblioteca Malatestiana, Cesena

280   Payment scene: funerary relief, from Neumagen, limestone, end of 2nd c.
          A.D., Trier Mus.

281   Teacher with his pupils: funerary relief, from Neumagen, limestone, end
          of 2nd c. A.D., Trier Mus.

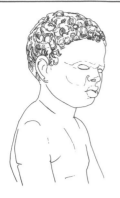

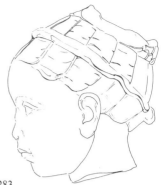

282
Boy, from Tarragona, bronze, 1st c.
A.D., Archaeol. Mus., Tarragona

283
Little girl's head, from Corinth,
marble, H. 22.5 cm., 2nd c. A.D., Mus.
of Fine Arts, Boston

284
Perfume vase, from Ostia, bronze, H.
15 cm., 2nd c. A.D., Vatican Mus.

285
Perfume vase, bronze, H. 6.5 cm., 2nd
c. A.D., Constantine Mus.

286
Statuette, from Rheims, bronze, H.
16 cm., 2nd c. A.D., Nat. Mus. of Antiquities, St-Germain-en-Laye

287
Lamp, bronze, W. 8.5 cm., 3rd c. A.D.,
Cabinet des Médailles, Paris

288
Ear-ring, from Boscoreale, gold and
glass paste, H. 3.7 cm., 1st c. A.D.,
Louvre

289
Ear-ring, gold and pearls, H. 2.3 cm.,
1st–2nd c. A.D., Hamburg Mus.

290, 291
Ear-rings, from Syria, l.: gold, H.
6 cm., r.: gold and pearls, H. 3.3 cm.,
3rd c. A.D., Hamburg Mus.

292
Ring, gold and cameo, D. 3.8 cm.,
2nd–3rd c. A.D., Louvre

293
Ring, gold and cameo, D. 3.2 cm.,
2nd–3rd c. A.D., Louvre

294
Wedding ring, gold and cameo, D.
2.7 cm., 2nd–3rd c. A.D., Louvre

295
Ewer: Victory slaying a bull, from
Boscoreale, gilded silver, H. 24 cm.,
end of 1st c. B.C., Louvre

296
Jug, from Krefeld, glass, H. 20 cm.,
3rd c. A.D., Römisch-Germanisches
Mus., Cologne

297
Victory slaying a bull: decorative
plaque, from Rome, terracotta, c. A.D.
100, Terme Mus., Rome

298
Victory slaying a bull: decorative
plaque, from Rome, terracotta, end of
1st c. A.D., Terme Mus., Rome

299
Ewer, nielloed silver, 4th c. A.D., Trier
Mus.

300
Ewer, silver, H. 38 cm., 4th c. A.D.,
Louvre

301
Pan handle, from Marwedel, silver,
1st–2nd c. A.D., Niedersächsisches
Landesmus., Hanover

302
Pan handle, from Pompeii, House of
Menander, silver, 1st c. A.D., Nat.
Mus., Naples

303
Pan handle, from Oberkassel, silver,
1st c. A.D., Rheinisches Landesmus.,
Bonn

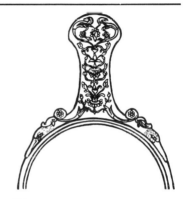

304
Pan handle, Nijmegen, silver, L. 7 cm.,
1st half of 1st c. A.D., Nijmegen Mus.

305
Pan handle: Cybele, from Beek, silver,
2nd c. A.D., Nijmegen Mus.

306
Pan handle, from Caspet (Great Britain), silver, 1st c. A.D., Louvre

307   Skyphos: foliated scroll with animals, from Boscoreale, silver, H. 15 cm.,
end of 1st c. B.C., Louvre

308
Skyphos: olive twigs, from Boscoreale, silver, H. 8 cm., beginning of 1st
c. A.D., Louvre

309
Skyphos: ivy branches, from Herculaneum, silver, H. 12 cm., beginning of
1st c. A.D., Nat. Mus., Naples

310
Kantharos: myrtle branches, Alesia,
silver, H. 11 cm., c. 50 B.C. (?), Mus. of
Nat. Ant., St-Germain-en-Laye

311
Kantharos: plane   leaves,   from
Boscoreale, silver, H. 10 cm., begin-
ning of 1st c. A.D., Louvre

312
Kantharos: Ariadne on a sea panther, silver, end of 1st c. A.D., Nat. Mus., Belgrade

313
Skyphos: still-life, from Boscoreale, silver, H. 6 cm., 1st c. A.D., Louvre

314
Kantharos: storks in their nest, from Boscoreale, silver, H. 13 cm., beginning of 1st c. A.D., Louvre

315
Kantharos, from Tivoli, silver, H. 10 cm., c. 50 B.C., Metropolitan Mus.

316
Cup, from Marwedel, silver, 1st c. A.D., Niedersächsisches Landesmus., Hanover

317
Cup, from Petroassa, gold and fine stones, W. 18 cm., 4th c. A.D., Nat. Mus. of Ant., Bucharest

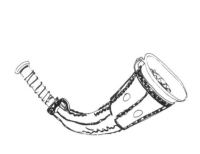

318
Vase in the shape of a horn, glass,
2nd–3rd c. A.D., Römisch-Germanisches Mus., Cologne

319
Flask with handle, glass, H. 17.8 cm.,
4th–5th c. A.D., Römisch-Germanisches Mus., Cologne

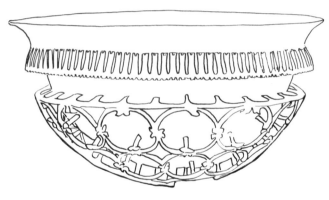

320   Cup with openwork relief decoration, glass, D. 18 cm., c. A.D. 300, private
coll.

321
Beaker, glass, H. 17.5 cm., 2nd half of
1st c. A.D., Römisch-Germanisches
Mus., Cologne

322
Vase decorated with shells, beginning
of 4th c. A.D., Römisch-Germanisches
Mus., Cologne

323
Oval salver, from Manching, silver, 2nd c. A.D., Prähistorische Staatssammlung, Munich

324
Oval salver, from southern Germany, tin-plated bronze L. 40 cm., 2nd–3rd c. A.D., Röm.-German. Mus., Cologne

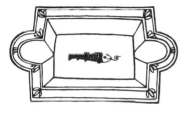

325
Rectangular plate, from Kaiseraugst, silver, L. 26 cm., c. A.D. 350, Augst Mus.

326
Rectangular salver, from Hildesheim, silver, L. 24 cm., 1st c. A.D., St. Mus., E. Berlin

327
Cup, from Mildenhall, silver, H. 11.5 cm., 4th c. A.D., B.M.

328
Goblet, from Kaiseraugst, silver, D. 7 cm., 4th c. A.D., Augst Mus.

329
Jug, terracotta, with barbotine deco-
ration, 2nd–3rd c. A.D., Römisch-
Germanisches Mus., Cologne

330
Jug, terracotta, with barbotine deco-
ration: gladiators, H. 25.8 cm., 2nd c.
A.D., Palatinate Mus., Speyer

331
Beaker with relief decoration, from
southern Russia, glazed terracotta, 1st
c. B.C., St. Mus., E. Berlin

332
Jug with applied thread decoration,
glass, 4th c. A.D., Römisch-Germanisches Mus., Cologne

333
Vase with inscription, Trier, painted
terracotta, 3rd c. A.D., Römisch-Germanisches Mus., Cologne

334
Vase with pricking-wheel decoration,
terracotta, 1st c. A.D., Römisch-Germanisches Mus., Cologne

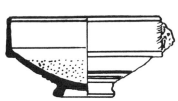

335
Krater, sigillated pottery, Augustan period, Italy

336
Lion-snouted mortar, terracotta, 2nd c. A.D., Lezoux

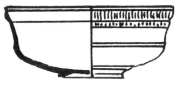

337
Straight-sided bowl, sigillated pottery, 1st c. A.D.

338
Hemispherical bowl, sigillated pottery, 1st c. A.D.

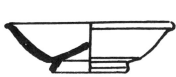

339
Ovoid vase with incised decoration, terracotta, 2nd c. A.D.

340
Sigillated pottery dish, 1st–2nd c. A.D., Lezoux

341
Boat decoration: wolf's head, from Lake Nemi, bronze, L. 52 cm., 1st c. B.C., Nemi Mus.

342
Boat decoration: lion's head, from Lake Nemi, bronze, L. 36 cm., 1st c. B.C., Nemi Mus.

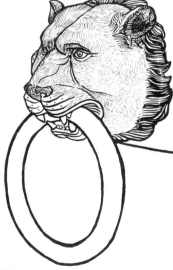

343
Boat decoration: head of Medusa, from Lake Nemi, bronze, H. 25 cm., 1st c. B.C., Nemi Mus.

344
Boat decoration: panther's head, from Lake Nemi, bronze, H. 32 cm., 1st c. B.C., Nemi Mus.

345   Couch decoration: mule, from Volubilis, bronze, H. 18 cm., 1st c. A.D.,
                              Archaeol. Mus., Rabat

346
Couch decoration: Silenus, from
Volubilis, bronze, H. 15 cm., 1st c.
A.D., Archaeol. Mus., Rabat

347
Couch decoration: Bacchus, bronze,
from Volubilis, H. 19.5 cm., 1st c. A.D.,
Archaeol. Mus., Rabat

348
Couch decoration: Silenus, from
Lixus, bronze, H. 12.7 cm., 1st c. A.D.,
Tetouan Mus.

349
Seat decoration: Constantinople personified, Esquiline, Rome, silver, H.
5.4 cm., 4th c. A.D., B.M.

351
Head of an Oriental (?): vase, bronze,
H. 19 cm., Louvre

350
Griffin, from Magdalensberg, bronze,
H. 40 cm., beginning of 1st c. A.D.,
Kunsthistorisches Mus., Vienna

352
Sick old woman: vase, from Vichy,
bronze, H. 9 cm., 2nd–3rd c. A.D.,
Louvre

353   Perfume vases in the shapes of animals, glass, 3rd–4th c. A.D., Römisch-
Germanisches Mus., Cologne

354
Lamp handle: Jupiter, Mor (Hungary), bronze, H. 20 cm., 1st–2nd c. A.D., Hungarian Nat. Mus., Budapest

355
Lamp with volutes and triangular handle, terracotta, 1st c. A.D.

356
Cordiform lamp with nozzle: man fighting lion, terracotta, 2nd c. A.D.

357
Cordiform lamp with nozzle: gladiators, terracotta, 3rd c. A.D.

358
Spouted lamp decorated with fleurons, terracotta, 4th c. A.D.

359
Spouted lamp, terracotta, 4th c. A.D.

360   Acanthus scroll, fragment from pediment, from Rome, marble, L. *c.* 2 m.,
         end of 1st c. B.C. (?), Mus. dei Conservatori, Rome

361   Acanthus scroll, marble, 13–9 B.C., Altar of Peace of Augustus, Rome

362
Scroll filled with animals, from Hildesheim, silver, 1st c. A.D., St. Mus., E. Berlin

363
Decorated pillar: acanthus scrolls, marble, 2nd c. A.D., Rome

364
Fantastic candelabrum, wall painting, 1st c. B.C., House of the Vettii, Pompeii

365
Decorated pilaster: labours of Hercules, Aphrodisias, marble, mid-2nd c. A.D., Archaeol. Mus., Istanbul

366
Decorated pilaster: scroll of roses, from Tomb of the Haterii, Rome, marble, H. 1 m., c. A.D. 100, Vatican

367   Decorated pilaster: Dionysus, marble, *c.* A.D. 200, basilica of Leptis Magna

368   Frieze, scroll, basalt, Kanawat (Syria)

369   Hunt scene: shallow cup, engraved glass, from Bonn, D. 17.6 cm., 4th c.
A.D., Rheinisches Landesmus., Bonn

370   Christian scenes, shallow cup, from Homblières, engraved glass, D. 21 cm., 4th c. A.D., Louvre

GLOSSARY

abacus   uppermost member of the capital: slab underneath the architrave or roof-support.

Achelous   river god vanquished by Hercules (Herakles).

acroterium (akroterion)   support and ornament positioned at the top and sides of a pediment.

Aigos   surname given by the Greeks to the posthumous son of Alexander the Great by Roxana.

alabastron   small, droplet-shaped perfume flask, narrow-necked with a round, flattened lip.

anta   pier produced by a thickening in a wall at its termination.

antefix   termination of covering-tiles decorated with a painted or carved motif.

apadana   hall of columns, particularly the audience chamber in an Achaemenian palace.

aryballos   small perfume flask. The body is sometimes angular but more usually globular. It has a narrow neck and a round, flattened lip.

askos   Greek term meaning 'wine-skin' and describing a bulging type of vase, often with a neck and an opening in the shape of an animal's head (duck-askos).

bracteate   panel of thin metal like a 'leaf', bearing an embossed decoration.

Brutus   according to tradition, the first consul of the Roman Republic, in 509 B.C.

bucchero   Archaic Etruscan pottery of glossy black paste.

bucranium   ox-skull ornamental motif.

canopus   type of terracotta cinerary urn with a lid in the shape of a human or animal head.

cella   cult-room in a Greek temple, containing the image of the divinity.

Chalcolithic   period during which both stone and copper were used in tool-making; between the Neolithic and the Bronze Ages.

chimaera   mythological animal with lion's head and goat's body.

cippus   small stone funerary monument, cylindrical or quadrangular, sometimes with a carved decoration or an inscription.

cist   bronze receptacle usually used for holding toilet articles or jewellery.

coroplast   artist modelling or moulding statuettes in baked clay.

deinos   type of round-bottomed cauldron resting on a support.

Diadoumenos   athlete fastening a victory fillet round his head. Famous work of the sculptor Polykleitos.

Glossary

Dionysermos composite figure, combining Dionysos and Hermes.

fibula metal clasp or buckle used for fastening clothing.

griffin fabulous animal with an eagle's head, wings and fore-quarters, and a lion's body, hind legs and tail.

Hathoric decorated with emblems of the goddess Hathor (cf. menat, sistrum).

hilani type of Syrian building with columned porch.

hypogeum underground section of a tomb, or a tomb cut into the rock.

instrumentum term describing all the utensils and instruments of daily life.

iwan construction of Iranian origin characterized by a large barrel-vaulted hall opening directly to the open air.

kantharos high-stemmed cup with a straight-sided bowl topped by two vertical handles.

kekryphalos net cap with which Greek women held their hair together.

kotyle Corinthian version of the skyphos; a deep, two-handled goblet with a lipless rim.

kourotrophos term used for a female divinity represented carrying or suckling a child.

kudurru boundary-stone decorated with reliefs and inscriptions.

kymation cornice-moulding on Greek temples, in the form of stylized leaves.

lagynos spoutless jug with a low, wide, angular body.

lebes vast bronze cauldron mounted on a tripod.

lekythos small perfume vase with a more or less cylindrical body and narrow neck. Usually employed in funeral rites.

libation ritual drink-offering.

loutrophoros type of elongated amphora used for the ritual marriage bath or funerary rites of the unmarried.

maenad female follower of the god Dionysos and often a prey to orgiastic ecstasies.

mastaba oblong Egyptian tomb (period of the Memphite dynasties) with sloping sides and a flat roof.

megaron Archaic type of Greek house, with a central hall between columns and an entrance framed by low walls or 'antas'.

meghazil 'spindle' in Arabic: the name given to two monumental tombs close to Tortosa.

menat magic necklace made of a heavy collar with a counterpoise resembling the goddess' torso: one of Hathor's insignia.

metope element in a Doric frieze (often placed along the entablature, just beneath the roof): square or rectangular panel between two triglyphs, at first painted and later carved in relief.

Moschophoros figure of a worshipper carrying a calf. Famous statue dedicated on the Athens Acropolis. The term is also used to describe Egyptian statuettes of this type.

naos chapel-like shrine located at the centre, or holy of holies, of an Egyptian (or Greek) temple. It contained the cult-image.

Natufian from the wadi in Natuf: early Neolithic phase in Palestine, also represented in Syria.

nemes funerary headdress of stiff linen worn by mummies and statues of deceased kings.

oenochoe vessel for pouring wine, with an ovoid body and vertical handle and often having a trefoil-shaped mouth.

olpe variant of oenochoe with a narrow, elongated body and long, vertical handle rising to the level of the rounded opening.

onos reel for winding yarn.

orthostat stone slab, frequently carved in relief, covering the lower part of a brick wall.

ostracon (*plural* ostraca)   fragment of pottery, or limestone chip, used instead of papyrus (which was very costly) for writing on.

paredrus   an element that forms a pair with another entity: thus Isis is the paredrus of Osiris.

pediment   triangular space formed by the gable of a two-pitched roof in Classical Greek architecture. It was often filled with sculptural figures.

pelike   variety of amphora with the body set plump on the base.

peplophoros   figure shown wearing the peplos (see below).

peplos   garment composed of a large piece of fabric folded under the bust.

Polykleitan   term used for works related to creations attributed to the Greek sculptor Polykleitos.

pothos   Greek word used to describe loving desire. Sometimes personified as a member of the retinue of Aphrodite, it has given its name to a famous statue by the sculptor Skopas.

pronaos   area in an Egyptian temple leading to the naos.

propylaeum   monumental gateway to a sacred enclosure.

protome   Greek word describing a representation of the head and neck, sometimes the bust, of a human or animal body.

psykter   small krater on a raised foot which was placed in a large vessel of cold water to cool the wine it contained.

pyxis   round lidded box.

rhyton   Greek vessel based on the principle of the drinking horn, often carved in the shape of an animal's head.

saluki   strain of greyhound found throughout western Asia and North Africa.

sigillated (pottery)   pottery decorated in relief by the use of punches or seals.

sistrum   type of ritual rattle, made of bronze, which Egyptian priestesses shook in honour of their goddess during cult observances.

situla   bronze receptacle in the shape of a bucket covered with vignettes and religious formulas, finishing with a lotus flower. It was used in offering libations to the dead.

skyphos   deep-bowled drinking goblet with two handles, usually set horizontally.

stamnos   large vase for keeping wine: high-shouldered, short-necked, with two horizontal handles.

stele   stone slab or pillar, usually inscribed or carved, used for commemoration, often at a grave.

strigil   bronze toilet utensil used by athletes to scrape off the oil with which they smeared themselves.

stylobate   base of a colonnade.

Tao Tieh   Chinese term used to describe a motif derived from a strongly stylized head.

temenos   sacred enclosure in the centre of which was the temple with all its annexes.

Tetrarch   one of the four co-regent princes in the system introduced by Diocletian for the government of the Roman Empire.

torus   rounded moulding at the base of a column.

triclinium   room with three couches; dining-room in Roman houses.

triglyph   rectangular tablet forming part of a Doric frieze, separating metopes; it was incised with vertical channels.

tyrannoktonos   Greek word meaning 'tyrant-killer'. Applied to two Athenian youths, Harmodios and Aristogeiton, murderers of the last tyrant of Athens. Famous statuary group executed by the sculptors Kritios and Nesiotes.

Villanovan   term applied to the culture in northern Italy during the Bronze Age, 12th to 9th century B.C., from which Etruscan civilization arose.

wadi   steep-walled dry valley in the desert.

ziggurat   stepped tower in Babylonia or Assyria.

This book was printed in spring 1981 by Hertig AG, Bienne.
The binding is the work of Mayer & Soutter S.A., Renens.
The setting was furnished by Febel AG, Basle.
The photolithography was provided by Schwitter AG, Basle.
Editorial: David J. Baker and Barbara Perroud-Benson.
Production, design and maps: Marcel Berger and Jasmine Kaenzig.

Printed and bound in Switzerland